GW01451558

The Campaign for Nuclear Disarmament

Short Histories

Agenda Short Histories are incisive and provocative introductions to topics, ideas and events for students wanting to know more about how we got where we are today.

Published

The Campaign for Nuclear Disarmament
Martin Shaw

Conservatism
Mark Garnett

Deglobalization
Edward Ashbee

Social Democracy
Eunice Goes

Thatcherism
Peter Dorey

The Campaign for Nuclear Disarmament

Martin Shaw

agenda
publishing

© Martin Shaw 2025

This book is copyright under the Berne Convention.
No reproduction without permission.
All rights reserved.

First published in 2025 by Agenda Publishing

Agenda Publishing Limited
PO Box 185
Newcastle upon Tyne
NE20 2DH
www.agendapub.com

ISBN 978-1-78821-777-4 (hardcover)
ISBN 978-1-78821-778-1 (paperback)

British Library Cataloguing-in-Publication Data
A catalogue record for this book is available from the British Library

Typeset by JS Typesetting Ltd, Porthcawl, Mid Glamorgan
Printed and bound in the UK by CPI Group (UK) Ltd, Croydon, CR0 4YY

Contents

Peter Kennard, "Broken Missile", photomontage (by kind permission of the artist)

I pondered all these things, and how men fight and lose the battle, and the thing that they fought for comes about in spite of their defeat, and when it comes turns out not to be what they meant, and other men have to fight for what they meant under another name.
William Morris, *A Dream of John Ball*

Acknowledgements

When I was asked to write this book, I was torn about whether to agree. The campaign against nuclear weapons is one of the most important in modern British history, and it was obvious that there was a major gap, since no academic account of it had been written in the present century. This meant, however, that writing it represented a large responsibility.

This was particularly true because I knew or met, at the time or later, many who took part in the 1958–63 movement, during which I wore a CND badge at school, I played a local organizing role in the 1980s movement and I took part in several related campaigns. I therefore felt accountable to my fellow activists, but I also knew that as a historian, I would need to evaluate dispassionately the difficulties and conflicts in the campaign's often turbulent history.

I took on the task, persuaded by my editor Alison Howson and even more by my wife, Annabel, who went on to share every stage of the journey. I have been encouraged by the assistance and support of both old friends and those who I have met through researching the book. David Cowell, Robert Crampton, Rob Fairmichael, Paul Oestreicher, Ted Parker, Ian Paul, Phil Shaw, Tony Simpson and Jonathan Usher responded to queries, made suggestions or provided information. Pat Gaffney, Kate Hudson and Angie Zelter gave their time to talk to me about their involvement, and Peter Kennard generously allowed me to use his "Broken Missile" design to publicize the project.

The support of other scholars was particularly important. I am grateful to Patrick Burke, Rhys Crilley, Ewan Gibbs, Chris Hill, James Hinton, Martin Levy, Mary Kaldor, Melinda Rankin, Sophie Scott-Brown, Dick Taylor and Frank Webster for sharing their work. Chris, James, Mary, Martin and Dick also read the manuscript, as did Hilary Fraser, Julian Harber, Jeff Michaels, Rick Rylance, Nigel Young and the publisher's anonymous reviewer. All of them made valuable and some very detailed comments that have improved the book, but none are responsible for its arguments, which are mine alone.

I am also grateful for the assistance of the Commonweal Library, University of Bradford, and the Cadbury Research Library, University of Birmingham, while without the University of Sussex Library, I could not have written this book.

Writing it has involved evaluating a large volume of information. While history is about a lot more than the facts, it is important to get them right, and the errors I have come across in other books – one even claimed that the Committee of 100 was the leadership of CND – have increased my alertness. However, some mistakes are bound to have crept in and I ask readers to let me know about them, and any omissions, in case there is a second edition.

I dedicate this study to all who have campaigned against nuclear weapons, as well as to my grandchildren who I hope will live to see a more peaceful world.

Martin Shaw
Devon

Abbreviations

ABM	anti-ballistic missile
ARROW	Active Resistance to the Roots of War
BCPV	British Council for Peace in Vietnam
CND	Campaign for Nuclear Disarmament
CP, CPGB	Communist Party of Great Britain
DAC	Direct Action Committee Against Nuclear War
EC	European Community
EEC	European Economic Community
END	European Nuclear Disarmament
GLC	Greater London Council
HCA	Helsinki Citizens Assembly
ICAN	International Campaign to Abolish Nuclear Weapons
ICBM	intercontinental ballistic missile
IKV	Interchurch Peace Council
INF	intermediate nuclear force
MAB	Muslim Association of Britain
NATO	North Atlantic Treaty Organization
NCANWT	National Council for the Abolition of Nuclear Weapons Tests
NMD	National Missile Defence
NPT	Nuclear Non-Proliferation Treaty
NVDA	nonviolent direct action
RAF	Royal Air Force
RSG	Regional Seat of Government
SALT	Strategic Arms Limitation Treaty
SDI	Strategic Defence Initiative
SDP	Social Democratic Party
SNP	Scottish National Party

START	Strategic Arms Reductions Treaty
StWC	Stop the War Coalition
SWP	Socialist Workers Party
TP	Trident Ploughshares
USAF	United States Air Force
USSR	Union of Soviet Socialist Republics (Soviet Union)
VSC	Vietnam Solidarity Campaign

Introduction

The danger of nuclear war, which almost disappeared from public consciousness at the end of the twentieth century, has returned in the third decade of the twenty-first. In the 1980s, when the threat came from a new stage in the nuclear arms race, mass movements protested across the Western world. Yet when a threat of actual use arose during a major war in Europe in 2022, public concern was muted. It was as though the protests of earlier decades had been forgotten. This book, which tells the story of the antinuclear campaign in Britain – one of the first places where it developed and was influential – offers a reminder that since nuclear weapons were invented, people have acted to prevent the catastrophe they could cause.

The world first became aware of this danger on 6 and 9 August 1945, when the United States of America destroyed the Japanese cities of Hiroshima and Nagasaki with atomic bombs, instantly killing tens of thousands and irradiating many more. Millions had already died during the Second World War, but most recognized the "atom bomb" as a radically new threat. Alarm grew much further as the Cold War sharpened and both the USA and the Union of Soviet Socialist Republics (USSR) developed thermonuclear hydrogen weapons or "H-bombs" – a thousand times more powerful than the Hiroshima bomb – as well as intercontinental ballistic missiles (ICBMs) to deliver them to each other's countries, opening up the prospect of a new age of warfare that could destroy human society.

In Britain, Clement Attlee's Labour government decided secretly in 1947 to develop its own atomic bomb, making it the third nuclear-armed state; the UK and Canada had helped the USA in the wartime Manhattan Project that developed the bomb, but the US McMahon Act of 1946 barred further nuclear collaboration.[1] By the time Britain tested its first bomb in 1952, under the Conservative government of Winston Churchill, antinuclear activism was beginning. In 1958 the Campaign for Nuclear Disarmament (CND) was founded and quickly generated a new type of mass protest movement, famously centred around marches from the Atomic Weapons Research Establishment at Aldermaston, Berkshire, to London's Trafalgar Square. Its slogan, "Ban the Bomb", and its new symbol soon spread around the world.[2]

Although intended as a short campaign, CND has now been at the heart of movements and campaigns against nuclear weapons, the Cold War and the wars and military activities of the UK state and the North Atlantic Treaty Organization (NATO) throughout two-thirds of a century and remains Britain's best-known peace organization. However, while CND has been the principal symbolic focus, a campaign existed before it was founded and later other groups also played major roles, especially in two periods that saw large-scale mass movements: the late 1950s to early 1960s and the early 1980s. In the first wave, the Direct Action Committee (DAC) and the Committee of 100, and in the second, European Nuclear Disarmament (END) and the Greenham Common Women's Peace Camp were also major centres of activism, often in cooperation but sometimes in conflict with CND. This book is about the campaign in the broadest sense, not just CND.

Obviously nuclear weapons are a global problem. The USA and Russia (before 1991, the USSR) have always had far larger arsenals and played more important roles in nuclear politics than Britain, as China also does today; and British nuclear forces have long been dependent on the USA. The campaign against nuclear weapons has been transnational but it has been organized primarily at the national level, often focusing on national issues – especially in Britain where "unilateral" nuclear disarmament has been to the fore. There has always been a tension between such aims and the global character of the problem, and a crucial question in the campaign's history has been how far it has managed to break out of national confines to become transnational. The period in the 1980s when this happened extensively across Europe was, as we shall see, one of the most important and, arguably, successful in the campaign's history.

This study therefore examines the British campaign's relationships with international power structures, as well as with its own state, and its roles in transnational as well as national protest. While the British campaign has not been the centre of the global antinuclear movement, let alone its organizing hub, it has made striking contributions and exemplifies wider developments. At the same time it has had profound impacts on British and world politics and society. For all these reasons, an up-to-date study is overdue.

Approaching antinuclear history

British antinuclear history has been written in different ways. Books by campaigners have presented informative and inspirational versions of a continuous "CND story" (Minnion & Bolsover 1983; Ruddock 1987; Hudson 2005, 2018), but from the beginning, many historians – including participants – have laid more emphasis on the campaign's contradictory and discontinuous character (Driver 1964; Taylor & Pritchard 1980; Taylor 1988; Hinton 1989; Liddington 1991).

The role of participant historians underlines the prominent role that intellectuals of various kinds have had in the campaign. Indeed, Christopher R. Hill (2018: 75–6) argues that CND's intellectuals began to write its history as soon as it was founded, exercising a disproportionate influence over its historiography, so that inequalities in private as well as public forms of evidence pose problems for historians working further downstream, even risking "a crooked picture".

This critique contains an echo of what E. P. Thompson – the best-known British left-wing historian of the twentieth century, who played a major role in the antinuclear movement – sought to address in his iconic *The Making of the English Working Class*, which he wrote during his first years of CND campaigning. He famously sought "to rescue the poor stockinger, the Luddite cropper, the 'obsolete' hand-loom weaver, the 'utopian' artisan, and even the deluded follower of Joanna Southcott, from the enormous condescension of posterity" (1963: 12). No antinuclear activist has suffered in quite this way, but it is certainly true that the Quaker stalwart of the local CND group, the anarchist school student who turned out with Youth CND and the young lesbian who was radicalized at Greenham Common have received far less attention than the intellectuals who articulated ideas and strategy at the national level. However, it is also true that many prominent participants – some of whom are or were remarkable individuals – have not had their biographies written. They are represented here by their actions and words, and I regret that space does permit me to profile them more fully.

Two related problems require attention. One concerns the differential ideological power of the campaign's "elite" groupings, which has affected how their relationships have been understood. The symbiotic relationship between the early campaign and the New Left, reproduced in the second wave with END, is reflected in the dominance of New Left perspectives at the expense of others, such as Gandhian pacifist direct action, which were profoundly influential in the movement's evolution – although these strands were, Nigel Young (1977) showed, closely linked in the international rebirth of radical activism.

Last but not least, four decades after its second peak the campaign as a whole has almost disappeared from the national and global "memory", as it is curated by the press, television and popular history. A young person today may not have heard of CND or, if they have, may regard it as almost as distant as the Chartists or the Suffragettes. International histories of the left sometimes compound the occlusion: for Michael Hardt (2023: 10), the antinuclear and civil rights movements of the 1960s "belong to a past world, not ours", and Britain is barely worth mentioning. Yet not only do nuclear weapons remain a huge problem but the role that the British campaign against them played in late twentieth-century politics should give it a place in any serious global as well as national history.

I seek, therefore, to rescue the antinuclear movement from various kinds of historical condescension, as well as to address the inequalities within its historiography – if not as much as I should like, since this is a short history. I also write from a perspective that is inspired partly by New Left ideas. It is difficult not to be: thinkers such as Stuart Hall, a pivotal figure in the first CND who went on to co-found cultural studies, Raymond Williams, that field's *éminence grise* who was also a CND activist, and Thompson with his influential version of "history from below" helped reshape the intellectual landscape.

Although the understanding of social movements has greatly expanded since their time, the advances to which New Left thinkers contributed enable us to look anew at the campaign, beyond its sectional perspective. For example, an analytical approach to the significance of television for the movement may not have been possible without a chain of thinking two of whose starting points were Williams'

(1962) and Hall and Paddy Whannel's (1964) work on communication and popular culture.

The book therefore tells antinuclear history in a particular way. I address its radical discontinuities and discuss it in the context of the social, political and cultural changes in which it has been caught up. Agreeing with Hardt (2023: 249) that "investigating international, transversal, and genealogical connections is a powerful method to begin study of social and political movements", I explore the complex links not only within antinuclear campaigns but also between them and other movements. I also bring the story up to date, exploring why, although CND has played a prominent role in more recent movements, such as those against the Iraq and Gaza wars, the antinuclear campaign itself has not yet been reborn as a mass movement. And while much of the general literature dates from the late twentieth century, I draw on recent research that often casts matters in new lights.

Despite the campaign's continuation in the last three decades, views of it in Britain mostly link it to the Cold War period. Ken Booth (1998: 37) warned that "the Cold War of the books" might "remain in the hands of those for whom the dominant memory will be that of a managed confrontation between ideological enemies in which Right triumphed". I bring together the very different story of the peace movement's contribution to its end, as well as the consequences of its eclipse as we moved into the darker times of the twenty-first century.

Notes on the text

This short history is organized chronologically around the two "movement" periods in which the campaign was most influential, and the chapters on these are longer, in proportion to the number of years they cover, than the others. Based on both primary and secondary sources, it aims to bring together the historical literature with new work on the campaign in the present century.

In order to reduce the intrusion of references into the argument, once a book or article is cited in a chapter, it can be assumed to inform the account thereafter and is not cited again unless the text makes reference to a specific quotation, fact or idea. For the same reason, some easily verified general background information is not referenced. Numbers of demonstrators are based on contemporary estimates and claims and should be treated as indicative rather than definitive.

Some remarks about terminology. "Britain" was used in the twentieth century to refer to both the United Kingdom of Great Britain and Northern Ireland (i.e. the state) and to society within its territory. I confine myself mostly to England, Scotland and Wales, where British nuclear politics has mainly been contested, rather than Northern Ireland, which together with the Republic of Ireland has a very different political and peace history that is mostly beyond the scope of this book. On the questions of naming, I generally follow contemporary usage, so that I reserve "UK" for formal descriptions of the state, at least until I reach the twenty-first century when it has been more widely used.

Similarly, "Communist" refers to Communist parties, their members and the regimes they controlled, not holders of communist views in general; "East" and "West" refer to the Soviet and US-led Cold War blocs, respectively; and "Eastern" and "Western" Europe refer to the European components of those blocs rather than eastern and western Europe in a general geographical sense.

1

Ban the bomb, 1952–63

On 17 February 1958, 5,000 people crammed into Central Hall, Westminster, and three overflow halls for the launch of CND; a thousand were turned away. The following day several hundred supporters sat down in Downing Street.[1] From its first public moment, CND became a mass movement rather than the elite pressure group that most of its founders envisaged. That Easter saw the first Aldermaston march from central London to the atomic weapon research establishment – from the following year, the direction would be reversed.[2] Public meetings were held in many cities and towns, so that by the end of the year there were over 200 local groups, as well as women's, scientists', artists', regional and youth sections. In 1959, CND expanded much further and by 1960 there were 459 groups. In August that year, the conference of the opposition Labour Party adopted unilateral nuclear disarmament as its policy. In two and a half tumultuous years, the new movement had brought nuclear weapons to the forefront in Britain, changing the face of its politics and culture, in some ways for ever.

The crisis of the late 1950s

This outbreak of antinuclear politics was, in retrospect, well prepared. The years after the bombing of Japan saw frightening new international tensions in which Britain was heavily involved, from the 1948–9 Berlin Blockade to the 1950–3 Korean War.[3] The possibility of nuclear war became a part of British life, and in this pre-H-bomb phase, the government actively prepared the public for it: annual publicity campaigns brought half a million people into the Civil Defence Corps by 1955 (Grant 2009: 4–5, 2016: 92–4). Although concern about atomic weapons was expressed by the Peace Pledge Union in 1945 and gradually grew in the late 1940s and early 1950s, the focus of pacifist, liberal and left-wing circles was mostly on other repercussions of the Cold War, such as the reintroduction of conscription in 1948, Britain's involvement in Korea and German rearmament in 1954. Quite a few of those who would warn of nuclear dangers in the late 1950s were content to accept them in the 1940s (Sedgwick 1959: 7).

If opposition to nuclear weapons was slow to develop, this was also because knowledge of Britain's involvement was limited. The Attlee government's 1947 decision to build a British bomb was so secret that it was made by a newly established committee from which senior ministers who had doubts about the idea were excluded (Ponting 1989: 181).

A rapid growth in the United States Air Force (USAF) presence in Britain was also not made public until 1950, although there was awareness in the affected areas. A 1947 US plan envisaged war against the USSR by 1955, with "the loss of Western Europe and the need for a massive atomic strategic air campaign launched from peripheral bases" (Duke 1985: 44–5).[4] That meant eastern England, where the government now allowed the USA to locate its B-29 bombers. Although originally intended as a temporary measure, a cluster of bases came under the control of the USA's new Strategic Air Command in 1948. After the discovery in 1949 that the USSR had obtained the bomb much earlier than foreseen, the first atomic-capable planes arrived, and work began on four new airfields including Greenham Common.[5]

By 1950, therefore, the USA was militarily capable of launching an atomic weapon from Britain (Young 2007: 135). Britain was once again its "Airstrip One" that George Orwell depicted in *Nineteen Eighty-Four* (1949), or as disarmers soon called it, its "unsinkable aircraft carrier".[6] Britain had no control over the US use of its nuclear weapons, and for those in the know, the question of their use "was terrifyingly real", the official historian concluded (Gowing 1974a: 310). Churchill warned in 1951 that "by creating the American atomic base in East Anglia, we have made ourselves the target, and perhaps the bull's eye of a Soviet attack" (Campbell 1986: 34, 11).

The issue came to a head in November 1950, when President Harry Truman said that there had "always been active consideration" of the use of the bomb in Korea. Over 100 MPs complained to Attlee, who was alarmed enough to rush to Washington for assurances about joint decision-making. But despite some window-dressing in parliament on his return, he left office in 1951 without any real constraints on the US use of its bombs (Duke 1985: 102, 106–17; Campbell 1986: 33).[7]

These elite developments began to be reflected in public opposition. In 1952 a small group of pacifists around Hugh Brock, assistant editor of the weekly *Peace News*, organized the first antinuclear protests, sitting down outside the War Office and at the new and unknown Atomic Weapons Research Establishment at Aldermaston.[8] They called their campaign "Operation Gandhi", after the great Indian advocate of non-violence whose *satyagraha* or truth-force method they embraced, and took the name Non-Violent Resistance Group in 1953 (Levy 2021: 14, 43–5, 55); but they gained limited attention.

Broader-based activism began in 1954, after both the USA and USSR had carried out H-bomb tests and as Churchill's government decided to produce its own H-bomb.[9] A Hydrogen Bomb National Campaign was set up with support from Labour MPs, and Dr Donald Soper, who chaired the first meeting, led his Methodist congregation in a protest march through London (Ormrod 1987: 199). Dr George Bell, Bishop of Chichester, known for opposing the area bombing of German cities in 1944–5, called for "the complete prohibition of atomic weapons" (Driver 1964: 187). In Oxford, students campaigned against the tests, while a Third Camp conference chaired by the socialist historian G. D. H. Cole explored Britain's abandoning the bomb to pursue a "positive neutralism" (Banks 1986: 5).[10] The following year, 11 eminent scientists, headed by Albert Einstein and the philosopher Bertrand Russell, launched a manifesto calling for an end to war because of "the risk of universal death" (Pugwash Conferences on Science and World Affairs 1955).

Despite self-censorship by the BBC and the "quality" papers, the sensationalist press increasingly highlighted the bomb's horrors. When, in 1954, crew members from a Japanese fishing boat, the *Lucky Dragon*, died of radiation sickness as a result of a US H-bomb test at Bikini Atoll in the Marshall Islands, the BBC began to reassess its coverage (Bingham 2012; Hill 2018: 61). Testing now became the focus of antinuclear action, and local initiatives in 1955 by members of the Cooperative Women's Guild in the Home Counties led to the formation of a National Council for the Abolition of Nuclear Weapons Tests (NCANWT) in 1956. This gathered an impressive list of sponsors, stimulated over 100 local groups and began to hold protests (Liddington 1991: 185). In 1957, women in NCANWT held a Black Sash protest modelled on women's protests against apartheid.[11]

The increasingly apocalyptic perceptions of nuclear war entering into British culture (Hogg 2012) were laying the basis for a mass campaign.[12] There was also more understanding of how strategic developments made Britain vulnerable. In March 1957, defence minister Duncan Sandys introduced a White Paper that shifted Britain's defence decisively on to a nuclear basis, confirming that "a full scale Soviet [conventional] attack could not be repelled without resort to a massive nuclear bombardment of the sources of power in Russia" (Driver 1964: 52–3), so that Britain would be the first to use nuclear weapons.[13]

In the same month, Prime Minister Harold Macmillan announced, after meeting President Dwight D. Eisenhower in Bermuda, that he had agreed to allow Thor intermediate-range ballistic missiles to be installed in Britain. Like their better-known 1980s successors, ground-launched cruise missiles, these were designed to use Britain as a base to strike the USSR. But unlike cruise missiles, which were supplementary to a "strategic" arsenal of ICBMs, in 1957 the latter were still years from being operational.[14] Thors would therefore be the cutting edge of a US nuclear attack and their deployment from 1958 to 1963 was Britain's highest-profile role in its nuclear war preparations.[15] Although they were to be manned by British troops, who alone were supposed to fire them, Thor warheads remained under US control. Many were not reassured by Macmillan's claim that there would be joint decisions on launching.

Rising concern produced a resolution at the 1957 Labour Party conference calling on the next Labour government to unilaterally refuse to test, manufacture or use nuclear weapons. In response Aneurin Bevan, for the leadership, said that unilateralism "is not statesmanship – it is emotional spasm", and would send a British foreign secretary "naked into the international conference chamber". Bevan – celebrated today as the founder of the National Health Service in 1948 – was the undisputed leader of the party's left and had supported unilateral disarmament up to the conference. His aggressive reversal, in pursuit of a *modus vivendi* with the party's leader Hugh Gaitskell, shocked the left, provoking the novelist, broadcaster and campaigner J. B. Priestley (1957) to pen an article in the *New Statesman* calling on Britain to take a moral lead and renounce nuclear weapons. The magazine was overwhelmed with mail, and its editor, Kingsley Martin, helped bring CND's founders together in early 1958 (Taylor 1988: 102–6).

Meanwhile, the Gandhian direct actionists had escalated their campaign. A Quaker from Malvern, Harold Steele, travelled to Japan in early 1957 in an attempt to enter the area of British H-bomb tests at Christmas Island (the first was carried out in May), and the committee that convened to support him soon became the Direct Action Committee Against Nuclear War (DAC). By November, it was preparing an ambitious 50-mile march from London to Aldermaston at Easter 1958 (Maclellan 2017; Levy 2021: 65–8).[16]

These developments all demonstrated that an antinuclear network with a growing social base, the essential condition for the emergence of a movement, was forming. However, there were also broader forces at work. Despite the social reforms of the 1945–51 Labour government, in many ways the British state remained authoritarian, while in society a conservative "normality" had been restored after the upheavals of the war. But this was starting to change in the mid-1950s: there was growing support for liberal causes such as the National Campaign for the Abolition of Capital Punishment, in which some of CND's founders were involved, and the beginnings of a cultural shift, widely recognized after the opening of John Osborne's play *Look Back in Anger* in 1956. Even gender attitudes were starting to change.

Then, during October–November 1956, the twin Suez and Hungarian crises disrupted the Cold War political divide, in which Labour and Conservative elites supported NATO while the small Communist Party of Great Britain (the CPGB, hereafter referred to as the CP) backed the USSR. In response to the nationalization of the foreign-owned Suez canal by Egypt's nationalist ruler Gamal Abdul Nasser, Prime Minister Anthony Eden involved Britain with France and Israel in an invasion that the USA disowned. Opposition to it united the Labour Party: Gaitskell called it "an act of disastrous folly whose tragic consequences we shall regret for years" and successfully demanded an unprecedented right of reply to Eden on television. People who would soon play important roles in CND, such as the Labour politician Michael Foot and the historian A. J. P. Taylor, appeared in novel, passionate debates on TV discussion programmes, while pacifists led by Soper appealed for civil disobedience in the form of a refusal to fight or to supply "this dreadful blunder" (Cadogan 1972: 165).

Suez aroused the social constituencies that would soon constitute the backbone of CND to demonstrate en masse in Trafalgar Square. Christopher Driver (1964: 32) recalled that, "amid the leaping emigration figures and the reports that 50 per cent of University reserves would refuse recall to the colours, it could be seen that nothing – political alignments, attitudes to authority, acceptance of war as a political last resort – could ever be quite the same again. And when the immediate fury over Suez had died down … the sap began to rise in [the] burgeoning popular movement for nuclear disarmament," which had been temporally eclipsed.

The Soviet invasion of Hungary, one of its satellite states, which overthrew a reforming, neutralist Communist government and suppressed the revolution its intervention sparked, was equally important for the emerging movement. This undermined the Stalinist domination of the British left and allowed it to escape Cold War politics, while moving people to support Hungarian refugees.[17] E. P. Thompson, who would play a significant role in the first wave of antinuclear politics and help initiate the second, had been involved as a Communist in the Yorkshire Peace Committee. In July 1956, he and his fellow-historian John Saville set up *The Reasoner* as an oppositional journal within the CP; after Hungary, they left the CP and started *The New Reasoner*, which soon raised the nuclear issue. Meanwhile student activists in Oxford established *Universities and Left Review*. In 1960, these merged to create *New Left Review* and a political current, the New Left, which played an outsized role in CND.

The movement gathers pace, 1958–60

Stuart Hall, the combined *Review*'s first editor, would later say that the twin crises symbolized "the break-up of the political Ice Age" (2010: 177), and 1956 has become the key year around which narratives of postwar Britain are plotted. Michael Randle, the young activist who was co-organizing the Aldermaston march, would later comment that after Suez and Hungary, the context of antinuclear activism changed utterly (Levy 2021: 68). Indeed, the emergence of the antinuclear movement marked an early beginning of the "long 1960s", which culminated in the revolutionary year of 1968 (Widgery 1976; Marwick 2005). Britain set much of the pace of change during the first half of this period but not in its "revolutionary" conclusion in 1968. However, the uniqueness of British conditions can be overstated: in France, opposition to the Algerian War laid the foundations for a parallel radicalization. Even the antinuclear movement was not a uniquely British invention: the West German Kampagne Kampf den Atomtod (Fight Nuclear Death) was founded in March 1958, at the same time as CND, and showed a similar combination of national and internationalist goals (Nehring 2011).

Although the DAC believed in nonviolent revolution, CND's founders were far from being revolutionaries. Many of the greatest in the liberal-left intellectual establishment were among the 50 who met in January 1958 in the London flat of Canon John Collins – a veteran campaigner who had helped found Christian Action, War on Want and the Defence and Aid Fund for Southern Africa – to set up an executive for the new campaign. This elected him as chair and Peggy Duff – an equally indomitable activist with a history in Labour politics, the anti-hanging campaign and NCANWT (which soon merged into CND) – as organizing secretary. Russell, then 85, a veteran of the anti-conscription movement in the First World War, became president. These would be pivotal figures in the campaign's first wave.

The executive decided that CND would not be a membership organization, attempted to co-opt the DAC and reluctantly embraced the Aldermaston march. Yet the DAC resisted co-option; between them and CND's founders there was a gulf "not merely of tactics and ideology but of age, background and political experience" (Driver 1964: 49). The DAC opposed war in general; the CND leadership restricted their outrage to the bomb. The DAC aimed to rouse public opinion through dramatic actions; the CND executive "was closer to the associational world of Edwardian England than to the forms of organization that dominated the student protests of the later 1960s", Holger Nehring argues, and some members even showed "outright disgust at social-movement politics" (2011: 132, 134). The executive believed that the Parliamentary Labour Party was the vehicle for achieving their aims, and since Labour's hegemony over organized centre-left opinion was near-total – it was as much complemented as challenged by the CP's influence in some affiliated trade unions – it made sense to try to make Labour a unilateralist party. The executive's views are well represented in David Boulton's (misnamed) collection, *Voices from the Crowd* (1964).

Initially these differences remained largely out of public view. CND's executive committed it to the radical unilateralist view that Britain should "renounce unconditionally the use or production of nuclear weapons and refuse to allow their use by others in her defence", as well as seek multilateral negotiations, which led to the severing of relations with the United Nations Association, which had supported NCANWT (Taylor 1988: 28). At the Central Hall launch, the rhetoric was militant and uncompromising. In response to Sandys' first-strike doctrine, A. J. P. Taylor laid out the full consequences of an H-bomb explosion, stirring his audience by suggesting that they shout "Murderers" whenever cabinet ministers spoke, just as the Suffragettes had shouted "Votes for Women" at their predecessors earlier in the century (Taylor 1988: 26–7; Driver 1964: 52–3).

In these early months, CND rode a wave of public shock about the nuclear threat. The Aldermaston March at Easter 1958, organized by the DAC (especially its chair, Brock, secretary, Pat Arrowsmith, and Randle) saw the first use of the nuclear disarmament symbol, based on the composite semaphore signal for the letters N and D, which its designer Gerald Holtom offered them a few weeks earlier (Holtom 2022: 36–50). The DAC took its stewarding seriously, tasking Randle with preventing Communist sympathizers from singing pro-Soviet songs in case the press got the wrong idea (Levy 2021: 70, 74). The CND executive was "somewhat nonplussed" by the march's success but had no alternative but to give its backing to further protests. If the early marches were modestly sized compared to those that came later, they were considered "very large by the standards of the time … in an age when most people prefer this sort of thing on their television sets" (Driver 1964: 59).

In the month of CND's launch, the government formally agreed to host the Thor missiles. Unlike cruise missiles, which would be concentrated at two bases, 60 Thors were to be distributed across 20 sites in eastern England with special Royal Air Force (RAF) squadrons operating three each. The first was formed at Feltwell, Norfolk, in September 1958 and soon missiles were flown in, but a visiting US senator found them stored in sheds "with no protection of any kind" (Duke 1985: 214). The sites were supposed to be secret, but the Cambridge left soon discovered the one at Mepal, Cambridgeshire. The Labour Party and Trades Council organized a march from Ely to the base, despite an attempt by the Ministry of Defence to get it called off since, under the

Official Secrets Act, the site did not exist. Peter Cadogan, a participant, later argued that this action "quite destroyed the security curtain" (1972: 167–8).

The DAC now focused its campaign on another base under construction at North Pickenham, Norfolk, and controversially tried to obstruct lorries entering and the operation of a massive concrete mixer; 45 were arrested and tried. They gained extensive publicity with these dramatic actions, which were a turning point in relations between the movement and the media. Yet even the sympathetic Labour MP Stephen Swingler criticized "pacifists making martyrs of themselves" and "adopting IRA tactics", forcing the DAC's April Carter to distinguish the group's non-violent obstruction from violence to either people or property (Hill 2018: 190–206; Levy 2021: 87–9). The DAC extended its campaign to Stevenage, where the Blue Streak missile was being produced, and Arrowsmith and Randle persuaded building workers to stage a token strike and demonstrate in the town centre (Randle 1987: 135).

The DAC's relations with CND became strained, worsening further early in 1959 when they ran a Voters Veto campaign during a Norfolk by-election, urging people not to vote for anti-unilateralist candidates, which annoyed CND-backing Labour politicians – a tactical error in Randle's later view (1987: 156). CND's leaders had to threaten to resign en masse to prevent a motion approving the North Pickenham civil disobedience being passed at its National Council, which only reluctantly approved a second Aldermaston March at Easter 1959 (Bulkeley *et al.* 1981). These disagreements anticipated more serious rifts to come, but for a time the urgency of the issue and the optimism and enthusiasm of the new movement mostly pulled CND together, especially in the localities.

After a successful second March,[18] the movement lost momentum as an election loomed and drew very little attention during the actual campaign in October 1959 (Butler & Rose 1960: 63). Although Macmillan arranged an unprecedented televised fireside chat with Eisenhower to shore up his defence credentials (Cohen 2019: 94–5), the nuclear issue played only a small role, and his victory was largely based on the new affluence: he had earlier claimed that most people had "never had it so good".[19] The movement was disheartened by the Tory majority of 100 but soon regained its strength, with an unprecedentedly large Aldermaston march in 1960. CND also radicalized further, as its 1960 conference ruled participation in direct action compatible with membership and committed it to oppose Britain's membership of NATO.

CND now grew in tandem with the Anti-Apartheid Movement, formed in 1959, which gained support from the same social constituencies; there was a large demonstration in Trafalgar Square, organized by the Labour Party, after the Sharpeville massacre in 1960. Opposition to "racialism" and "colour bars" was also growing, reflecting the growing importance of anticolonial resistance for British dissent (Gopal 2020: 395–436). One of CND's founders was Fenner Brockway MP, the "Member for Africa" who had championed Kenyans against the British repression of the Mau Mau insurgency and steered the Movement for Colonial Freedom from 1954. A short-lived but influential Campaign Against Racial Discrimination, of which CND activist Dr David Pitt was chair, was also established, in 1964 (Elias 2020: 293–5).

The nuclear context was shifting. In March 1960, Macmillan cancelled Blue Streak and committed instead to buy the Skybolt missile system from the USA. This development undermined not only the claim for the "independence" of Britain's nuclear systems but also the idea that British disarmament, in isolation, could make a major difference (Freedman 1980: 8–9, 15). In return for Skybolts, the USA would use Holy Loch, on the west coast of Scotland, to house its nuclear-armed Polaris submarines, which would replace the Thor missiles but without their dual keys. The controversy over Britain's centrality to US nuclear preparations soon re-emerged when the shooting down of a US U2 spy plane over the USSR, which caused a major Cold War crisis in May 1960, was followed by the downing of a second plane that had taken off from Brize Norton in Oxfordshire (Duke 1985: 220–3).[20]

Macmillan kept the Polaris deal secret until November 1960, so these changes did not register in the Labour Party when the conflict over unilateralism came to a head at its Scarborough conference in October. The unilateralists had already been strong at the 1958 conference, but trade union block votes (which vastly outweighed those of constituency parties) defeated their resolution. In 1959 key unions, led by Frank Cousins of the Transport and General Workers Union, swung behind unilateralism and over a third of all resolutions at the Trades Union Congress supported it; but because of the election there was no Labour conference that autumn. By the 1960 gathering, sufficient block votes were mandated for two unilateralist motions to be virtually guaranteed success, and these were duly adopted in the teeth of fierce opposition from the party leadership. "In the aftermath of the election defeat", Richard Taylor comments, "Gaitskell could not stem the tide of revolt." However, nobody in CND "had a clue as to what to do with the victory", Stuart Hall later told Taylor (1987a: 111, 115).

Indeed, CND's success soon proved pyrrhic. The votes were predetermined, but in an emotive speech, Gaitskell presented unilateralism as a challenge to his leadership, vowing to "fight and fight and fight again to save the Party we love". His speech was also well calibrated: his original commitment to a British bomb had been exposed by the Blue Streak decision, but he took the opportunity to shift his ground, attacking unilateralism for entailing NATO withdrawal, even if neither the conference motions nor the proposing speeches recommended this. Ultimately his determination proved decisive: his position was reinforced by a new anti-unilateralist pressure group led by right-wing Labour MPs, the Campaign for Democratic Socialism, and at the 1961 conference in Blackpool, five of the six biggest unions fell in line in order not to split the party before the next election.

The 1960 victory resulted chiefly from the commitments of some union leaders. Although CND supporters were informally encouraged to join local Labour parties to influence its policy, not enough had done so (many were not "political") and around two-thirds of constituency parties voted with the leadership. Ironically, the effects of CND's "entrism" may have been greater in 1961, since the constituencies actually moved in its direction, as they continued to do in 1962 and 1963 when it was too late (I owe this hypothesis to Nigel Young, one of the entrists).

The civil disobedience campaign, 1960–2

This reversal consigned the CND leadership's orientation to near-irrelevance for almost two decades. Following it, leading Labour unilateralists such as Michael Foot supported compromise policies while some rank-and-file CNDers who had joined the party left it. The antinuclear movement as a whole moved in radically different directions.

Some experimented (unsuccessfully) with independent antinuclear candidates through an Independent Nuclear Disarmament Election

Committee, which further antagonized the Labour left. CND also intervened strongly, but without a candidate, in the Orpington by-election in March 1962, holding a public meeting and delivering a manifesto written by the journalist James Cameron to every house (*Sanity* 1962, March: 4). The H-bomb was a "hot topic" in the campaign and although the victorious Liberal candidate, Eric Lubbock, was not a unilateralist, he criticized Britain's bomb and was a vehicle for CND-inclined voters to help oust the Conservatives, in a victory that launched the "Liberal revival" (Membery 2021: 161–3, 168–9).

A more substantial section moved in an extraparliamentary direction. In the spring of 1960, an American postgraduate student at the London School of Economics, Ralph Schoenman, had begun to persuade some DAC and New Left activists of the need for a new mass civil disobedience campaign, as he put it the following year, to "put the government in the position of either jailing thousands of people or abdicating" (Taylor 1988: 206). He then approached Russell and together they prepared to establish the new group. As Collins became aware of the plans – just before the crucial Labour conference vote – there were acrimonious exchanges between him and Russell, leading to the latter's resignation as CND president.

On 22 October 1960, the Committee of 100 was established, with Russell now as its president, including a younger, more avant-garde set of intellectuals such as the filmmaker Lindsay Anderson, novelist John Braine, critics John Berger and George Melly and the playwrights John Arden, Shelagh Delaney, John Osborne and Arnold Wesker, as well as all but two members of the DAC. Indeed, the Gandhian group effectively merged into it, although it continued to act independently into 1961; Randle, who had taken over as DAC chair, became the Committee's secretary.[21] As well as developing different methods of action, the Committee involved an English version of the participatory democracy that was emerging in the US civil rights movement, in contrast to the formalistic meetings of CND (Young 1977: 408 n116).

The formation of the Committee caused a permanent rift with the leadership of CND. However, Peggy Duff later commented: "the ordinary rank and file people just didn't want to have to choose between Canon Collins and Russell … for them it was all part of the campaign against nuclear weapons. Those who could sit, sat, and those who couldn't went along and cheered them. And everybody marched. And

Bertrand Russell sits down at the Committee of 100 demonstration, February 1961

Source: Sally and Richard Greenhill / Alamy Stock Photo.

the relationship at grass roots level was always pretty good. It was always at the top that they fought" (Taylor 1988: 63).

The Committee's campaign began with a sit-down of thousands in Whitehall on 18 February 1961, just three years after CND's Central Hall launch. Russell attached a declaration to the door of the Ministry of Defence, and when the police displayed "gentle, almost Gandhian characteristics", he commented: "We do not want forever to be tolerated by the police. Our movement depends for its success on immense public opinion and we cannot create that unless we rouse the authorities to more action than they took yesterday" (Taylor 1988: 200).

But the real action was at Holy Loch, where *Proteus*, the US Polaris submarine depot ship, arrived the same day (Steven 2008: 59). A six-week march from London that mobilized churches, trade unions and Quaker meetings along the way was reinforced by large numbers of Scots. Around 4,000 people sat down and DAC kayakers attempted to board the depot ship for the submarines.[22] The anti-Polaris campaign was "the nearest to major political success that CND ever got", Nigel Young later argued, but the CND leadership "in a post-Scarborough paralysis, almost entirely failed to respond" (1977: 418 n56).[23] It was a decisive moment for the movement's resonance in Scotland: as Janey and Norman Buchan (1983: 52) put it: "What had been a terrifying abstract was now only too real, visibly menacing. We had a particular target which was of immediate and direct relevance."

Russell's wish for a vigorous official response was soon fulfilled. In summer 1961 tension between the USSR and the West over Berlin, culminating in the East German construction of the wall dividing the city, increased the credibility of the Committee of 100's message of urgency. As it planned further demonstrations in September in London and at Holy Loch, the authorities pre-emptively took 37 of its members to court, of whom 32 – including the aged Russell – were imprisoned for refusing to be bound over to keep the peace.

It seemed as though someone in Whitehall had decided to give Russell a martyr's crown. He used the court to claim that it was "a profound and inescapable duty to make the facts known and thereby save a thousand million lives. … Non-violent civil disobedience was forced upon us by the fact that it was more fully reported than other methods of making the facts known, and that caused people to ask what had induced us to adopt such a course of action" (Taylor 1988: 223). His statement from prison posed the nuclear threat in all its starkness: "Our ruined, lifeless planet will continue for countless ages to circle aimlessly around the sun, unredeemed by the joys and loves, the occasional wisdom and the power to create beauty which have given value to human life. It is for seeking to prevent this that we are in prison" (Russell 2009 [1967]: 620).

The Committee's demonstrations became more militant. At Easter 1961, a section led by Schoenman took off from the Aldermaston march to sit down outside the US embassy in Grosvenor Square, and after arrests were made fought something approaching a brief pitched battle with the police outside West End Central police station (Taylor 1988: 201). This infuriated Collins, who condemned it on behalf of CND.[24]

The Committee's London demonstration on 17 September 1961, at a moment of high public alarm because of the Berlin Wall and US and Soviet resumptions of H-bomb tests, was its largest, estimated at 12,000, and uniquely ITV set aside most of the afternoon for live coverage (Carroll 2010: 175 n11; Randle 1987: 138). The crowd in Trafalgar Square – where the government had unprecedentedly refused permission for a rally – tried to break through police cordons, with jeering, jostling and isolated fighting; there were allegations of police assault. There were 1,314 arrests and the episode marked, Taylor argues, "the final break between the Gandhian pacifist practice of the DAC vis-à-vis the police, and the new militancy of the Committee of 100 with its mass resistance perspective" (1988: 226–7).

After this the Committee felt strong enough to plan an ambitious series of mass actions designed to temporarily immobilize key airbases, as well as in regional cities, in December 1961. As these approached, protestors bound for the USAF base at Wethersfield, Essex, the main target, found that the coaches that were to have taken them had been cancelled. The Committee's offices were raided and Randle and five other key workers arrested and charged under the Official Secrets Act. The state had taken the movement's measure and was determined to stop its advance.

Although protestors sat down in six places and 848 were arrested, the Committee did not immobilize any airbase. Most agreed it had failed, and the bubble of enthusiasm underlying its expansion burst. It became preoccupied with an internal reorganization and (having rejected Arrowsmith's proposal to return to Wethersfield) held a mass sit-down in central London in March 1962. "Nobody could call the demonstration a failure," *Peace News* commented, "[y]et there was something missing in the atmosphere … a certain coldness, a lack of creative feeling"; civil disobedience had almost become "a ritualized process akin to the later Aldermaston marches" (Taylor 1988: 240). The hope of building a mass nonviolent movement that would seriously disrupt the state disappeared, and in Cadogan's view the Committee "found itself in the fatal position of 'looking round for issues' round which to maintain a movement on a scale matched to the crises" (1972: 171).

The Committee's protests led to legal cases and prison sentences, and some activists became ingenious barrack-room lawyers. But the Official Secrets trial that began on 12 February 1962 was of a new order, leading to 12- to 18-month sentences for the six arrested over Wethersfield.[25] The defendants compared the nuclear threat to the Nazis' extermination of the Jews, citing the judge in the trial of the Holocaust organizer Adolf Eichmann, in Israel the previous year. Randle was able to explain why he believed there was a moral duty to break certain laws in order to prevent such acts, and Pat Pottle (who conducted his own defence) got Air Commodore Graham Magill, the Air Ministry's director of operations, to admit that if necessary he would press a button knowing that it would annihilate millions of people (Driver 1964: 162–4; Levy 2021: 134–9).

Randle later claimed that this gave the Committee the "moral and political edge" (1987: 140), but the trial's net effect was negative. The movement lost several leaders for a sustained period, the sentences were a serious deterrent to further disobedience and the outcome exposed the inadequacy of direct action alone, at least on the scale that was then possible, for seriously challenging the state. The Committee had outpaced CND in 1961 but now it too was at an impasse.[26]

The Cuban Missile Crisis and movement decline, 1962–4

In October 1962, the superpowers faced off over the installation of Soviet nuclear missiles in Cuba, within easy striking distance of the USA.[27] Eventually the Soviet leader, Nikita Khrushchev, ordered a retreat while President John Kennedy also opted for a negotiated solution. Yet for a week – in the first "televisual" world emergency (Cohen 2019: 151) – it seemed as though the predicted nuclear holocaust was imminent, and the disarmament movement, in common with many across the world, held its breath. People experienced the crisis "in their whole being", Randle recalled, leaving London in order to be in the countryside when the bombs fell or deciding to be with their loved ones (Levy 2021: 258). Amid relief at the outcome, opponents suggested that public opinion had been excessively influenced by the movement's "scaremongering";

yet the classic account of the crisis calls it "the defining event of the nuclear age and the most dangerous moment in recorded history" (Allison & Zelikow 1999: 1).

Cuba exposed the claim that the "independent deterrent" gave Britain influence, but it also threw the movement into disarray.[28] Russell fired off telegrams to the two leaders, laying more of the blame on the USA, but disarmers were divided on that issue. Even if the movement had been proved right about the nuclear danger, Cuba still created a feeling of powerlessness and irrelevance. Some provincial demonstrations had a spontaneity that they had lost in the capital, but with the resolution of the crisis the sense of urgency evaporated, marking for many the beginning of CND's decline (Driver 1964: 141, 147–8). The sense that after all the nuclear powers *could* manage their extraordinarily destructive weapons was reinforced in 1963 when the USA, USSR and UK signed the Partial Test Ban Treaty and a secure "hotline" between the White House and the Kremlin was established.

The crisis prompted a shift in CND policy. While still advocating the renunciation of British nuclear weapons, tests and bases, its new *Steps Towards Peace*, written by Stuart Hall (2017 [1962]), gave prominence to disengagement in central Europe, withdrawal of all nuclear weapons to the USA and USSR and the establishment of "nuclear-free zones". These ideas, which anticipated some themes of the 1980s movement, were accepted by the leadership partly because they appeared to be part of a process of reconverting the mass movement to a pressure group. But they were rejected by many members for whom unilateralism was "a principle and not merely a tactic" (Taylor 1988: 93–4). The conflict over the proposals induced depression in the movement and Hall later told Taylor that he regretted them. The Committee of 100, which abandoned its original London-centric model for decentralized regional committees, was also divided, as some activists published a call for more radical action, *Beyond Counting Arses*, in early 1963 (Carroll 2010: 162–4).

Yet the movement was by no means finished. Its ideas were still spreading in many local areas, as the number of CND groups topped 900, and even into the factories, where Arrowsmith worked with shop stewards to organize industrial workers against the bomb, with modest success. In January 1963, a major nonaligned peace conference was held in Oxford, organized by Peggy Duff. The Soviet-backed World Peace Council had been invited to observe it but was uninvited after delegates

from several countries warned they would not attend if its representatives were permitted to take part. Soviet delegates were stranded in
their London hotel while shuttle negotiations with Oxford continued,
ultimately unsuccessfully. The conference formed an International
Confederation for Disarmament and Peace, for which Duff would later
work after leaving CND. The European Federation Against Nuclear
Arms, which War Resisters International had helped set up in 1959,
was subsumed into the new body.

Meanwhile, two young air force technicians, Mike McKenna and
Ted Parker, called in *Peace News* (1 February 1963) for the formation
of a "forces CND"; they were court-martialled, given eight months
in military prison and discharged (Parker 2021: 17–53). Many more
activists campaigned over the impossibility of effective civil defence
against nuclear weapons: the days when a thick layer of rescue services
surrounded the core goal of protecting state administration had gone.
The Home Office (1963) put on sale a 9d (4p) booklet, *Advising the
Householder on Protection against Nuclear Attack,* showing how to build
an indoor fallout shelter, how to put together a survival pack and what
to do if a warning sounded. NATO's Fallex 62 simulation had predicted
that nuclear war would leave 15 million dead in Britain, and CND now
launched Fallex 63, which showed the effect of nuclear attacks on 60
military targets and cities. A huge amount of local work made it a very
effective campaign.

The movement's last big impact in 1963 further exposed government
preparations for the aftermath of nuclear war. A Spies for Peace group,
originating in the radical element of the Committee of 100, published
full details of the government's plans for Regional Seats of Government
(RSGs) to administer the country (Carroll 2010; Walter 2023: 123–37).[29]
They then targeted the RSG at Warren Row near Reading and, finding
it unlocked, took papers from that they used as a basis for a pamphlet,
Danger! Official Secret! RSG-6, which they distributed on the year's huge
Aldermaston march. A demonstration veered from the march towards
Warren Row, and the actor Vanessa Redgrave gave its location to 80,000
people from the platform at the final rally. The CND leadership had
lost control of the march to the more anarchic movement fostered by
the Committee, and it was also losing its Labour support: with an election due in 1964, few MPs took part and several withdrew from CND's
National Council.[30]

Police guard an entrance to RSG6 in Berkshire, where nuclear disarmament demonstrators protest, 15 April 1963.

Source: PA Images / Alamy Stock Photo.

Spies for Peace had an impact across the country and the report was duplicated in many localities. David Cowell, in a communication with the author, remembers a demonstration at the RSG at Dover Castle, "a very civilized occupation of the entrance, with one policeman in attendance". Sheila Rowbotham was at her friends' house in Oxford when a man knocked on the door: "convinced this was a plain-clothes policeman, I was non-committal when he asked for copies of 'Spies for Peace'. To my great chagrin, he turned out to be a left-wing trade unionist who wanted to give them out at the Cowley car plant, where he worked" (2000: 67).

The Committee had also been losing its broad base, with the "big names" including Russell withdrawing; the initiative now lay with DAC veterans, anarchists and the libertarian-Marxist Solidarity group. It briefly took on a new lease of life following a protest against the visit of King Paul and Queen Frederica of Greece in July 1963, after the assassination of a prominent peace activist and MP, Grigoris Lambrakis. Committee activists were again arrested and jailed, but this time one, the cartoonist Donald Rooum, was able to show that a brick had been planted on him in West End Central police station, resulting in four officers being charged with conspiracy to pervert the course of justice. The linkage of democratic issues and antinuclear politics anticipated the direction that the revived movement would take in the 1980s, but it was not appreciated by CND purists who saw it as a weakening of the campaign's focus (Taylor 1988: 267–8; Levy 2021: 151–3). But by this stage, it was widely recognized that the movement was declining.

Analysing the mass movement

The first mass antinuclear movement spanned six full years, from early 1958 to late 1963, a period of maximum Cold War tension and Britain's greatest prominence in US war preparations – exactly the period when Thor missiles were deployed in England. These years of intense activism had huge impacts. As the official nuclear historian acknowledges, both Labour and Conservative governments had "wished to conceal information and avoid publicity at all costs" (Gowing 1974b: 126), but the movement forced nuclear issues into the open, creating an educated minority public opinion. Indeed, Hill (2018: 49) even argues that the movement can be defined as an "information ecology", an alternative conduit of information, which was the primary "currency" of its politics. Its campaign around civil defence was a success: government planning "largely become a laughing stock" and was forced into greater secrecy (Grant 2009: 136, 146, 149). There was, moreover, majority public support for some of the movement's secondary aims, such as halting atmospheric testing, not introducing Polaris and preventing proliferation. Opinion in Britain and elsewhere was certainly a factor in the Test Ban Treaty.

However, it is going too far to say that "the movement became a victim of its own success" (Wittner 2009: 112): no section of the movement believed that it had achieved its goals. Polling suggested that it had increased support for unilateralism but never to more than a third of voters. Its support was deep but not wide enough. Driver (1964: 236) estimated that around half a million people (1 per cent of the population) were involved. While this seems low – allowing for the turnover of people from day to day as well as year to year, the Aldermaston marches alone may have attracted that number, while more must have attended local meetings and protests – the movement was certainly an activist minority, drawn from particular social groups. It had spread across the UK, with a particular resonance in Scotland and Wales, where it contributed to the emergence of the idea of "nations of peace" and the slow emergence of distinctive civic nationalisms (Hill 2016). In Ireland, there were two campaigns (North and South); the main annual public activity of each "was to send representatives on the Aldermaston march" (Prince 2006: 863).

Although manual workers formed the majority of society and CND influenced the manual trades unions, Frank Parkin (1968) showed that they were a small presence in the movement, which represented an expressive "middle-class radicalism", in contrast to the instrumental radicalism of the working class. While the Buchans claimed that "the mobilization of opinion in Scotland was more widely based, more representative of the people in general, and therefore, in a word, more working class in character than the early days of CND elsewhere" (Buchan & Buchan 1983: 52), even there the movement was mainly middle class in character (Hill 2016). Randle concedes that the exclusion of mass working-class support may have been a price the movement paid for the radicalism of its demands and style of action (1987: 151).

Moreover while mass immigration from the Caribbean and the Indian subcontinent peaked during these years, and 1958 saw white riots in Notting Hill and Nottingham, people of colour were almost entirely absent. Stuart Hall, who had come from Jamaica as a student in 1951, was an important figure but even he was only beginning to connect to the Caribbean population in London. While CND-supporting members of the Universities and Left Review Club became involved in community politics in Notting Hill, the campaign as such had little connection to the new minorities (Hall & Schwarz 2018: 257–9; Clark 1972: 178–9). However, in 1959 David Pitt, the Aldermaston march's original medical officer, was Britain's first parliamentary candidate of African origin, with active CND support (Duff 1971: 160; Taylor & Pritchard 1980: 72).

Although for the *Daily Mail*, the 1958 Aldermaston crowd were "mainly middle-class and professional people behaving entirely against the normal tradition of their class" (Driver 1964: 55), the movement was not even supported by the majority of the "middle class" as then understood. Its base was chiefly in a narrower, higher-educated section, particularly those in the welfare and creative professions, as well as, of course, students, especially in the expanding humanities and social sciences. A later sociologist, John Mattausch (1987), would see them as "state-class radicals" who not only *came* from the groups expanded by the postwar growth of the state but whose radicalism *derived* from their experiences of and commitments to its welfare rather than warfare side. Nevertheless, CND reflected a substantial section of the population: between 20 and 25 per cent regularly supported unilateralist positions (Berrington 1989: 21–3).

Anticipating the twenty-first-century realignment in which the much more numerous university-educated became the strongest base for left-wing politics, Parkin saw this group as "a permanent source of potential opposition to certain commonly accepted socio-political values" (1968: 178). They were the natural source of recruits to movements such as CND, their radicalism heightened by the discrepancy between their high educational and relatively low economic statuses. Radicalism was a generational rebellion for some, but many young disarmers were in accord with radical parents. Activism also reflected the cultural radicalization of the late 1950s, as lower-middle-class writers and artists filled the Committee of 100, contrasting with the older higher-status professionals who founded CND.

Women were generally more pro-disarmament than men but were underrepresented in CND; although Duff and Jacquetta Hawkes were very prominent, only in 1964 did it get a female "chairman", Olive Gibbs. There were few women in more than backroom roles in the New Left, whose university element originated in Oxford, which then had few women students (Davison & Gilbert 2020: 142).[31] The Committee, typified by its "angry young men", was also about two-thirds male (Carroll 2011: 166). However, for some women activists its more egalitarian milieu was conducive to political involvement (Carroll 2004), as was the DAC, where Pat Arrowsmith and April Carter played major roles. The

Cooperative women's role in triggering the chain reaction that ended in the formation of CND was written out of the first drafts of the movement's history (Hill 2018: 75). Indeed, what distinguished the movement from earlier peace movements, Jill Liddington argues, was "how marginal women-centred peace activities had become" (1991: 189–90).

In terms of gender (which was not discussed as such at the time), some of the movement's language now seems antiquated. Russell's (1961) Penguin Special was called *Has Man a Future?*, and worse, Collins described CND's energy as "virile" (Driver 1964: 235). But despite this sexism, as it would soon be called, the movement challenged the dominant military masculinity deriving from the world wars (Burkett 2016: 422). Links between women's experiences of CND and the revival of feminism in the late 1960s have been largely neglected, but it represents a missing link in the transition from the conventional gender roles of the immediate postwar period (Wittner 2000: 197).

CND had been set up by middle-aged people and "spawned an incredible number of committees", Duff (1971: 154, 160) complained. There was a lot of hard, repetitive work, summed up by "the old duplicator going thud, thud, thud, through the early hours of the morning". And if the March was the heart of the campaign, its legs were the hundreds of local groups, through which most joined and supported the movement. These not only mobilized for national and regional demonstrations (CND's regions included national councils in Scotland and Wales) and implemented campaigns (as over civil defence) but also organized myriad local meetings, protests and events, often with considerable invention. Although these were well reported in local newspapers – then more influential than today – they have been under-researched.

Yet the movement, in the local groups as well as on the march, was hardly stuffy: it was full of youth and imagination. CND's two largest sections were the university and youth campaigns. CND was the biggest political society in many universities, and Youth CNDers included some young workers and apprentices as well as pupils. Youth CND, which produced the first widely circulated movement newspaper, *Youth against the Bomb*, grew "not through, but in spite of, the adult campaign" (Young 1977: 399 n9). Moreover, the Committee of 100 involved a "different type of protestor", the radical activist who was prepared to face prison (Carroll 2011: 95).

For young people, the movement was a space of freedom, even intoxication. As Driver rather quaintly put it: "The generation of Aldermaston is an emancipated one, and where its parents have not consented to emancipation it emancipated itself, using the money its predecessors never had to buy travel, jazz, and long conversations in coffee bars." A pupil expressed this more colloquially: "You need to get out of yourself, have an urge to express yourself, you gotta prove you're alive and not dead inside in this age of mass culture – for some people it's speed, for some it's religion, for me it's CND" (Driver 1964: 59, 41). The DAC earnestly discussed whether its women should wear trousers and its men grow beards (Levy 2021: 83), and there was even a public school rebellion, although it was very peaceful compared to the one in the 1968 film *If*, directed by Lindsay Anderson. (However, supporters were still in a minority among the young, most of whom still left school at 15. This was the early baby boom generation who in their late middle age, dubbed "boomers", would mostly support Brexit in 2016.)

The movement drew on the youth culture that developed in the mid-1950s among the first generation of teenagers, but this was transformed as first the "jazz revival" and then, via skiffle, the "folk revival" set the tone. The latter, typified by the Ian Campbell Folk Group and later Bob Dylan and Joan Baez, saw folk clubs spreading to most towns, often in tandem with local CND groups (Campbell 1983: 116; Brocken 2003; Parker 2021: 66–8). "Protest songs" such as Ewan MacColl's "The H-Bomb's Thunder" inspired the March: "Men and women, stand together / Do not heed the men of war / Make your minds up now or never / Ban the bomb for evermore" (Widgery 1976: 99). In 1962–3, the irreverence of television's *That Was the Week That Was* also chimed with CND.

For the young, it was the movement's indiscipline and sometimes carnivalistic atmosphere that was attractive. The march, with the camaraderie of sharing crowded floors in local halls and singing over 50 miles and several days, was widely felt to be a new type of protest, which was copied in scores of countries. Watching it in 1958, the American pacifist Bayard Rustin – who had links with the DAC activists and was one of the speakers in Trafalgar Square – is reported to have kept saying: "All these young people, it's unbelievable" (Driver 1964: 55). He would go on to organize the 1963 civil rights march in Washington, DC, at which Martin Luther King proclaimed: "I have a dream".

Aldermaston was by no means the only march – in 1960 there was one from Edinburgh to London and another, coast-to-coast, from Liverpool to Withernsea, East Yorkshire, and there were many local efforts – and not all protests were marches. Some were outside nuclear sites such as the Polaris base and East Anglian air bases. Others included "bombing" towns with information on the effects of a nuclear weapon dropped on their centres. A protest subculture developed, with "new transactions of culture and politics that were to redefine the very nature of 'protest' itself" (Hill 2018: 148–9). The combination of many different styles, ideas and personalities fostered tolerance, although one supporter told a conference: "In CND I have to mix with so many odd people that the sooner we ban the bomb the better" (Duff 1971: 126).

The new type of activism reinforced the movement's dominant moral driver. Most of it, Duff (1971: 129–31) concluded, "was absolutist and compulsive". Many really believed that a nuclear war could start any minute, so the movement "wanted to get rid of nuclear weapons, all of them. It wanted to do it very quickly. This explains the way it behaved. It was in a tremendous hurry." But most were also "basically very British, conservative and rather naive. They thought banning the bomb was a fairly simple matter and they never recognized the revolution in British politics it required. They wanted to get rid of the bomb, leave NATO and abandon the American alliance without upsetting the pattern of life in Sutton, Totnes, or Greenwich, SE3."

Civil disobedience often engaged people in a way that was similar to the March but it also challenged this attitude. While Russell backed it mainly for its publicity value, for the DAC activists it had more intrinsic value: as Alan Lovell explained, they aimed to make an emotional impact and "attack [the] deep-rooted beliefs and attitudes in people" (Whannel & Hall 1961: 19). This was all the more true as the Committee of 100 moved from obstructing only targets such as launch sites, as Russell advocated, to embrace a wider range of confrontations.

The importance of emotion made it difficult, however, to turn the movement into a disciplined, strategically driven collectivity. Unilateralism became "a sort of religion, almost an ideology", even "a way of life", rather than unilateralists being "multilateralists who meant it" as Hawkes put it (Duff 1971: 203–4). Yearly, Duff reflected, "we saw at the end of the march the image of failure to come: the failure of CND to create something stronger, more enduring and victorious … the failure of politics in Britain to change. … It wanted a revolution – and there were times … when the smell of revolution was in the air, insistent, compulsive and heady, like Paris in May 1968." The movement

> frightened its own leadership, scared the politicians stiff, and ranged against itself all the careful, unimaginative, conservative forces of all the establishments, including its own. They fought it, and fought it, and fought it again, and beat it. It didn't last. How could it? It came up against all the hard inanities and harsh realities of politics. It had no programme, no ideology, no plans for alternative policies, let alone alternative governments.
>
> (Duff 1971: 143)

The movement and the media

It was largely through the changing mass media that the movement educated the public. It emerged in the last years of a broad liberal and left-wing national press: sympathetic newspapers were more numerous than they would later be, including the liberal *News Chronicle* (before it closed in 1960), the Labour *Daily Herald* (before it became the *Sun* in 1964), the Cooperative Sunday *Reynold's News* (which closed in 1967), the Communist *Daily Worker* (which became the *Morning Star* in 1966) and of course the *Guardian* (which dropped "Manchester" from its name in 1959). Three weeklies, *Peace News*, the *New Statesman* and the Labour-left *Tribune* for which Duff had worked also played supportive roles. Therefore, although Hill (2018: 89) is right to highlight the successive closures in the left-wing press, most of these occurred after the movement had peaked, not "as it blossomed".

Even if the other, mostly Conservative, papers (the majority in terms of circulation) were largely hostile, the movement often received substantial coverage. Its negative tenor may have undermined the movement's appeal – "yearly we read the press with impotent fury", Duff (1971: 142) complained – but it still alerted potential supporters to campaign activities. However, neither the press nor BBC radio, hitherto the other national news medium, was the movement's prime arena. This was the time when television finally took off in Britain: set ownership grew massively with the coronation of Queen Elizabeth II in 1953 and was further boosted by the launching of a second channel, ITV, in 1955.

BBC television initially chose to educate the public about nuclear weapons through current affairs and lectures rather than film; its broadcasts seemed contrived in favour of the government and tended to camouflage and minimize nuclear dangers (Hill 2018: 63). Yet television soon served to empower radical action by enabling ordinary citizens to assess political issues through a visual medium. Suez accelerated the transformation of news broadcasting, and Independent Television News led the way in the effective reconciliation of news and picture values into a single programme. ITV, especially the Manchester-based Granada, was also less deferential towards the government.

In this context, mobilizing a mass movement was contingent on coordinating activities with news broadcasting. By 1958, Hill judges, the state's "monopoly of information" about violence – as important as the monopoly of violence itself – had been broken, leaving the stage set for a news media contest over nuclear information (2018: 77). CND and the Committee of 100, supported by many journalists and artists, were well-positioned to take advantage of the possibilities. An influential cross-section was emerging between middle-class radicalism and the media, creating an "infrastructure of dissent" that was to shape media and movements throughout the 1960s.

Macmillan was worried about this development. As early as March 1958, he asked his minister of information, Charles Hill, to counter CND, mobilize church and intellectual support and kill pro-CND stories. The government tried to characterize CND as Communist but this was largely unsuccessful, not least because the party was initially lukewarm towards it. Meanwhile, the new television drama included plays about nuclear war by CND supporters such as J. B. Priestley and Marghanita Laski, which Mervyn Jones believed "probably woke up more people than all the meetings put together" (Hill 2018: 103).

The DAC, with their North Pickenham protests, were the first to fully recognize the possibilities of the relationship between the methods of protest and media coverage. They stressed action's power to communicate and mobilize, and their campaign, at scale and over weeks, represented a new, even alien departure for the press and police as well as protestors. The success of direct action was coming to be measured largely by its public rather than its practical effect.

The DAC even commissioned a film, *Rocket Site Story* (*West Side Story* had opened the previous year), which it supplied to television. The rest of the movement also developed direct means of communication, including the much-discussed 1959 documentary *March to Aldermaston* and even a Committee of 100-linked "pirate" radio station, the Voice of Nuclear Disarmament. A black-and-white CND monthly, *Sanity*, was launched in 1961; it was mostly poorly illustrated, but some of the Campaign's propaganda was sharply designed and aimed at the media as well as the public (Cohen 2019: 124–33).

The CND badge was another key product, allowing those (such as the writer's 14-year-old self) who were attracted by the movement's mediated presence to participate daily in it without ever joining a march. Although pinned badges had long been used to signify political affiliation, in Britain this appears to have been the first widely worn plastic version, pioneering what became a universal feature of late twentieth-century campaigns – although the Campaign's first badges were made by Eric Austen from clay, so that if "we all went up in nuclear fire, the badges would survive and remain as our memorial" (Duff 1971: 115–16).

Above all, it was the Aldermaston marches that represented the communications transformation that the movement involved: they were effectively made for television news. Initially, the visibility of the marches and marchers was hugely positive for the movement: the DAC's radical practice of bearing witness coincided with the CND leadership's aim of appealing for public support. But eventually tensions over representation increased: as Stuart Hall commented, there were "two styles of politics, conveniently symbolized by the Front and the Back of the March" (Taylor & Pritchard 1980: 57).

The March's inclusive, carnivalistic character facilitated bottom-up initiatives. If they were to remain newsworthy, actions had to become ever more radical in form, which encouraged the emergence of more militant groups and disruptive imagery and tactics. The movement's *political* dynamics were increasingly entwined with *media* dynamics that prioritized shock and subversion. But the outcomes were contradictory: the coverage could be large but it often focused on the form of the protest, even trivializing and personalizing it, rather than on the issues.

Both CND and the Committee of 100 recognized the importance of the media but views of how to engage with it were part of the split between them. The Schoenman-led breakaway of a few hundred to the

US embassy in 1961, with its physical conflict, captured media attention to the virtual exclusion of CND's huge, peaceful march.

Ideology and politics, strategies and outcomes

There is much to support the idea that the campaign was as much a social as a single-issue movement. Many supporters felt that its participatory environment was an achievement in itself; two decades later, up to a third even believed that it had achieved its goals although in political terms that was manifestly not the case (Taylor & Pritchard 1980: 30). However, Hill's conclusion that it cohered "around communication rather than ideology" (2018: 2, 84) is more problematic. Ideology was important to many sections of the movement and entered deeply into its strategies and tactics. The movement both drew on long-established traditions of ethics, politics and activism and created its own distinctive ideas as well as styles of politics.

If the connections with the earlier women's antiwar movement were limited, there were echoes of the anti-conscription movement when the mooted reintroduction of conscription was opposed in 1964 (Driver 1964: 238). The absolute pacifism of the 1930s Peace Pledge Union (PPU) had been discredited during the Second World War, and in any case many absolute pacifists were sceptical about the focus on nuclear weapons: the PPU and the Fellowship of Reconciliation both officially withheld support from CND on the grounds that if successful, it might encourage conventional war (Levy 2021: 71; Ormrod 1987: 205). However, a less organized pacifism now enjoyed a renaissance: almost half of movement participants later described themselves as pacifists (Taylor & Pritchard 1980: 24).

The most influential version was the DAC's, which adapted Gandhi's ideas and practices, developed in the struggle against British imperialism, but appropriated them to a specifically British form of morality (Scalmer 2011). For Randle, indeed, its ideas also derived from the Independent Labour Party, Guild Socialism and the libertarian left in general (1987: 147). The renewal of British anarchist thinking was also important, as the DAC took direct action beyond the traditional anarchist "propaganda by deed" (Whannel & Hall 1961: 21; Walter 1962; Scott-Brown 2022: 10–15).

DAC activists were also influenced by their fellow pacifists in the USA, led by the veteran A. J. Muste. Some of them, including Gene Sharp, who spent time in London as assistant editor of *Peace News* from 1955 to 1958, and Rustin, who had been pivotal to the nonviolent resistance to segregation organized by the Congress of Racial Equality in the late 1950s, were the first Western activists to develop a distinctive Gandhian approach. However, the DAC may have organized according to a different logic from the Mahatma's original truth-method: "tactically driven, media-oriented, no longer unfailingly peaceful in spirit", in the words of Sean Scalmer (2011: 7).

Indeed, in the Committee of 100 the DAC's approach combined with Russell's radicalized liberalism and what Driver (1964: 112) calls Schoenman's "intellectual extravagance" to create a sustained movement aiming to force the state to back down. Yet Randle later (1987: 150) questioned whether they "had a strategy at all": "Perhaps in one sense we did not", he concluded, but they were better at pinpointing the weaknesses of CND's Labour-path strategy.

"Civil resistance" was a crucial idea, developed also in Sir Stephen King-Hall's (1958) case that since there was no defence against the bomb, military defence was no longer feasible. Civil resistance was taken seriously by the emerging group of defence intellectuals, with the director of the Institute for Strategic Studies, Alastair Buchan, contributing a supportive foreword to a 1964 *Peace News* pamphlet on *Civilian Defence* (Driver 1964: 246–7).

Established religious and political traditions also played significant roles. CND was largely secular, and the Committee of 100, overall a "very irreligious" group (Carroll 2011: 87), was even more so. Yet Christian ideas were an important source of antinuclear and especially pacifist beliefs: "nonconformist, mostly middle-class Christians were Gandhi's keenest supporters", even if tight-knit Black church communities in the USA were "ultimately more significant" for the spread of his ideas (Scalmer 2011: 7). The campaign's Easter focus had a clear Christian reference – the CND sign was always black and white to express funereal symbolism, while spring daffodils adorned the front banner of the "March for Life". Indeed, Christians were important at all levels – especially Quakers, members of the Society of Friends, who made up over a quarter of them (Taylor & Pritchard 1980: 23). As well as Donald Soper, the Anglican Pacifist Fellowship had been involved in the early antinuclear campaign.

In May 1959, Christian Action (which Collins had chaired since 1951) and the Friends' Peace Committee jointly sponsored a large meeting in the Albert Hall involving well-known radical Christians such as Mervyn Stockwood and Trevor Huddleston. Christian CND was formed soon afterwards and, although sometimes semidetached from CND at large, pursued antinuclear arguments across the churches and organized pilgrimages over Whitsun (Pentecost) (Ormrod 1987: 194–202; Driver 1964: 197–216; Flessati 1997: 25). A group of Catholic ethical thinkers brought together by Walter Stein (1961) developed a "nuclear pacifist" position.[32]

Left-wing political traditions were more directly influential and all in different ways also followed the nuclear pacifist approach, that is, they were "pacificist" – a term popularized by Martin Ceadel (1987) because "pacifism", originally a broader idea, had come to be identified with absolute pacifism (Ceadel, 2002: 11, traces it to A. J. P. Taylor). This was the attitude, too, of most of CND's founders, many of whom were left-wing liberals who saw nuclear weapons as a distinct problem rather a symptom of more fundamental issues. Labour itself had always contained pacifists but it had never been a pacifist party, and the unilateralism of its left, while motivated by genuine concern for disarmament, was also bound up with its animosity towards Gaitskell and waned after his death in 1963.

The political strands that were most influential were those to the left of the Labour mainstream, which saw disarmament as part of socialist transformation. The CP, still the largest force on the left despite its post-1956 losses, initially opposed unilateralism – seeing it as dividing the existing peace movement – but changed its position as it recognized CND's rapid growth, including in the unions (Taylor 1987b: 163–8). The CP's participation actually helped its membership recover: it was paradoxical, Rip Bulkeley *et al.* (1981) noted, that "one of the main organizational beneficiaries of CND, a movement conceived in moralistic opposition to nuclear war, should be a party still tightly wedded to the politics of one of the world's two nuclear superpowers".

Groups from the Trotskyist tradition were also involved in CND, especially the Socialist Labour League (SLL), which grew after the CP's split and focused its campaign against the Labour leadership on this issue throughout 1957; one of its members seconded the first unilateralist resolution at that year's Labour conference. However, like the

CP, the SLL defended Soviet nuclear weapons because they belonged to the "workers' state", albeit a "degenerate" one. The smaller International Socialism group, with its slogan "Neither Washington or Moscow but International Socialism", was more in tune with movement thinking and played a role in the New Left but was marginal in CND. Later, the most influential role was that of an even smaller group, Solidarity, in the Committee of 100. Many Youth CNDers became involved in wider politics through the Young Communist League, the Labour Party's Young Socialists, in which all the Trotskyist groups were involved, and the Young Liberals, who underwent a radical, community politics phase.

The New Left could also be said to align with pacifism, but it represented a novel form of politics, reinterpreting as well as partly transcending Marxism as then understood. "More than any other element in the politics of unilateralism this group belonged to its time", Christopher Driver argued, developing "the political and military case for CND beyond the naive oversimplifications of Canon Collins' short-term campaign to rid Britain of nuclear weapons" (1964: 73–4). Although a critical engagement with Marxism was at its heart, "many of the people who flocked to the 'Partisan' Coffee House and to the N[ew] L[eft] Clubs in the early days were drawn not to Marxism, humanistic or otherwise, but to a 'new kind of politics'" (Taylor & Pritchard 1980: 68).

The New Left's key international idea was "positive neutralism". In the prevailing interpretation, this combined the new hopes raised by colonial independence (which the first of Britain's African colonies, Ghana, gained in 1957) with those for reform in the socialist states (raised by the revolts of 1956), and saw Britain linking states as diverse as India, Yugoslavia, Austria and Israel (Worsley 1960).

Yet although imperial paternalism was being unlearned, the New Left tended to idealize both the postcolonial regimes, many of which were authoritarian and little interested in disarmament, and the Non-Aligned Movement, which even when formalized in 1961 was only a loose framework. The New Left's vision captured an important set of connections but it too romanticized Britain's role: as Alasdair MacIntyre (1960) argued, "the colonial revolution divide[d] Britain from those states which on this view she should aspire to lead".

There was also, however, a European version of the New Left vision. Although Stuart Hall argued in 1958 that Britain needed to be present while NATO reconstructed its policy (Driver 1964: 81), E. P. Thompson

(1958) was already arguing for an "active neutrality" in which Britain would build "something like a 'Bandung' group of uncommitted nations in Europe", aimed at dismantling the blocs but relaxing tension and exerting a mediating influence in the meanwhile.[33] Soon Hall also broached a similar movement *across* boundaries, "WITHIN, as well as BETWEEN, governments and countries" (capitals in original). Britain's real allies, he argued, were those Germans, French and others who were challenging their governments as CND was its own (1960: 7–8). This was, he argued, "a revolutionary way of looking at foreign foreign policy" – it anticipated END's later idea of a pan-European peace movement.

If the New Left showed strategic ambiguity, as Richard Taylor argues (1987b: 182), they were exploring the scope for new forms of politics in an unprecedented situation; although some such as Thompson were political veterans in their thirties, many, such as Hall, were recent graduates. Moreover, while the New Left's roots were socialist and communist and the DAC's pacifist and anarchist, there was more affinity between them than is often understood. *Universities and Left Review* board member Alan Lovell, contributing its first discussions of movement tactics (1959), was a DAC activist (and soon a Committee of 100 member) who made it clear that direct action did not preclude the kinds of political moves the New Left advocated, even inside the Labour Party.

It was the DAC that made the greatest practical efforts to link opposition to nuclear weapons with anticolonialism, in its "Sahara Project" against French nuclear tests in Upper Volta (now Burkina Faso), from 1959. The DAC based itself in Ghana with support from its first president, Kwame Nkrumah, who like them was influenced by Gandhi. The project's links with Nkrumah were facilitated by African-American and anti-apartheid networks and produced a pan-African conference in Accra, proposed by one of its members, the Rev. Michael Scott (who had been expelled from South Africa). However, it failed to develop sustained direct action and finally folded when Nkrumah was overthrown in 1966 (Hill 2019; Levy 2021: 93–102).

Ultimately NATO withdrawal proved the most influential part of the New Left agenda. Adopted by CND in 1960 on a motion from the London Region, which had just published Hall's (1960) pamphlet advocating this, it was a logical conclusion from the fact that NATO was a nuclear alliance and Britain's role ultimately tied it into a nuclear policy even if its own bomb was discontinued. Yet this made it a very high-stakes challenge to the state: as Peggy Duff later reflected, "CND was now asking for a revolution in the foreign and defence policy of Britain" for which the conditions did not exist at the time (1971: 202). The policy also gave a new weapon to the movement's opponents, as Gaitskell showed in 1961.[34]

Underlying the movement's dilemmas, some historians have emphasized the "moralizing" approach to nuclear weapons shared in different ways by the CND leadership, Russell, the DAC and the New Left. Taylor (1988) sees this as a fundamental reason for the failure to develop an adequate political strategy, since it lent itself to the idea that nuclear weapons could be resolved without tackling the underlying problem of the Cold War – or indeed the structural concentration of power in what a sociologist who influenced many activists, C. Wright Mills, called the "power elite" (Mills 1958, 1959).

James Hinton goes so far as to argue that CND's ideology of moral leadership was an "imperialist pacifism". One banner actually proclaimed: "Britain's unilateral action ended the slave trade: let Britain lead again." Unilateralism partially reflected the strategic situation in the mid-1950s, when the UK was the only nuclear weapons state apart from the USA and USSR – although by the end of the decade, France and China were also developing nuclear programmes that they were unlikely to abandon. But it also spoke to the nostalgia for a more glorious past, "which simmered below the surface of British political consciousness, on the left as much as on the right". Yet the fusion of morality with politics in the simple unilateralist demand was central to the movement's mobilization: it was difficult to imagine that a movement of such vigour could have been built around anything less. Unilateralism "enabled pacifists to move towards political engagement, and it lent moral vision to the politics of the left" (Hinton 1989: 156, 181, 232, 161).

Ultimately, neither of the two main strategies – the CND leadership's for a unilateralist Labour government and the Committee of 100's for a civil disobedience movement so massive that the state was forced to concede – was likely to succeed in the circumstances of 1958–63. Although the timing of the 1959 election before CND built its maximum support was unfortunate and its 1960 Labour conference victory premature, the failure of the leadership strategy was inevitable given the fundamental importance of nuclear weapons for the Labour leadership and the state, both of which were deeply committed to the Atlantic alliance.

Equally, while the Committee's failure was precipitated by tactical overreach at Wethersfield, it never got near to mobilizing the kind of support that might have achieved its goal. It had effectively adopted a revolutionary strategy, but its actions mostly remained within "the tradition of minority dissent rather than the tradition of majority revolution", as Nicolas Walter put it (1962: 109). Despite the antinuclear minority being large and vocal, the wider apathy that E. P. Thompson (1960) diagnosed as the obstacle to social change had not been overcome.

The movement's failure therefore resulted more from the enormity of the challenges it faced, given its unilateralist agenda, than from its divisions. Duff (1971: 200) concluded that "issue-orientated campaigns carry within them the seeds of their own extinction, unless [their goals] can be rapidly attained"; but the movement's could not. The movement had educated the public and transformed Britain's nuclear culture, but it had set itself an almost impossible task, at least in what Perry Anderson (1965: 10) judged were "the most adverse historical circumstances" of the late 1950s.

2

The campaign and the new movements, 1964–79

By 1964 the antinuclear movement was waning. Its influence had been, Stuart Hall later claimed, "ENORMOUS … politically it was *very, very* influential", but paradoxically, the bomb was "the one thing [it] couldn't do anything about" (Taylor & Pritchard 1980: 109, emphases in original). It had major international impacts, especially by stimulating "CNDs" in other countries, from Ireland to Australia. But its principal effects, which form the main focus of this chapter, were to pave the way for other campaigns and movements, which in turn would lead nuclear disarmers to embrace opposition to wars and nuclear power and other goals. The shifts in radical politics that the movement helped produce, which accelerated rapidly towards the revolutionary year of 1968, would in turn challenge some of its core beliefs, particularly its commitment to nonviolence.

CND and the Wilson government's nuclear policies

Diluted effects of the movement could be seen in the British political mainstream in 1964. CND contributed to the climate that helped a new Labour leader, Harold Wilson, narrowly win that October's election. The party's manifesto criticized Polaris in CND's terms: "It will not be independent and it will not be British and it will not deter", and many CND members campaigned for it (Parker 2021: 68–9). The Liberal revival, a mild form of middle-class radicalism, largely accounted for Labour's victory – since its share of the national vote barely increased while the Liberals' rose markedly at the Conservatives' expense – and as we saw at Orpington, disarmament had played a part in this. Yet defence was not prominent in the election. The Tory leader, Sir Alec Douglas-Home, tried to make it an issue – a poster showed a lolling protestor holding a CND sign, with the strapline: "meanwhile the Conservatives have signed the Test Ban Treaty" – but with little success (Butler & King 1965: 129–30).

In office, Wilson appointed the first minister for disarmament, the *Times* journalist Alun Gwynne Jones, who as Lord Chalfont appeared twice in *Sanity* in 1965. Wilson also cut back civil defence in 1966 and 1968. However, from CND's point of view, Labour offered no real change. Wilson advocated alliance control over NATO's nuclear weapons, but CND opposed what would have been a multilateral nuclear force. With its activism in decline, there was little to prevent civil servants and military chiefs from convincing Wilson that cancelling Polaris would be a mistake: he accepted the system, although reducing the number of submarines from five to four. Like Attlee in 1947, he confined the decision to ministers who agreed with him: Foreign Secretary Patrick Gordon Walker and Defence Secretary Denis Healey. Previous governments had claimed that Britain's weapons were a contribution to a combined NATO deterrent, but Healey – who had earlier dismissed them as "a virility symbol to compensate for the exposure of its military impotence at Suez" – now promoted the idea of having "more than one centre of decision for the first use of nuclear weapons" to justify keeping Polaris (Duke 1985: 209; Freedman 1980: 26). Indeed, according to Henry Kissinger (1988: 219), in 1969 he even advocated the "demonstrative" use of nuclear weapons in a conflict situation if warnings failed.

Wilson also set up a committee, so secret that its existence was not acknowledged in the official list of cabinet committees (Ponting 1989: 183), to explore upgrading Polaris' capabilities, beginning the project to develop new "Chevaline" warheads. It was approved by cabinet through a brief mention in a paper on another topic, to which the disarmers Michael Foot and Barbara Castle offered only token dissent. The option was chosen for political rather than for strategic reasons, to avoid the political threat to the Labour government of openly enhancing Britain's nuclear weapons (Freedman 1980: 54). Continued by Edward Heath's Conservative government after 1970, Chevaline was finally authorized when Wilson returned to power in 1974, but its existence was kept from parliament and the public, with its costs disguised, until 1980, after his successor James Callaghan was defeated by Margaret Thatcher.[1]

CND, the anti-Vietnam War movement and 1968

With nuclear weapons policy conducted out of public view – between 1965 and 1980 there was not a single defence debate in parliament – the situation was not promising for CND as it moved into a post-movement phase. Collins resigned as chair, and although the executive had stated in 1959 that CND was not to be a permanent body, in 1966 it adopted national membership, becoming "an organization rather than a campaign" (Duff 1971: 225). Aldermaston marches continued to be held but were diminished affairs, and *Sanity* (1965, July: 7) reported the *Guardian*'s verdict that CND was "alive – but not kicking". At the local level, however, many groups still flourished (Parker 2021: 65–9), and Christian CND experienced a resurgence (Ormrod 1987: 208–10). During 1966–8, demonstrations took place at Barrow-in-Furness and Birkenhead against the launches of each of the UK's Polaris submarines.

During 1964–5 there were renewed arguments in CND about the relationships between unilateral and multilateral action and even about NATO withdrawal. Debates carried on until the 1970s about broadening the aims of the campaign, either to cover the whole foreign and defence field or to a wider programme emphasizing that the money spent on the bomb could improve social conditions. The "ploughshares" idea – transforming arms-making into production for peace – appeared as a campaign theme at a Scottish CND conference (*Sanity* 1965, September). In 1965, CND took a position not only on the Vietnam War but also on the crisis in Rhodesia, unconvincingly linking the settler regime's Unilateral Declaration of Independence to nuclear war (Phythian 2001: 144). But "most of the local groups wanted to campaign on the Bomb and only on the Bomb. Too many of them did not want to get involved in 'politics'" (Duff 1971: 207).

Also in 1965, Peter Watkins produced *The War Game*, one of the most powerful films ever made on nuclear war – John Lennon described it as "like getting your call-up papers for peace" – for BBC television. In a case of suppression almost unparalleled in British broadcasting history, it was stopped from being shown by the chair of the BBC's governors, Lord Normanbrook – who had recently retired as cabinet secretary after involvement in nuclear decision-making – and Director-General Hugh Greene, after the government had made its preference clear. There was also pressure from Mary Whitehouse's National Viewers and Listeners

Association (an early sign of a right-wing version of middle-class activism which would soon become more important). However, the film embarrassed the BBC by winning the Academy Award for Best Documentary Feature of 1966 and was widely shown by CND from then onwards. The decision remains a source of historical controversy (Chapman 2006; Wayne 2007).

From 1965, the Vietnam War became the main focus of CND activity. Unlike fellow Labour prime ministers Clement Attlee over Korea in 1950 and Tony Blair over Iraq in 2003, Wilson avoided openly committing British troops. However, he gave political and covert military support to the USA's attempt to prop up the South Vietnamese regime against the National Liberation Front (Vietcong) insurgency supported by North Vietnam. CND helped set up the British Council for Peace in Vietnam (BCPV) and unofficially supported Richard Gott's independent antiwar candidacy in the January 1966 Hull North by-election – but he won just 253 votes (0.5 per cent).[2] Meanwhile, ex-DAC activists were part of a peace team that went to North Vietnam to draw attention to the USA's indiscriminate bombing (Levy 2021: 162–3).

CND soon found it difficult to maintain a simple antiwar position. Duff was already under fire in letters to *Sanity* in September 1965 for appearing to support the Vietnamese armed struggle, and by mid-1966 Malcolm Caldwell, who would become chair in 1968, was able to claim that the line that CND should be neutral between the Vietcong and the USA had "gone completely". And while CND opposed China's explosion of an H-bomb, Caldwell told the readers of *Sanity* (1967, August): "What the Chinese bomb means to the exploited peoples of the world is hope: hope that American global imperialism can be stopped in it tracks … so that we can all build a better and more human life." However, these positions drew strong criticisms from those who felt that it betrayed CND's core values (Phythian 2001: 145, 147–8).[3]

Duff resigned as general secretary in February 1967, as the organization, which had just staved off a deep financial crisis, launched a national membership target of 3,000. Although CND was effectively addressing a wider range of foreign policy issues, she linked her departure partly to CND's insistence on relating everything, including Vietnam, to the bomb. She regarded the nuclear danger in the war as "pretty remote", but it was later shown that US military and administration officials discussed nuclear options in Vietnam, especially during January–February

1968, even if these were squashed with President Lyndon Johnson who was privately furious about them (Duff 1971: 207; Tannenwald 2006: 704).

Meanwhile, the war helped fire up student protests. Nicolas Walter had remarked that "the middle class has no tradition of direct action" (1962: 109), but CND and the civil rights movement had changed that. A mass student movement, originating in southern Black colleges in the USA, spread to elite universities and other countries by the mid-1960s (Marwick 2005: 788). In the London School of Economics (LSE), Hal Draper's *Berkeley: The New Student Revolt* (1965) was required reading in the Socialist Society founded by International Socialism and Solidarity supporters. In 1966 the LSE saw the first sit-in in a British university, and by 1967 sit-ins were commonplace on campuses: a mass movement was forming around the intersection of international and university issues.[4]

In the rump Committee of 100, where there had never been a simple consensus on nonviolence, the "tactically nonviolent" increasingly outweighed the Gandhians. Terry Chandler was even described as "turning pacifism into a military activity", as the group moved on from nuclear issues to the Vietnam War, increasingly engaging in "subversive stunts" (Carroll 2011: 108, 112–20). In April 1967, it undertook its last major action, the occupation of the Greek Embassy after the colonels overthrew democracy, and some LSE students took part. The doorman was presented with flowers (the "Summer of Love" was beginning) and the music of Mikis Theodorakis (which symbolized resistance) was to be broadcast from the embassy's balcony. However, the protestors were soon arrested – the idea that the police could not intervene on Greek territory proved illusory – and spent a night in the West End Central cells, during which Wilson precipitously recognized the dictatorship. Charges of riot and affray were laid against 42 people, and at the Old Bailey in October, despite reduced charges following a plea bargain, the judge singled out Randle, Chandler and Del Foley for prison sentences (Levy 2021: 183–7).[5] The Committee of 100 itself folded in 1968.

Meanwhile the anti-Vietnam War movement mushroomed. Johnson had hugely escalated the US campaign, saturation-bombing Vietnam with napalm while his forces even committed massacres (most notoriously at Mỹ Lai in 1968). In 1963, Bertrand Russell had set up a Peace Foundation, of which Schoenman was secretary, and in 1966 it established an International War Crimes Tribunal, which included Jean-Paul Sartre.[6] Together with the Trotskyists of the tiny International Group (soon renamed the International Marxist Group), the foundation also set up the Vietnam Solidarity Campaign (VSC), which organized a demonstration to the US Embassy in October 1967.

Although Duff asked, "Can't we just have one Vietnam Campaign?" (*Sanity* 1967, December), the Tet Offensive carried out by the National Liberation Front (NLF) in January 1968 strengthened the VSC, which supported the Vietnamese armed struggle, at the expense of the BCPV's "peace" campaign. This radicalization alienated many of CND's and the Committee of 100's pacifists, although some, such as the poet Adrian Mitchell who wrote "Tell Me Lies About Vietnam", embraced the new movement.

VSC's tactics deepened the divisions. Already in 1965, a BCPV-CND vigil outside the US embassy in Grosvenor Square had involved confrontation and 78 arrests, but VSC's March 1968 demonstration was a turning point. The organizing committee had vetoed Tariq Ali's proposal to "occupy the imperialist fortress", but it was indicative of the mood. Some marchers came prepared to provoke the police, who responded aggressively when the demonstration got close to the embassy. *Peace News* called the fighting "ugly, scary and sad", but a Solidarity pamphlet, *The Death of CND as Performed by the Grosvenor Square Demonstrators under the Direction of Themselves Alone*, celebrated it as an answer to the "ritualization" of Aldermaston, noting that the violence had brought the march via television into millions of homes. This march has been seen as the most violent in postwar Britain at the time (Ali 1987: 177–82; Rowbotham 2000: 169; Solidarity 1968; Hill 2018: 238).[7]

VSC aimed for a much larger march on 27 October 1968. "Defeat US aggression, Victory to the NLF and the Vietnamese Revolution, End Labour complicity in the war", read the poster with a backdrop of the Vietnamese flag that it plastered across London. Until this point, each demonstration had built on the drama and shock value of the last, but the May events in France altered everyone's perspective. An expectation of greater violence – even revolution – was hyped by the hostile press, the Rolling Stones' Mick Jagger and Keith Richards wrote "Street Fighting Man", whose words drew criticism, and the government approved a new police Special Operations Squad to infiltrate the antiwar movement.

On the face of it, CND and VSC were diametrically opposed over this demonstration. Dick Nettleton, CND's general secretary and a CP member, argued that violence on London's streets would distract from the violence in Vietnam, while VSC claimed that its protest was "no peace march" (Halloran, Elliott & Murdock 1970: 66). Yet VSC now faced CND's dilemma of orderly protest versus civil disobedience. It negotiated a route which avoided Grosvenor Square, as Ali later put it, to make the march a show of "strength" rather than "force", without the "punch-up" to which that inevitably led (Ali 1987: 220; Undercover Policing Inquiry 2023a: 12). Alongside the Stones' lyrics, the 27 October edition of the new revolutionary paper the *Black Dwarf*, which Ali edited – and which included CND supporters such as Adrian Mitchell and the designer Robin (Rueben) Fior on its board – reprinted a stern text by Friedrich Engels, warning that conditions had become unfavourable for street fighting.[8]

In the event the march, James Halloran and his fellow sociologists commented, "was similar to that of the last day of the Easter marches" (1970: 71). Only a Maoist-led breakaway went to the embassy, diverting media attention from the main protest as Schoenman's had in 1961. This great anticlimax punctured the movement's growth. As the war itself also entered a stalemate – although it was to continue until 1975 – it proved VSC's peak. Yet the demonstration remobilized the student movement: in the LSE an occupation to house the Vietnam protestors from across the country provoked the authorities to install new security gates, which the student left then forcibly removed, in response to which the director closed the LSE for 25 days in early 1969, leading to nationwide protests.

In this case, the student movement mirrored the escalation towards physical force seen in the Vietnam protests, and this was celebrated by some activists (e.g. Hoch & Schoenbach 1969).[9] However, force was directed at property rather than people, and a survey by two LSE sociologists concluded that despite the dramatization of student violence by both activists and their opponents, most events represented as such were "not very violent" (Rock & Heidensohn 1969: 109). Subsequent occupations remained mostly nonviolent, including the last big wave initiated at Warwick in 1970, where occupiers in the university's registry waded through the political files which it kept on students.[10]

If critics sometimes conflated the deliberate breaking of rules with violence, the abandonment of a nonviolent ethos had facilitated this elision. Even if the rhetoric of the VSC and student movements was not always matched by deeds, they interpreted direct action quite differently from the antinuclear movement. And it was not only Gandhian pacifism that had been superseded: the New Left had also been overtaken. It had begun to decline as early as 1962, when its clubs were fizzling out and the *Review* came under the more theoretically oriented editorship of Perry Anderson. There was an attempt to revive the original New Left in 1967–8, in a May Day Manifesto movement involving Raymond Williams, Stuart Hall and E. P. Thompson, but this fell flat (Rowbotham 2000: 174–5; Davison & Gilbert 2020: 147–8). The Anderson-led *Review* was rather more in tune with the new intellectual climate, famously displayed in the Dialectics of Liberation congress – where Black Power met antipsychiatry – at the Roundhouse, London, in July 1967 (Levy 2024).

Richard Taylor and Colin Pritchard found in their 20-years-after survey that there was "no evidence to support the hypothesis that [antinuclear] Movement activists became the core of the new far-left groups that emerged in the late 1960s" (1980: 111). The truth in this is that the core of these groups had formed earlier, while most recruits were students who arrived after CND's peak. However, some had been in the movement: a survey of student marchers in October 1968 showed that 58 per cent had belonged to or actively supported CND or the Committee of 100 (Halloran, Elliott & Murdock 1970: 53–4); both airmen discharged from the RAF three years earlier were active in the LSE Socialist Society by 1966 (Parker 2021: 17–37); and another LSE activist, Alan Fowler (2024), describes going home to the north-west and taking part in CND campaigning with Nettleton and his wife.

Indeed, the new politics that CND had initiated reached its peak in the events of 1968. These were less momentous or violent in Britain than in other countries, but even here 1968 was, David Widgery argued, "a particularly unruly year to write about", defying "all attempts to tidy it away" (1976: 341n). The problem of encapsulating it in conventional categories was that its political dynamics were parts of a larger social explosion which the anarchist Jeff Nuttall (1968) named "bomb culture" and the historian Arthur Marwick (2005) later called a "cultural revolution"; this idea was current because of the Great Proletarian Cultural Revolution initiated by Mao Zedong in China in 1966, which many on the left, not just the tiny Maoist groups, idealized and conflated with the cultural ferment in the West. As with the Aldermaston march, for what was called the "counterculture" it was emotion as much as politics that seemed to have radical potential (Whiteley 2011). However, to E. P. Thompson much of it seemed "excessively self-absorbed, self-inflating and self-dramatizing" (Rowbotham 2000: 169).

It is easy to see the imagery and rhetoric of revolution as "largely fictitious: a cultural construct born out of mediated politics" (Hill 2018: 6). A police officer who infiltrated the VSC in Camden, London, concluded that although its members "were notionally revolutionary, none of them was capable of achieving revolutionary aims by force" (Undercover Policing Inquiry 2023a: 12).[11] Yet the VSC campaigned in solidarity with the Vietnamese revolution and the Marxists who led it recognized, as their October 27 decision showed, the difference between protest and revolt.

Moreover, the revolutionary ideas that resonated with a layer of student and other radicals could have real consequences. In Northern Ireland, CND banners were carried on the first marches organized by the Civil Rights Association set up in 1967, itself inspired by the US civil rights movement. The key Derry activist Eamonn McCann had marched with CND and the movement had been "an important stage in the political education of many other Northern Irish radicals" (Prince 2006: 863). However, their decisive political formation was through contact with the international revolutionary left in London and on the Continent. The direct action orientation of Peoples Democracy, the group they established in October 1968, while nonviolent, was partly designed to provoke the sectarian Northern Ireland state. Their success in this led, however, to their being eclipsed not only by constitutional nationalists but also by militant Republicans, who in conflict with Loyalist organizations opened up a new phase of war.

The new social movements and the antinuclear campaign

British society was also polarizing, as the mass response to Enoch Powell's "rivers of blood" speech showed in April 1968. This proved to be the beginning of a reaction to the 1960s that led to a turbulent new decade. Globally, in what Michael Hardt (2023) calls the "subversive seventies", positive and ambivalent attitudes to violence played a major part in the new extraparliamentary left.

In Britain, the countercultural paper *International Times* summarized in 1972, "the revolution began as a dove, with a CND sign above its breast. It became a peacock, fanning out a psychedelic rainbow of bells, beads and Beatles. But for many it became a hawk, whose outlook was that of the Angry Brigade, and even the Irish Republican Army" (Hill 2018: 3). Yet although the revolutionary and student left espoused solidarity with armed movements around the world, the tiny Angry Brigade, Britain's only homegrown armed group – which carried out bombings during 1970–2 (Weir *et al.* 1985) – was even more marginal than urban guerrilla groups elsewhere. Street violence resurfaced in campaigns to block the National Front, but it did not lead to a wider adoption of violent tactics.

Although the low-level civil war in Northern Ireland was the only armed conflict within the UK in the late twentieth century, the antinuclear movement's involvement with it was limited compared to its activism over Vietnam. CND called for the withdrawal of British troops from Derry following Bloody Sunday (30 January 1972), but it was decided not to include the issue in the 1972 march (Phythian 2001: 149). Pacifists from the British Withdrawal from Northern Ireland Campaign urged soldiers not to go to Ireland, and Pat Arrowsmith was imprisoned for 18 months for handing out leaflets at an army base; she went on hunger strike in solidarity with Irish prisoners (*Sanity* 1974, 6: 2). However, while Bruce Kent defended these campaigners in *Sanity* (1975, October–November: 13), Ireland did not became a major focus for CND, although a new movement, the Peace People, emerged there in 1976.

In 1970s Britain, the left's ambivalence towards violence proved a political dead end, as many members of the antinuclear movement believed it would. The principal legacies of 1960s activism were not violent actors, or even new parties, but more peaceful social movements, especially for environmentalism and women's, gay and Black liberation. Indeed, there were "masses of other movements, on behalf of the homeless, for penal and educational reform, to protect consumers, to safeguard the environment" (Marwick 2005: 791). Of particular relevance to disarmers, the Campaign Against the Arms Trade was founded in 1974.

Prominent single-issue campaigns included the Stop the Seventy Tour, set up in 1969, which nonviolently disrupted the games of the apartheid South African rugby team, leading to the following year's cricket tour being cancelled (Hain 1972). Former antinuclear activists were involved in virtually all them, with Committee of 100 supporters the most likely to be involved in community politics. Nonviolent direct action became a universal tool known by its acronym: indeed, Randle would later claim the most tangible effect of the DAC and the Committee was "to establish a tradition of NVDA [nonviolent direct action] within the political culture" (1987: 157).

Of the larger movements, the environmental was the most closely related to the antinuclear campaign, and its most important organizations, such as Friends of the Earth and Greenpeace, all date from the early 1970s. Indeed Greenpeace was originally "an antinuclear group with an environmental emphasis" (Zelko 2013: 8), set up to stop nuclear tests. The forerunner of the Green Party, the PEOPLE Party, was set up in 1972, becoming the Ecology Party in 1975 and the Green Party in 1985; in West Germany in the same period, the Greens emerged as a major "anti-party party", which would be very important for the anti-nuclear movement in the 1980s. In Britain, the electoral system helped block that possibility.

CND increasingly reflected the new thinking about the world as smaller, more vulnerable and more deeply connected; the planetary destruction that nuclear war would cause was no longer a single issue but part of a larger problem (Burkett 2012: 632). By 1978, a third of 1960s nuclear disarmers, especially pacifists and direct actionists, were active in various environmental campaigns, although these were not necessarily perceived as very radical: "environmentalists might be described as active moderates with an element of anti-party politics about them" (Taylor & Pritchard 1980: 45).

This shift had consequences for how nuclear power was perceived. The early CND had largely embraced the "atoms for peace" philosophy, which was first outlined by Eisenhower in 1953 and used to justify the UK nuclear power programme from 1956. Under this very heading, *Sanity* (1962, December: 1) had hailed a campaign by scientists and trade unions for a switch from military to peaceful nuclear production. Some CND members, notably Professor John Fremlin, a tenacious letter writer in *Sanity*, continued to support nuclear power in the 1970s and after.

But for most disarmers, nuclear energy came to symbolize global eco-logical threats, particularly because of a growing awareness of French nuclear testing in the Pacific. The smiling sun "Nuclear Power – No Thanks" logo, designed in Denmark in 1975, became as ubiquitous as the CND sign. Campaigners objected to nuclear power not only because it generated the radioactive material used in nuclear weapons but also because populations were threatened by radioactivity from reactor components and waste, which it was necessary to store for unimagina-bly long periods. The 1979 accident at Three Mile Island, Pennsylvania, increased awareness of these risks. The antinuclear energy campaign was particularly influential in Scotland, where a Scottish Campaign Against the Atomic Menace was founded in 1976 and opposed the building of a nuclear plant at Torness (Ross & Gibbs 2024). Many thousands of demonstrators occupied the construction site in both 1978 and 1979.

The other new movement in which many disarmers were involved was Women's Liberation. As a social movement it was almost the oppo-site of the antinuclear, founded mainly out of fundamental concerns with women's oppression rather than an issue agenda, although it had plenty of issues, from equal pay to childcare and abortion, as well as campaigns and protests about them. The new feminism originated in the USA in the mid-1960s, but in Britain it was not until late 1968 that a movement began. It spread rapidly at the grassroots level during 1969, initially through "consciousness-raising" groups, the first National Women's Liberation Conference was held in 1970 and the movement expanded throughout the decade. The general social, cultural and polit-ical influence of what came to be called second-wave feminism was huge, but it also influenced and was influenced by parallel movements for gay and Black liberation, although the idea of "intersectionality" had not yet been invented.

When the Women's Liberation Movement came to reflect on its ori-gins, Jill Liddington (1991: 199) argues, it tended to record "not CND and the Committee of 100, but … a reaction to the chauvinism of the Marxist left or underground press. As a result, links between women's experiences of CND and the revival of feminism only six years later have been largely neglected." Feminism revived with scarcely any knowledge of its anti-militarist past, and its wholesale redefinition of violence left "little space for *military* violence", or of *non*violence "as an empower-ing feminist strategy for confronting militarism"; it reacted against "any stereotyping of women as naturally *more* caring, *more* peaceful, *less* violent than men" (emphases in original). In these senses, the new feminism was at odds with earlier feminism and pacifism, but links began to be made: feminists started to connect to peace politics, while women in pacifist circles tried to make sense of women's liberation. In the late 1970s, Liddington concludes, there was a shift away from socialist feminism "towards an emphasis on female-centred culture and a hatred of male violence".

For much of the 1970s, CND itself was largely marginalized in the new movement scene. In 1970, its belated attempt to relate to the counterculture, a "Festival of Life", was not very successful; in 1971, it had barely 2,000 members; and in 1972, after a revival of the Aldermaston march attracted only 300 people, there was discussion about whether it should disband (Young 1977: 437 n39; Hetherington 2005). It lacked the closer relevance of other sectors to the wider political crisis: by the end of the decade, Britain was experiencing what Stuart Hall (1979) called the "Great Moving Right Show", which culminated in Margaret Thatcher's victory in that year's election.

However, CND survived, partly because of the cultural capital that remained from its heyday: policy-relevant knowledge, campaigning experience, networking and recognition. Capable activists, although much reduced in numbers, linked the campaign into national and international civil society. In opposition in 1970–4, the Labour Party provided an increased focus for activity: its conference called in 1972 for the withdrawal of all nuclear bases and in 1973 opposed any nuclear defence policy. Dan Smith, appointed CND general secretary that year at the age of 22, worked to improve its parliamentary links (Tønnesson 2022). In 1974, a "Study War No More" campaign over military links in British universities gained attention. In 1975, it held a teach-in instead of an Easter march. In that year's referendum, it opposed British membership of the European Economic Community (EEC) as the harbinger of a military union, but *Sanity* published pro-EEC views (1975, June–July: 2, 7). And CND was still not the whole antinuclear movement: pacifists who had gone through the DAC and Committee of 100 continued to organize, partly through War Resisters International, of which Michael Randle had become chair in 1966.

CND's survival was partly because of the organized interests that were invested in it. Mgr Bruce Kent, who became CND chairman[12] in

1977 and general secretary in 1980, later said that two groups kept it going: the Quakers and the Communist Party (Kirby 2013: 19). The CP largely controlled the national office, *Sanity* and major committees, and helped keep CND noticed in the trade unions and other milieux where it had influence. Yet Nigel Young (1977: 155) saw its stranglehold as compounding the decline: for him, the CP "bored from within in every sense" and was out of sympathy with the spirit of the campaign.

CP influence could be seen in CND's greater emphasis on NATO withdrawal and its ambivalent response to the Soviet invasion of Czechoslovakia in 1968. Unlike over Hungary, the British party criticized Soviet actions, but under its influence CND's conference – anticipating arguments over Ukraine half a century later – passed a resolution blaming NATO for "provoking" the invasion, because it had "inspired the creation of the Warsaw Pact, to preserve whose unity the Russians invaded" (Phythian 2001: 154 n25). However, the CP did not have it all its own way: the ex-DAC activist April Carter, who had worked with Czech dissidents in 1968, became chair in 1970.

Personal linkages, an under-researched part of CND's history, connected the campaign into a wide range of networks. Kent had been involved in the Catholic peace group Pax Christi since he was asked to become its chaplain in 1958, had been chaplain to the University of London, visited South Africa with a Quaker-inspired trust, chaired War on Want and became involved with the Campaign Against the Arms Trade and Preservation of the Rights of Prisoners (Kent 1992: 155–6, 168). Smith, when he left the general-secretaryship in 1976, became a researcher, helping to produce critical reports on defence policy together with Labour MP Robin Cook (who was defence correspondent of the *New Statesman* and a contributor to *Sanity*), Mary Kaldor and others, and wrote a book whose timely publication aided the second wave of the movement (Cook & Smith 1979; Kaldor, Smith & Vines 1979; Smith 1980). However, when it came to NATO, instead of the full withdrawal that CND advocated, Cook and Smith argued for a "partial disengagement … possibly of a rather unambitious kind to begin with" (1978: 27).

Small beginnings in academia provided institutional bases for disarmament research, which helped reinforce the campaign. A School of Peace Studies was founded at Bradford in 1973 (O'Connell 1986; Rogers 2000), as a result of a public appeal and Quaker support, and an Armament and Disarmament Information Unit at Sussex in 1978, in which Kaldor – who had international links through working at the Stockholm International Peace Research Institute – was involved. Despite the Cold War polarization between "war" and "peace" studies, the slowly growing fields of International Relations, defence studies and defence economics were becoming useful milieux for disarmament academics. The late 1970s also saw widely noticed trade union projects exploring the conversion of military to civilian production, notably at Lucas Aerospace (Wainwright & Elliott 1982) and Vickers. Kaldor was a consultant to the latter, and these also fed into the Labour reports.

Détente and CND

CND continued its campaign against the national "deterrent" in the 1970s, but developments in Cold War politics reinforced its marginality. Nuclear alarm waned, so that it seemed that the campaign had lost its relevance. Dean Rusk claimed that US administrations deliberately lost the Vietnam War "rather than 'win it' with nuclear weapons" (Wittner 2009: 111). The Partial Test Ban Treaty was followed in 1968 by the Nuclear Non-Proliferation Treaty (NPT), in which non-nuclear states agreed not to seek nuclear weapons in return for the recognized nuclear weapons states committing themselves to disarmament.

What came to be known as "détente" reinforced the belief that the superpowers would avoid nuclear war. However, this "did not mean a complete relaxation of tensions [but] rather a new form of competition" (Colbourn 2022: 51). Instead of disarming, the USA and the USSR were simultaneously intensifying their nuclear arms race *and* seeking to jointly manage it. By 1974, their combined nuclear stockpiles had reached the equivalent of a million times the destructive power of the Hiroshima bomb. Both were expanding their ICBM capabilities and seeking to develop anti-ballistic missile (ABM) systems.

Negotiations between the superpowers continued throughout the decade. They had jointly pledged in 1967 to limit their competition and in 1969 talks for a Strategic Arms Limitation Treaty (SALT) began in Helsinki. In 1972 a SALT I (interim) treaty and an ABM treaty were agreed. In 1974 the basic framework for a SALT II agreement, limiting the numbers of missiles, bombers, ICBM launchers and multiple independently targeted re-entry vehicles on ballistic missiles, was adopted. Although there was disagreement on US plans to deploy air-launched cruise missiles, in June 1979 President Jimmy Carter and Soviet leader Leonid Brezhnev signed the SALT II treaty in Vienna.

Alongside these talks, transformations were under away in Europe: East–West economic, political and cultural ties had increased since the 1960s; the *Ostpolitik* of West German Chancellor Willy Brandt helped normalize relations between the two Germanies; and many Western Communist parties were moving in a "Eurocommunist" direction, increasingly independent of Moscow.

From 1973, Britain, together with all European states including the USSR as well as the USA and Canada, was involved in the Conference on Security and Cooperation in Europe. This produced the Helsinki Final Act of 1975, with three substantive "baskets", outlining principles such as respect for sovereignty, the inviolability of borders, non-intervention and self-determination; economic, scientific and technological coop-eration; and measures to improve human rights and freedom of move-ment, journalistic conditions and cultural exchanges. A fourth dealt with monitoring and future relations. The agreement, especially its third basket, would later play a critical role in the unwinding of the Cold War (Snyder 2011).

It principle, the SALT and Helsinki talks strengthened CND's case, especially since the UK was not party to the former negotiations (although it could have been included in a further round, SALT III). However, détente weakened all public and media concern about nuclear weapons. Even a worldwide US nuclear alert in October 1973, because of intelligence that the USSR was about to send troops to Egypt in its war with Israel – possibly the most dangerous nuclear confrontation since Cuba – prompted little public discussion, although US forces in Britain were put on high alert without the UK being consulted (Wittner 2009: 114; Duke 1985: 267).

Despite this unpromising situation, CND started to revive in a small way in the mid-1970s. Demonstrations continued at the Polaris base at Holy Loch, where Kent conducted an exorcism in 1973. After three years' discussion and editorial cuts, in 1976 the BBC allowed CND to present an "Open Door" television programme, which Duncan Rees, the general secretary from that year, credited with its recovery. CND's chair, John Cox, who would soon publish a widely read book on nuclear politics, *Overkill* (1977), was able to tell the 1976 conference that it had got over "that dreadful period of being a huge organization declining. We are now a small organization that is growing" (Rees 1983: 72). Countrywide weeks of action during 1976–8, involving showings of *The War Game*, stimulated the campaign further, almost doubling the number of local groups and leading to 600 new national members in 1978, compared to only 100 in 1972.

Polaris remained CND's main target. Its Chevaline upgrade remained secret, but (because of the very long lead times in nuclear weapons procurement) by 1978 secret discussions were already beginning on a full replacement. Prime Minister Callaghan decided, together with the now-usual informal group of senior ministers, that like Polaris this should be submarine-based and favoured following precedent by purchasing the Trident system from the USA. No decision had been made by the time Labour lost office in 1979; Margaret Thatcher, when she took over, formed an official cabinet committee to take Trident forward, but it was still not publicly known (Ponting 1989: 184–5).

With these discussions behind closed doors, it was NATO nuclear weapons developments that finally triggered a serious revival of CND. A new US "enhanced radiation warhead" refocused the campaign after protests in the Netherlands in 1978, where a petition against it reached 1.2 million signatures, an impressive number given the size of the population and the need to collect signatures by hand. The weapon, popularly known as the "neutron bomb", maximized lethal radiation but minimized blast damage to buildings. Designed for the battlefield, it drew attention to the risk that a conventional war in Europe could quickly go nuclear: the first strong sign of the specifically European concerns that would soon dominate nuclear politics.

Although the Stop de Neutronen Bomb campaign was initiated by the Dutch Communist Party and partially funded by East Germany (de Graaf 2003: 13), the opposition widened to other parties and groups. Support for the Interchurch Peace Council (IKV) grew rapidly (Evert 1980: 43–52) and it increasingly overtook the CP-backed campaign. The IKV, with its slogan "Free the world of nuclear weapons, and begin with the Netherlands", developed a determined unilateralism based on church pronouncements from the previous decade: Pope John XXIII's 1963 encyclical *Pacem in Terris* and a 1962 pastoral letter of the Dutch Reformed Church.

CND's petition, with a quarter of a million signatures, did not match the Dutch, but Europe-wide opposition led President Carter to abandon the neutron bomb's deployment. CND Vice-Chair Cathy Ashton (1983: 75) later argued that the campaign had shown that "united action within Europe was capable of producing results". And the Dutch campaign was not the only sign of new concerns about nuclear weapons: the Swedish prime minister, Olaf Palme, called for a "nuclear-free Europe" in 1978 (Coates 1987: 11).

This campaigning revival coincided with crucial geopolitical and arms race developments in which détente gave way to new tensions. Although the Cold War was an unequal contest in which the USA (and even more, the West) had an immense superiority in wealth, technology and international alliances, the Soviet leadership aimed to achieve military parity by devoting a higher proportion of its gross domestic product to military expenditure. In the late 1970s, their improved intermediate-range missile, the SS-20, was seen as destabilizing by Western elites, which also felt threatened by increasing Soviet support for revolutions in an "arc of crisis" from Afghanistan through Iran, where the Shah was overthrown in 1979, and the Arab world to the horn of Africa (Halliday 1983: 21).

On 12 December 1979, NATO decided to install 464 intermediate-range, Gryphon ground-launched cruise missiles – deemed slow and therefore not first-strike – in Britain, West Germany, Italy, the Netherlands and Belgium. Meanwhile, 108 Pershing II ballistic missiles – capable of striking Moscow in minutes – would be introduced into Germany. One week later, the USSR decided to send its troops into Afghanistan to support the Communist regime there, which was threatened by rebellion.

These twin developments, symbolically reminiscent of the Hungary–Suez coincidence, marked a dramatic cooling in East–West relations. With an aggressive conservative coalition including a "New Right" ascendant in Washington, the political mood around SALT II ratification was implacably hostile and Carter withdrew it. However, even Fred Halliday (1983: 14–15), who saw this as the onset of a "Second Cold War", emphasized that, unlike in the first, the hotline continued to function and East–West talks continued on intermediate-range weapons and conventional force reductions and in the Conference on Security and Cooperation in Europe.

Indeed, the deployment of what would be called "Euromissiles" did not result from new tensions *in* Europe. It principally reflected the continent's role in NATO's rarefied strategic thinking during what Mary Kaldor (1990) later called the "imaginary war" between the blocs, and especially the anxieties of West European leaders. NATO's military doctrine, "flexible response", adopted in the late 1960s, was deliberately vague about when it would use nuclear weapons in the European "theatre". Now, with strategic nuclear forces constrained by SALT, West German and some other leaders feared that the SS-20s threatened to leave the USA unable to respond, weakening its nuclear guarantee to Western Europe and potentially decoupling Europe's security from North America's; already in 1977, German chancellor Helmut Schmidt had gone public with his concerns.

The idea of a distinct "Eurostrategic balance" gained currency, and European leaders' interest in offsetting the putative Soviet advantage coalesced around a deployment of cruise missiles. Although the Carter administration disputed the idea of an increased Soviet threat, "it was increasingly clear that perceptions mattered almost as much as capabilities", Susan Colbourn (2022: 83, 88, 91) comments. The problem was "highly psychological and political" and NATO's "dual track" decision (missile deployment plus unspecified arms control) "had far more to do with the politics of the alliance than anything else".

The distribution of the proposed deployment was also obviously political. West Germany, the UK and Italy were committed, but the Netherlands and Belgium agreed only with reservations, in the hope of deferring if not cancelling the deployment. The Dutch pressed for the idea of cutting the deployment to zero, should the Soviets make sufficient cuts to their arsenal, to be included in the communiqué.

It was also obvious that the deployments would be sensitive in Britain, Germany and Italy as well as the Low Countries. What leaders saw as maintaining Europe's nuclear guarantee, publics could see as preparing to fight a "limited" nuclear war in Europe. Yet despite the recent opposition to the neutron bomb, neither NATO nor its opponents envisaged that its decision would provoke a massive peace movement. The USA had long deployed a wide range of "theatre" weapons in Europe: in Britain, Lawrence Freedman of the Royal Institute of International Affairs pointed out, there had been American nuclear weapons for decades and the number of F-111s had been increased as recently as

1977 without protest (1980: 125). Indeed, the International Institute of Strategic Studies had suggested in 1976 that the USA was considering the deployment of cruise missiles in Britain (Duke 1985: 275), and the missiles were mentioned in *Sanity* in 1977, but they had not become a campaigning issue.

Although Freedman now worried that cruise missiles might be "more positively identified", no one foresaw that a mass movement of the early 1960s type could develop, this time right across Western Europe and with a pan-European focus. Still less did anyone envisage a movement that would profoundly affect not only the nuclear arms race but also the very structure of the Cold War international system.

3

Against the Euromissiles, 1979–87

In Britain, the alarm about the NATO decision was sounded by E. P. Thompson (1979), fittingly in the *New Statesman* and elsewhere, 21 years after J. B. Priestley's essay that launched CND. He expressed the core argument that would be made across Western Europe in the next four years: "*why*, since there is already terror enough, ten times over, ballistically poised at both end of Power's great divide, do we need this intermediate additive of terror at all? Ah, it is a safeguard to *prevent* the ultimate horror of a Soviet/US nuclear war! It is to 'localize' nuclear war: that is, to keep nuclear war local to us, and to West and East Europe, and away from America" (emphases in original). Attacking the secrecy and lack of democratic accountability, as well as a reported British decision a month earlier to replace Polaris by Trident, Thompson returned to the case for active neutrality that the New Left had advanced 20 years earlier.

He followed this clarion call with private overtures to prominent left-wing Labour MPs Tony Benn and Eric Heffer. However, it was after Ken Coates of the Bertrand Russell Peace Foundation rang him that the first steps were taken towards a pan-European campaign against the cruise and Pershing missiles. Coates had worked with East European and Soviet dissidents over the previous decade and had been calling for a new European initiative: NATO's decision and Thompson's outcry gave him the target that he had been lacking. With input from Coates, Mary Kaldor and Dan Smith, Thompson then drafted an Appeal for European Nuclear Disarmament, which was widely discussed and circulated for signatures in Britain and elsewhere before being publicly launched in London, Oslo, Paris, Berlin and Lisbon on 28 April 1980 (Coates 1987: 11–14; Burke 2004: 39–52).

The Appeal (European Nuclear Disarmament 1980) provided a political framework that would inspire much of the campaigning across the continent throughout the 1980s, and endorsing it was the basis for being involved in the END process. Unlike CND's constitution, which framed the nuclear problem as one that should be solved first by national action, it developed a European approach and addressed the political under-pinning of the nuclear arms race, the Cold War. Aiming to free Europe "from Poland to Portugal" from nuclear weapons, the Appeal called on the USSR to halt the production of SS-20s and the USA not to develop new missiles for Europe. It also argued for ultimately dissolving both military alliances.

The Appeal called for a Europe-wide campaign of protest, a "trans-continental movement" with wide-ranging exchanges of views, and defended the rights of citizens to take part in the movement and every kind of exchange, setting it against the repression of the Soviet bloc. This was partly a tactical move to emphasize END's independence from official Soviet peace campaigns (Rankin 2017: 64), but it would prove one of its most important ideas. The Appeal's iconic passage urged: "We must commence to act as if a united, neutral and pacific Europe already exists. We must learn to be loyal, not to 'East' or 'West', but to each other, and we must disregard the prohibitions and limitations imposed by any national state."

The ideas behind END were elaborated theoretically by Thompson in "Notes on Exterminism, the Last Stage of Civilization" (1980: 23, 24, 30). The title referenced Vladimir Illych Lenin's famous "Imperialism, the Highest Stage of Capitalism", and the article attacked the "immo-bilism" of the Marxist left in relation to the Cold War (see also Shaw 1981). Thompson argued that the USA and the USSR did not *have* military-industrial complexes; they *were* such complexes, societies centred on their weapons systems, their development conditioned by the "reciprocal" logic of weapons competition and the ideological "addiction" of both ruling elites to a conflict that was leading the world towards extermination. END was initiating a counter-thrust, a "logic of process leading to the dissolution of both blocs". Thompson argued that the new movement could tame the nuclear arms race by unravelling the Cold War system that underlay it. END's new third camp would not be a group of states outside the blocs but linked movements within and across them.

Thompson's ideas were soon widely shared. Ann Pettitt, who would soon initiate the Greenham protests, describes a friend, Jean McOllister, who went with her to meet Russian peace activists, who was "already thinking outside the Cold War and turning it, in her mind, into a historical phenomenon" (Pettitt 2006: 168). But these were not the only ideas in END, let alone in what was soon called the "peace movement". Both drafters and signatories interpreted the Appeal in different ways. For many, arms control *was* its central purpose and East–West campaigning secondary. Indeed, many grassroots activists were probably unaware of the Appeal.

Although END made the first call for a pan-European movement against the missiles, neither then nor at any stage did it constitute that movement or even its centre. While END was launching its Appeal, IKV was already a mass movement and a West German movement was rapidly developing, uniting in November 1980 through the Krefeld Appeal that eventually gathered five million signatures (Burns & Van Der Will 1988: 207–9, 225). There were soon many movements, and although the missiles crisis was manifestly an international issue and transnational linkages were integral to all of them, each fought it out primarily within its own national context.

A new movement explodes

In Britain, grassroots groups were organizing even as Thompson penned his *Statesman* article. By January 1980, an East Anglia Campaign Against the Missiles and a Campaign Against the Oxfordshire Missiles had already formed to oppose feared deployments at RAFs Lakenheath and Upper Heyford respectively. Public nuclear controversy also escalated before the Appeal was launched. In the first Commons defence debate for 15 years, the Conservative defence secretary, Francis Pym, finally revealed the Labour government's secret Chevaline project (Salisbury 2021: 125–8). In February, the BBC's *Panorama* broadcast leaked parts of the official civil defence film on nuclear war: "Arrangements will be made to treat any people who are ill or injured", it promised vaguely, before giving instructions on moving the body of anyone who died "to another part of the house" (Beckett 2016: 82–3). In March, the government published *Protect and Survive*, which proposed that people hide under a table or the stairs to protect themselves from nuclear fallout. The pamphlet was "the best gift CND ever had from any government", activist Philip Bolsover later wrote (1983: 89).

In June 1980, the government announced that 96 cruise missiles would be stationed at RAF Greenham Common. A Campaign Against Cruise was quickly formed in nearby Newbury, involving Joan Ruddock, chair of the local Labour Party, who would soon become chair of CND. On 15 July, timed to coincide with the 80th birthday of Queen Elizabeth the Queen Mother, which would dominate the TV news, the government also announced that it planned to purchase the Trident missile system, despite the First Sea Lord dismissing it in 1979 as "a cuckoo in the [naval] nest" (Johnson 2006: 69n). This was a major additional provocation to the burgeoning campaign.

With END taking the national and international lead and diverse local initiatives, CND was not, in the first half of 1980, the organization of the movement. A new Oxford group called itself Campaign Atom, Meg Beresford recalled, because it was "*quite* sure that CND was a defunct organization" (Liddington 1991: 214, emphasis in original). In West Yorkshire, the movement took off after a 700-strong meeting in Bradford in early June at which Thompson gave a passionate speech; a regional END organization was set up, working with local peace groups.

E. P. Thompson speaking to a CND rally at the War Memorial Park in Kenilworth following a march through Coventry, 26 May 1984

Source: Trinity Mirror / Mirrorpix / Alamy Stock Photo.

Peace Studies, from which the organizers of the meeting came, was soon training speakers for the movement. Some groups, such as the Hull group that I co-founded, were local ENDs. In the women's movement, anti-nuclear power ecofeminism quickly developed into antimilitarism, and Women Oppose the Nuclear Threat was set up in Leeds.

Bruce Kent later acknowledged that CND was slow to grasp what was going on (1992: 169–72). He recalled that when he took over as general secretary in January 1980, he discovered that "not a few 'active' members were actually dead", while campaigning consisted largely of sending out ancient copies of *The War Game* to local groups: "after every outing they got shorter and shorter as broken pieces of 16mm film were sliced out". Nor was the left alert to the missiles: in a "debate of the decade" in March (Hain 1980), none of the dozen prominent Labour, far-left and feminist speakers mentioned them. However, in June, Labour's national executive called the first national demonstration of the new movement, a 20,000 strong rally.

By September 1980, there were over 300 local peace groups with a membership of over 40,000. Many were not affiliated to CND, but it was nevertheless a major beneficiary of the upsurge; it had scheduled a demonstration in Trafalgar Square in October and this mobilized an impressive 80,000 people. National CND membership more than doubled in 1980, as it did every year until 1985 when it reached 110,000. The number of local groups topped 1,000 in 1982. Soon life was breathed into CND's semi-dormant structures, its paid staff rapidly expanded, and Kent and Ruddock were celebrities, voted Man of the Year and runner-up as Woman of the Year respectively by BBC radio listeners in 1983. *Sanity*, relaunched as a monthly in 1982, became a lively, information-packed magazine.

CND and END were closely entwined, with many fulfilling roles in both. Even John Cox, CND's leading Communist, who saw the "US = USSR" approach as "dangerous", backed END's appeal because its campaigning thrust was anti-NATO (1980: 11). END saw itself as supplementing rather than supplanting CND and chose not to be a membership body. Kent was an original signatory of the END Appeal and Thompson wrote the iconic pamphlet *Protest and Survive* for CND and the Russell Foundation, which was quickly expanded into a bestselling Penguin Special (Thompson & Smith 1980). Most of the anti-missile groups eventually affiliated to CND but some kept their original names;

for example, Hull END, officially the Hull Campaign for European Nuclear Disarmament, functioned as CND's local group.

In one sense END was a pressure group within CND, but there was also a loose functional specialization. CND was the main centre of national campaigning and grassroots coordination, while END prioritized European linkages, although CND also had international contacts. END published research and provided a distinct intellectual focus, in *END Bulletin* and later *END Journal* as well as reports. It took advantage of CND's national reach, while CND used END as a resource.

Compared to the early 1960s, there had been a big shift in what Raymond Williams called "the structure of feeling", giving expression to the political sentiments of millions who had not known the original CND (Inglis 1995: 164–5). The radical middle class, much enlarged in the intervening years, had new feminist and environmentalist values that now informed the peace movement. Like the trade union movement they were provoked by the rise of Thatcher, and in 1980–1, her reactionary new conservatism was becoming highly unpopular amid recession and rising unemployment.

The movement's novel European approach also chimed with cultural shifts. Younger generations had grown up with fuller connections between Britain and the rest of Europe, absorbing continental ideas and lifestyles. There may have been what James Hinton (1989: 187) called an "old imperial pacifist suspicion of continental Europe", but CND's opposition to UK membership of the EEC in the 1975 referendum reflected more than that: Thompson, for example, had argued against it despite a deep commitment to a free and democratic Europe, which he traced to his part in the liberation of Perugia and the memory of his brother Frank, a British officer, who was executed in 1944 while working with the Bulgarian resistance (1985b, 1947). In any case, attitudes towards European integration were beginning to change faced with the reality of Thatcherism.

In a few short years, the critical intellectual culture around nuclear issues that had begun to form in the 1970s bore fruit in a vast range of publications, way beyond those that emanated from CND, END and Spokesman, the Russell Foundation's prolific publisher. These ranged from posters, pamphlets and popular texts to serious investigations, for example about the societal and environmental consequences of nuclear war (Rogers, Dando & Van den Dungen 1981; Schell 1982; Openshaw,

Steadman & Greene 1983), the threat of a "nuclear winter" (Greene, Percival & Ridge 1985), civil defence and the US military apparatus in Britain (Campbell 1982, 1986), the linked risks of nuclear energy and war (Bunyan 1981; Durie & Edwards 1985), the "nukespeak" that euphemized nuclear weapons (Chilton 1982) and the danger that the conventional bombing of nuclear power stations would turn them into nuclear weapons (Ramberg 1982). A considerable academic literature elaborated on the movement's themes, from critiques of the idea of "limited nuclear war" that lay behind NATO's missile strategy (Clark 1982) to studies of military technology, warfare and capitalism (Kaldor 1982a, 1982b; Shaw 1984).

Professional groups such as Scientists Against Nuclear Arms played an important role, while musicians, graphic artists and novelists such as Martin Amis took up the cause. There was also an Ex-Services CND, and the British Nuclear Test Veterans Association often featured in the CND press and local meetings. Indirectly, the movement stimulated the spread of peace studies in schools, but by 1984 this has had become a target of right-wing intellectuals and was eventually squeezed out by the national curriculum that the Thatcher government implemented in 1988 (Behr, Megoran & Carnaffan 2017: 6–7).

In a major contribution to the movement's strategic orientation, the Alternative Defence Commission (1983) produced a comprehensive report on *Defence without the Bomb*, later reinforced by a second study (1987). Ex-DAC activists were at the heart of this initiative, hosted by Bradford Peace Studies: it was proposed by April Carter with support from Adam Roberts, a former assistant editor of *Peace News* who had become an International Relations academic at Oxford. Michael Randle became its coordinator and Howard Clark was also involved. Senior Bradford academics James O'Connell and Paul Rogers were chairs in turn, and the commission was broadly based, with contributions from Kaldor, Smith, Joseph Rotblat and Walter Stein as well as Labour and union figures. For its staff, however, one of its contributions was to put nonviolent civil resistance back on the agenda (Levy 2021: 224–31).

The movement quickly gained wide political support: the grassroots of both the Labour and Liberal parties strongly opposed the new missiles. The CP, which had dominated CND in the 1970s, now became a fairly minor force, although it "worked relatively harmoniously" within the new movement (Taylor 1987b: 172). However, Labour's upheaval after its 1979 defeat, in which the veteran unilateralist Michael Foot became leader and the left – led by Tony Benn, who had long radicalized since he opposed unilateralism in 1960 – increasingly dominant, was a mixed blessing.

The left attacked the party's record in government for the non-implementation of its radical policies, including nuclear disarmament, but this provoked a reaction from the party's right. A "gang of four" senior politicians left in 1981 to form a new Social Democratic Party (SDP): Labour's opposition to the EEC was a major factor, but anti-unilateralism was decisive for two of the gang – Bill Rodgers, who had co-founded the Campaign for Democratic Socialism in 1960, and David Owen, Labour's last foreign secretary – who some CND supporters labelled "Dr Death" for his combative backing of nuclear weapons. Although the up-and-coming Liberal MP Paddy Ashdown was a prominent anti-missile campaigner, his party leadership was less sympathetic and quickly formed an electoral alliance with the SDP, complicating the electoral calculus from CND's point of view.

Christian peace activity also grew rapidly. A May 1979 protest at Westminster Abbey, where the 30th anniversary of NATO was being commemorated, had brought together activists from the Anglican Peace Fellowship, Pax Christi, the Fellowship of Reconciliation and the Quakers, and Christian CND had begun to revive. It organized a 900-strong conference, "Profess and Survive", in Coventry Cathedral in 1981, where Kent described the Church as the movement's "sleeping giant" (Flessati 1997: 28). Using the Christian calendar for peace witness, it organized vigils, pilgrimages and Peace Pentecosts linking military bases. Christian CND claimed in 1983 that 23 per cent of CND members were practising Christians, and its groups brought the nuclear debate into local churches.

Stimulated by the Dutch churches that supported IKV, the Church of England's Board for Social Responsibility produced a report, *The Church and the Bomb* (1982), which concluded that Just War principles forbade the use of nuclear weapons. An opposing "Christian Conservatives" conference was hastily convened, with pro-nuclear arguments branded as a "theology of deterrence" (Ormrod 1987: 213).

Although many local clergy and congregations were supportive of *The Church and the Bomb*, the Church's Synod refused to accept its recommendations. Generally, the churches did not provide a peace platform

as they did in the Netherlands and Germany. None of the denomina-
tions apart from the Quakers reached a formal unilateralist position,
although the General Assemblies of the United Reform Church and
the Church of Scotland opposed nuclear weapons (Kalden 2017: 261;
Flessati 1997: 43; Ormrod 1987: 210–15). The Catholic Church was led
by the anti-communist Pope John Paul II, and Bruce Kent credited the
Catholic civil servant Michael Quinlan, later permanent secretary at
the Ministry of Defence, with steering Cardinal Basil Hume to support the government. Kent became increasingly disillusioned with his
bishops, who were squaring "official Church teaching with what our
Government was actually doing … they did nothing to stop Cruise or
Trident". He ended up leaving the priesthood in 1987 (Kirby 2013: 7;
Kent 1992: 197–206).

The results of surveys by Peter Nias, of END supporters in 1982 and
CND members in 1985, showed that they largely mirrored the social
profile that Parkin had established in the 1960s (Byrne 1988: 56–7).
While both groups were primarily educated middle-class radicals,
ENDers were older and even more highly educated: over three-quarters
had degrees, compared to just over half of CNDers, itself a much larger
proportion than in the general population. Although many trade unions
were committed to unilateral disarmament, polling showed that most
members supported Britain's possession of nuclear weapons, while participation in the movement by manual workers remained low and there
was no serious trade union action to prevent the deployment of nuclear
weapons (Marsh 1989: 107).

Almost a third of END supporters were academics, and despite the
larger role women were playing at all levels in the wider movement,
ENDers were mostly men (Burke 2004: 62–5), probably reflecting the
fact that despite its radicalization since the 1960s, academia was still
very male-dominated. Likewise, despite the advances of antiracism in
the labour movement and popular culture in the 1970s, people of colour
still remained underrepresented; for example, there was "white guilt"
about the absence of Black women at Greenham Common (Roseneil
1995: 95). A leading activist also complained about CND's "lack of
impact among young people in the 1980s", compared to the first wave
(Hinton 1988: 11).

A survey in 1985, after the movement's peak, asking "Who mobilizes
political actions?", found that 2 per cent named CND: a small minority,

but it was "the only single-issue organization capable of significant mobilization of political activity" (Marsh 1989: 106). Extrapolated nationally, this would imply that over 1.1 million were mobilized, which given repeated large demonstrations, multiple local actions and the turnover of participants could be an underestimate.[1]

John Mattausch (1987: 139–40) argued that in view of its minority standing, the antinuclear campaign was not a mass movement. However, it attracted broad support from particular sections of society, which is what most movements do; those which attract support right across a society are exceptions. It also appeared to have significant effects on public opinion: polls during 1982–3 showed consistent majorities against cruise missiles in Britain, and some showed rising support for unilateral nuclear disarmament. According to Gallup, in September 1980 only 21 per cent supported it, but two years later this had grown to 33 per cent, although it later fell back (Berrington 1989: 23–5).

As in the first wave, the movement depended on its ability to orchestrate media coverage through demonstrations and direct action. The range in the national press had narrowed since the 1960s, making television even more crucial. CND soon complained that its huge marches received minimal coverage and opportunities to express its ideas were few. In a letter to BBC staff, END supporters itemized BBC television's "sins" both of omission and commission: they received a response when 50 members of the BBC's film library publicly declared their intention to form an antinuclear group. But the upper echelons remained reluctant to "air CND-type views": the BBC withdrew an invitation to Thompson to deliver the 1981 Dimbleby lecture, with the director-general overruling his staff (Aubrey & Thompson 1982: 85–6).

The movement reached ever further into popular culture. The folk music of the 1960s had given way to a broader scene, and pop groups quickly picked up the antinuclear vibe, creating songs "laden with atomic tension" (Knoblauch 2017: 101, 105–11). A previously irregular festival organized by Michael Eavis in a Somerset field became the Glastonbury CND Festival in 1981. This proved both the making of the event and a regular source of income for CND, peaking at £137,000 in 1987. "The CND symbol that sat like a magic eye at the pinnacle of the Pyramid Stage was a beacon to the tribes who stood in opposition to Thatcher and all she represented", Billy Bragg later wrote (Eavis & Eavis 2019: 101, 93).

The Pyramid Stage with the peace symbol restored, 50th Glastonbury Festival, June 2022

Source: Guy Bell / Alamy Stock Photo.

Speaking at the festival, Thompson (1984) likened the crowd to a medieval army with its tents across the fields. "This has not only been a nation of money-makers and imperialists", he told them, "it's been a nation of inventors, writers, a nation of theatre, musicians, an alternative nation, and it is this alternative nation which I can see in front of me now." This passage was replayed through the Pyramid Stage speakers when Jeremy Corbyn addressed Glastonbury in 2017.

Local groups in a decentralized movement

The alternative nation's new expression, the peace movement, existed mainly at the grassroots. By the time most groups had affiliated to CND, there were around three local members for every national member – the national campaign was even described as a "clearinghouse" for the groups (Rochon 1988: 91). However, it was more than this: it was the movement's essential pan-UK organization and sole representative forum, which also provided its regional framework, including national councils in Scotland and Wales and Northern Ireland CND, which (having gone into abeyance in the mid-1960s) had been re-established in 1979 (INNATE 2023: 7).

However, CND was only one of the peace movement's centres; in different ways, END and the Greenham camp also fulfilled this function. Indeed, the movement was more than any of them or even their sum. It is best thought of as a network of networks, structured on local, regional, national and international levels around clusters of activity such as mass protest, direct action and campaigning in the institutions, and also around different beliefs and cultural orientations. The parts were largely autonomous, deciding their own plans of activities and relating to each other more in an ad hoc way than through CND's structures. One of its strengths compared to the 1960s was a greater tolerance of different modes of action and a recognition that they could be complementary.

Local groups played a key role in maintaining this unity, supporting all the main types of activity and their centres. For example, between 1980 and 1984 Hull END sent protestors to London, Greenham and Barrow-in-Furness (where Trident submarines would be built), was involved in a trans-Pennine march and actions at the Fylingdales and Menwith Hill surveillance bases, supported activists at peace camps and, in line with its END orientation, developed links with the peace movement in other northern European ports, with some members attending conventions on the continent.

CND should be understood as a "form of life", Mattausch (1987: 19) argued, and each group had its own. Groups did not merely provide the bodies for national activity; they were cultural milieux and organizing centres in their own rights, often with major presences in their areas through press, radio and even television coverage. The Hull group, like

"Bridges Not Bombs" protestors, led by the author with his son in a pushchair, approaching the Humber Bridge on Easter Saturday, 10 April 1982

Source: author.

many in larger cities, acted as a focus for the campaign in the surrounding towns, initiating a subregional Humberside CND which organized a "Bridges Not Bombs" march of over 2,000 people across the newly opened Humber Bridge in 1982 and a march against the Falklands War. Local peace festivals brought together environmental, feminist and left-wing groups, speakers and musicians, sometimes with celebrities such as the actor Julie Christie, Humberside's main speaker in 1983.

The groups' often frenetic activism (*Sanity* listed 18 events in the Sheffield area alone in April 1983) was supported by their own structures, which Ann Pettitt, the initiator of the Greenham protests, criticized as "suffocating beneath an avalanche of newsletters" (2006: 31). Mattausch's study of two groups in a Scottish city showed that officers were not typical of the members, most of whom did not regularly take part in meetings or actions; they had a stronger "commitment to campaign" engendered by their prior participation in bodies such as churches and party politics (1987: 25, 137).

Another study, of Aberystwyth, Wales, found that activists were geared to the older end of the age range, with a significant number whose activity began in the first wave. Christianity was a driving force for the involvement of 21 per cent and almost 40 per cent were members of Labour or Plaid Cymru. Membership was part of a "seamless web" of political commitments rather than being the result of them: "feminism, socialism, libertarianism, environmentalism and Welshness stake out much of the territory in which peace groups move" (Day & Robbins 1987: 229). Hull END more or less fitted these patterns: well networked in local institutions, many activists were involved in the Labour Party and trades unions, regional MPs such as John Prescott and Bob Cryer spoke at its meetings, and it included prominent Quakers, notably Alec Horsley, the retired founder of the regional firm Northern Foods, who had supported CND and the Committee of 100 in the 1960s.

Civil defence played a critical role at the local level. Here at least, Kent was right to claim that "more than anything" it made CND a movement again (Salisbury 2021: 132–3). Campaigners in almost every city and town published leaflets and pamphlets exposing the local impact of a nuclear weapon (today, you can generate a DIY map of the local impact of various types of nuclear weapons online). Another widely used tactic was the symbolic "die-in": 2,500 people lay down in Glasgow's George Square in May 1983, in the culmination of one of Scotland's largest protests. Raymond Briggs' satirical comic book, *When the Wind Blows* (1982), popularized the anti-civil defence case: it depicted an elderly couple, the Bloggs, following official advice, erecting a lean-to in their house and stockpiling supplies. After the bomb drops, they die slowly from radiation poisoning while dutifully waiting for help that never arrives.

In the era of "think globally, act locally", the civil defence issue worked with a new initiative, the municipal "nuclear-free zone", as groups' entry-point into local politics. After the first was declared in Manchester in 1980, around 200 local authorities covering over half the UK population eventually followed suit. Although nuclear-free zones, sometimes meaning nuclear power-free, had been proposed internationally, the new British campaign inspired cities across the world (Schregel 2017: 209–10). This movement was boosted by the new municipal socialism, a New Leftish version of Labour politics, to which peace was integral; it was most prominently represented by the Greater London Council (GLC) under Ken Livingstone but spread to other cities, notably Sheffield (Payling 2014). The GLC employed the investigative journalist

Duncan Campbell, who published the most extensive exposé of civil defence (1982).

The issue provided a focus for demands on councils, with the bunkers that higher-level authorities were required to maintain serving as local manifestations of nuclear war.[2] The Hull group's first march, already attracting 500 people in December 1980, was to Humberside's bunker outside the city, and Sheffield's bunker was where local officials gathered in Barry Hines' 1984 film, *Threads*, as nuclear war broke out. Shot on a shoestring with CND members among the extras, this film was a grim update of *The War Game*, which itself continued to be widely shown by groups and finally appeared on television in 1985.

In Bridgend, South Wales, the anti-civil defence campaign was more than symbolic or politically instrumental. A severe and pro-tracted struggle developed with direct action on a par with that at Greenham Common, from which it received support. In December 1981, Mid-Glamorgan County Council, despite passing a nuclear-free resolution, approved a contract for a "civil emergency centre": a nuclear bunker. On 24 January 1982, in "a direct challenge to the wartime machinery of local councils and the Government's nuclear war plans for Wales", as its chronicler Tony Simpson put it (1982: 11), CND occupied the construction site at the Waterton industrial estate and established a peace camp, backed up with extensive leafleting and weekly rallies of hundreds. On 6 March, after 43 days, protestors occupied a 30-foot section of shuttering for the bunker walls until concrete was poured on to the bodies of two of them in front of television cameras. Twelve days later, the council gave in and voted against the bunker. For many, the victory was a symbol of Welsh radicalism: during the occupation the last Welsh county declared itself nuclear free. Paul Flynn of Wales Against Nuclear Arms presented the declaration of a nuclear-free Wales, by 22 local authorities, to the European Parliament.

The Cruise imperative and the unilateralist conundrum

Initially, END and the local anti-missile groups agreed that stopping the cruise missile deployments was the priority even if ultimately there were larger goals; but as the nuclear-free zone movement demonstrates, the movement's agenda tended to broaden. Indeed, the conjunction of

Trident with "Cruise" (as it was universally called) necessarily gave the movement a secondary, distinctively national target, which was especially important in Scotland where the submarines would be based. Polling showed that a majority of the public were favourable towards its positions on both issues.

The movement faced, however, the question of the relationships between these issues and its commitments inherited from the 1960s. As Raymond Williams (1980: 35) argued, campaigns against Cruise and Trident need not involve "the full unilateralist case", support for which rarely rose above 30 per cent in polling. There were multilateralists among END's supporters, and apart from IKV, few of the new movements were unilateralist: the German united around the specific aims of stopping Cruise and Pershing II and the American worked for a "nuclear freeze" (Thompson 1985a: 37). Likewise, stopping Cruise did not necessarily entail an immediate UK withdrawal from NATO, which was even less popular than unilateralism. The dissolution of the nuclear alliances that END envisaged could plausibly be seen as a medium-term goal.

At the level of political mobilization, the movement generally followed END's logic. The platform for CND's 1981 demonstration was "No Cruise! No Trident! No SS-20s!" and its 1982 conference overwhelmingly voted it "essential that CND's major effort next year ... be devoted against the Cruise missile programme". There was also strong support for the idea of equally opposing Soviet and US nuclear weapons: a survey of 41 local groups formed in 1980 found that 30 were both anti-US and anti-Soviet, while only 11 were anti-US but "silent about the Soviet Union" (Mattoo 1992: 63). Yet anti-Americanism was still a significant element (Burke 2004: 104).

Unilateralism also remained influential. A simple and powerful idea, easily grasped as a logical consequence of the shared moral imperative against nuclear weapons, it was imbued in CND's tradition and culture as well as in many of its ideological strands, direct actionist, Christian and Labour alike. Although some leaders such as Ruddock were new to the movement, most including those of END had been involved in or supported CND during the first wave, and they often used unilateralist language. In *Protest and Survive*, Thompson not only couched his call to cancel Cruise as a "unilateral" demand but also urged that "we must dispense with the expensive and futile imperial toy of an 'independent' deterrent" (Thompson & Smith 1980: 60).

The tensions between unilateralist beliefs and the demands of political strategy played out in a new context in the 1980s. There was consensus about both the Cruise priority and the larger objectives of abolishing British and ultimately all nuclear weapons, but the movement often failed to distinguish short- and long-term objectives. As the government's plans for Trident firmed up, the British deterrent was pushed to the fore. Although it was clearly easier to win public opinion to stop Trident than for a full British renunciation of nuclear weapons – especially since anti-unilateralism was the preferred government and press attack line – the unilateralist framing was deeply embedded in CND's arguments against the deterrent's new form.

The recommendations of the Alternative Defence Commission (1983: 275–8) attempted to address these tensions. It proposed that a unilateralist government might pursue a "conditional NATO option", in which Britain would remain in the alliance in the short term with the aim of raising the nuclear threshold, phasing out battlefield and theatre nuclear weapons and "decoupling European NATO from the US nuclear deterrent". Only if NATO resisted these demands would Britain begin a process of withdrawal. The commission recognized that the most important aspects of managing the transition were political and diplomatic, to ensure that Britain's actions "were not misunderstood and did not create unnecessary panic and instability". However, some members were unable to support the conditional NATO option. Randle (1983) argued instead for an in-depth "defensive deterrence" reinforced by nonviolent resistance.[3]

These proposals acknowledged that abandoning nuclear weapons, while morally straightforward, could be anything but in practical terms. They addressed concerns that thoughtful critics had long expressed. Christopher Driver (1964: 82), for example, had pointed out that the removal of nuclear weapons could "upset the balance of power in the world so radically" that it could make war more likely; he was concerned that the movement's populist case "never rested on such nice calculations of military probability". Recently, Lawrence Freedman (1981: 3) had argued in a critique of END that abolishing nuclear weapons and alliances would "unsettle" the international order.[4] Kaldor (1981: 1) responded that END was not "an arms control proposal but a political objective": the overcoming of the Cold War itself.

The Alternative Defence Commission's recommendations helped shore up the movement's political defences, emphasizing that its policy was "not 'unilateral disarmament' ... but unilateral *nuclear* disarmament", as Thompson (1985a: 36) later put it. END had never seen NATO withdrawal as a priority, since other European movements were not arguing for their countries to pull out. However, CND's 1982 conference had been "split down the middle" when making NATO withdrawal a campaigning issue was proposed (Burke 2004: 105). Although leading CNDers had opposed this on the grounds of the political damage it would cause, and a narrow decision in favour was not implemented, the conditional NATO option did not become CND's policy offer.

Indeed, although presented as a road map for a unilateralist government, the Alternative Defence Commission's favoured option could easily be interpreted as a departure from unilateralist purity, as Steps for Peace had been in 1962. Yet the commission's semidetached status meant that the conflict to which those had given rise was avoided. Indeed, in contrast to the 1960s, the movement avoided turning its differences into hard-and-fast divisions. The disagreements that mattered, as we shall see, were as much within particular sectors, such as END and the women's peace movement, as between factions in CND's decision-making bodies. The movement's attention wandered during three years of intense activity – "we all had nodded off on our marching feet once or twice", Thompson acknowledged (1985a: 90) – but as much because of its decentralized nature and the diversity of its activities as its differences.

Ultimately the strategic situation that had brought the movement into existence helped maintain its focus. The 1983 deadline for Cruise and Pershing II deployment loomed over the movement as it did over NATO, giving it a timescale as well as a target. And there was another built-in deadline that it talked less about: the electoral one. Whereas the first movement was formed in 1958 with a general election nearing, the 1980 movement arose shortly after Thatcher's 1979 victory, with no election expected before 1983–4: precisely when Cruise would come to a head. Given the Conservatives' commitment to the missiles, any realistic chance of stopping them depended partly on the Labour and Liberal parties, but the movement was only one influence on their electoral prospects.

Greenham Common and direct action

It was direct action – initiated not by CND or END but by women activists in Wales – that particularly helped keep the focus on Cruise. In 1980, Ann Pettitt, who had taken part in a student sit-in at Bristol, been involved in Women's Liberation and squatting in London and then moved to rural Wales, took the initiative to form an antinuclear campaign in Carmarthen. This initially opposed nuclear power – radioactive waste dumping was an issue in neighbouring mid-Wales – but when the group turned to nuclear weapons, Pettitt, having read *Protest and Survive*, realized that since the cruise missile system was ground-based, it "was get-at-able in a way that no other system was … . Straight away I realized how vulnerable it was to … just people lying in the way" (Liddington 1991: 223–4).

Later she read in *Peace News* about a women-led peace march from Copenhagen to Paris, and had the idea of a march to Greenham Common. After John Cox helped obtain a £250 loan from CND, 36 women, 4 men and 3 children set off from Cardiff on 27 August 1981 on a 110-mile "Women *for* Life on Earth Peace March '81", with a pink banner showing a sprouting tree and a CND symbol. In Bristol, many feminists turned up their noses at their "women-led" rather than "women-only" march and even the CND group didn't want to get involved, for fear of being criticized by the feminists. But elsewhere they found warmer welcomes as they snaked their way across southern Wales and England. They entered Bath singing "Take those toys away from the boys" and "No more Hiroshimas", and leafleted along the way.

The first aim of the march, Pettitt (2006: 42) recalled, was "to gate-crash the closed world of the media debate on defence issues". But despite considerable pre-march publicity, they now received minimal coverage. "It was this realization that the media were ignoring them that prompted more confrontational tactics", Liddington (1991: 230) notes. "One evening, at a stop-over in Wiltshire, someone mentioned the suffragettes. Why not chain themselves to the fence at Greenham?"

When they arrived early on 5 September, mistaken for cleaners by the sole policeman at the main gate, four women chained themselves to the fence and supporters from Newbury Campaign Against Cruise soon turned up. Letters to the US base commandant and the minister of defence were read out, the latter demanding a televised debate. Jeered at by US servicemen and taking it in turns to be chained, some decided to stay; a nurse, Helen John, who was somewhat older than most of the women (many were mothers of young children), was the most determined. Enough remained to form a small peace camp, with camping equipment supplied by local supporters. Initially the police refused to move them on as no obstruction was being caused, and although the authorities erected a high-security fence, they feared evicting the campaigners.

The camp dug in through the autumn and winter. Growing conflict with the authorities increased its national backing from women's peace groups and the wider movement, and a national support network was built up built around telephone-trees (the movement's main system for spreading news quickly, through cascading phone calls). But Greenham remained low-key and marginal to most women in both CND and the women's movement in late 1981 (Liddington 1991: 235–7).

In February 1982, the camp became not just women-led but women-only: the men were asked to leave. There was tension within the peace movement around this exclusion: if most activists increasingly recognized the special nature of the camp, women who were not prepared to work in a separatist way felt rejected. Annie Tunnicliffe (1983) argued in *Sanity* the following year that "hierarchies have a way of establishing themselves, especially when there is a pretence of no hierarchy, no system", and her critique resonated with readers – nine out of ten letters supported her (*Sanity* 1983, May: 27). Yet in the camp, many felt that anarchy worked, enabling increasingly daring tactics of which there were many examples by the time Tunnicliffe's article appeared.

Greenham also became more mystical and spiritual. A rich symbolic culture evolved that articulated the camp's closeness to nature; imagery of snakes and spiders abounded. Mary Daly's *Gyn/Ecology* (1978) was widely read and its critique of phallic myths internalized. Participants not only objected to being called "ladies"; many also called themselves "Wiimmiin", "Wombyn" or "Womyn", and in court often swore to "The Goddess" instead of God. For them, Cruise was more effectively blocked by these practices than by mainstream peace politics or feminism. But as one activist put it, "for every woman who revelled in the association of ecofeminism with earth Goddesses, there was one who winced", and many recoiled from what they saw as pseudo-religious ideology (Feigenbaum 2008: 120). Later, Donna Haraway's (1985) idea of the feminist cyborg became identified with Greenham and counterposed to the idea of the goddess (Feigenbaum 2008: 122–34).

"Reversing traditional roles, women have been leaving home for peace, rather than men leaving home for war", Women for Life on Earth (1982) wrote to women across the country in October, together with plans for a national demonstration on 12 December, the third anniversary of NATO's decision to introduce the missiles. Meanwhile bruising legal conflicts, as the authorities tried to remove the camp, made it reminiscent of the suffragettes' historic battles. In November, 11 women charged with the sentry-box occupation pleaded it lawful as a prevention of genocide. Expert witnesses including Thompson and the Bishop of Salisbury supported them, but in this and other cases, 23 women were imprisoned.

The December 1982 action, Embrace the Base, saw tens of thousands, including many from other European countries, completely encircling it with candles glowing in the dark; they humanized the fence by attaching photographs of their families to it until every square foot was covered. The scene had been "organized on a shoestring with the simplest of modern technology: the telephone, the photocopier, and the postal system", but that day the Greenham Women and Cruise "were at last in every living room that had a television" (Pettitt 2006: 150). They became a global symbol of antinuclear protest.[5]

This was followed the next day by the first of a series of large-scale blockades and sorties into the base, bequeathing iconic images such as the ring of women, silhouetted against the dawn, who danced on top of missile silos on New Year's Day 1983. The women seemed to have found an answer to the quandary of direct action: large-scale arrests occurred, but the state chose not to bring the full panoply of the law down upon them as it had against the Committee of 100. Indeed, the judiciary could barely cope with the growing number of women defying the law.

Greenham now emerged from the obscurity into which media neglect had cast it and became a spectacle, occupying "the central theatrical arena" of the whole movement against Cruise, "dramatically staged against a variety of backdrops: the High Court, Newbury Council Chamber and magistrate court, Holloway [prison]", as Liddington puts it (1991: 235–6, 252). However, coverage often blurred the women's committed nonviolence, representing it as "disruption" and "attacks" on the camp and even the "peace" of the local area; the women saw even the

Guardian's reporting as negative. The force the police used against the protestors was rarely depicted, while editors searched endlessly for "balance", for example presenting the tiny Women and Families for Defence, founded by the *Sunday Express* diarist Lady Olga Maitland, as the equivalent of the large women's peace movement (Glasgow University Media Group 1985: 197, 206–15).

However, the Greenham community developed its own culture that enabled its resistance. Songs, adapted from and inspired by the women's music of the 1970s as well as a wider repertoire, were developed through singing round the campfires and played a powerful role in constructing Greenham identities. There were more nuanced if sometimes critical accounts in movement journals such as *Peace News* and the feminist magazine *Spare Rib*, as well as in camp-based newsletters, which because of the camp's DIY ethos were even handwritten. New visual technologies were also beginning to alter activists' communications: videocassettes of the 1983 film *Carry Greenham Home*, made by student film-makers Beeban Kidron and Amanda Richardson from their footage of Embrace the Base, were widely circulated, prefiguring today's activist digital video (Feigenbaum 2008: 54–113, 222–70).

The camp became the centre of an expanding women's peace network, indeed "the most visible form of women's activism ... in Britain in the 1980s" (Roseneil 1995: 4–5). While Greenham was rooted on the perimeter of the base, it was also a wider symbolic community, and in turn depended on the larger movement, including CND at local, regional and national levels. In December 1982, CND's conference recognized women's independent action and voted five Greenham women onto its National Council, but mistrust continued to fester between the camp and CND.

The centrality of Greenham made it the focus of extensive debate, both during the campaign against Cruise and after. Although criticized by some feminists for promoting an essentialist idea of women as naturally more peaceful (which echoed the maternalism of prewar women's peace campaigns), it nevertheless helped create a women's peace movement that combined many strands of feminist opinion (Liddington 1991: 259; Jones 1983). The priority for the emotional, or what one participant called "intelligent feelings", was at the heart of Greenham politics and offered a distinct, powerful approach to the development of the movement (Feigenbaum 2008: 12–15).

Greenham Common, where 30,000 women demonstrators linked hands to form a human chain around the base, 1983

Source: Sally and Richard Greenhill / Alamy Stock Photo.

For many participants, Greenham also offered a new model of women's communal living, forms of consciousness and identities. Its ethos included the autonomy of women, opposition to hierarchy, respect for diversity and individuality, personal responsibility, communality, environmentalism, reflexivity and valuing the non-rational, as well as nonviolence and the inseparability of means from ends. In particular, Greenham became a place where lesbian identities were constructed and reconstructed, as confident younger lesbians often undertook the more audacious actions. The meaning of this was positive, Sasha Roseneil (1995) argues, enabling not only personal transformations but also the community of the camp, which sustained it as a powerful peace protest.

In a period in which homosexuality remained very controversial, this side of the Greenham ethos was a lightning rod for the right.[6] For the Tory press, the Greenham women were unfit mothers, dirty, hysterical and lesbian (Young 1990: 45–88). For one of the many local critics, they threatened the ideal of the "natural, feminine woman with all her motherly, family instincts" (Moores 2014: 213). The *Sun* called them "manhaters" and the local Newbury paper consistently delegitimated the camp. However, extreme antifeminism may have limited the ability to mobilize local opposition of one hostile group, Ratepayers Against the Greenham Encampments. This represented a Thatcherite version of middle-class activism, linked to national "new right" networks and consisting of shopkeepers, businessman, former military officers, retired professionals and housewives (Moores 2014).[7]

The camp remained defiant. Neither the arrests, the right-wing hostility nor the media framing appeared to detract from public opposition to Cruise deployment, which rose to 67 per cent of women and 55 per cent of men in one January 1983 poll. A report commissioned by the government suggested that "young women" were "perhaps the most important" group that it needed to win over (Salisbury 2021: 175). By late 1983 the camp had multiplied itself into different colour-named sites at each of the base's nine gates, representing different ideas, styles and issues way beyond nuclear weapons. These included violence against women, nuclear dumping, animal liberation and veganism, aid and development, and a Christian vigil, and each attracted different groups to spend time there.

Greenham put women at the heart of the antinuclear movement in a way that would have been unimaginable in the first wave. In this sense, it was a product of the 1970s women's movement, as was CND's often reluctant acceptance of it. It was also a radical innovation in practice, since it concentrated campaigners for many months – and, as it turned out, years – in a particular place. This enabled much more distinct life forms to develop than in local CND groups or even close-knit non-place-based groups such as the DAC.

Greenham subverted the military idea of the camp, counterposing an open, humane community to the fenced-in encampment of armed men and weapons. Although Resurrection City, a civil rights tent city in Washington, DC in May–June 1968, was a loose precedent, it was Greenham that introduced the "protest camp" into the repertoire of social movements, and it later played a major role from Occupy to Tahrir Square (Feigenbaum, Frenzel & McCurdy 2013: 2–40). Greenham helped inspire a wave of peace camps, including at Faslane and Lossiemouth in Scotland, Molesworth (first set up by the Friends of Reconciliation and supported by Christian CND), Lakenheath, Upper Heyford, Dawes Hill, Naphill, Capenhurst and Burtonwood in England, Bishopscourt in Northern Ireland and (as we have seen) briefly at Bridgend in Wales.

Greenham was a product of and hugely reinforced the movement's direct action tradition. A wave of NVDA had already been developing in 1981, when a network of CND trainers was created; soon workshops were organized at Bradford University. Thirty years earlier NVDA had been the method of a particular group, the DAC; it had then become the strategic option of the Committee of 100, mostly opposed by CND; now it was a common repertoire that a network of groups, mixed as well as women's, utilized to create diverse actions, often with integral CND support.

Direct action was clearly understood in nonviolent terms, since violence was understood as belonging to the state and aggressive masculinity – the flirtation with it in the 1960s and 1970s was not repeated. However, confrontational tactics, which had been controversial even within the DAC when they were first used, were now completely normalized, even if only a minority participated. A 1985 survey showed that 56 per cent of CND members believed that NVDA strengthened the campaign while only 22 per cent thought it weakened it; 30 per cent were prepared to take part (Byrne 1988: 126).

Indeed, it was now increasingly central to the movement and new mass actions developed: in April 1983 Lakenheath was blockaded, and between 31 May and 3 June 1983 one of the largest ever civil disobedience actions took place at Upper Heyford, with 5,000 blockading the base where eight nuclear-armed F-111s were on permanent standby; there were 752 arrests.

However, not all NVDA was mass action. In the spirit of carrying Greenham home, in 1984 Angie Zelter founded the Snowball Civil Disobedience Campaign in Norfolk, whose method of disobedience was the individual cutting of one strand of wire from the fence of the nearest base. "Cutting a single strand", she later explained, "was to limit the amount of damage done and to be perceived as purely symbolic from an individual's point of view, unthreatening in a physical way to the authorities, but serious enough to warrant prosecution" (Zelter 2021: 28). The action snowballed locally until 50 were tried in Fakenham in 1986, and by 1987 it had spread to 42 bases, with around 2,500 arrests, some leading to imprisonments when people refused to pay fines (Bove 2007).

For the Special Branch in 1983, NVDA was "without doubt the most influential force within the peace movement" (Undercover Policing Inquiry 2023c: 3–4). They emphasized the effectiveness of the decentralized preparations for large NVDA actions: there was "no central organizing committee" for NVDA, only an initiating group that could be "one of several hundred" participating groups. Within each of these, close relationships created trust and minimized the risk of infiltration, which the police successfully carried out in national CND: they had full details of the 12-hour shifts allocated to different CND regions for the Upper Heyford blockade, from an informant who attended a London Region council six weeks beforehand; details were passed to the Home Office (Undercover Policing Inquiry 2023b).

NVDA was also, the Special Branch argued, a double-edged sword for the "structured hierarchy" of CND, who had tried to influence it by providing training. This had "only served to exacerbate the problem" since the trainers were "drawn mainly from the feminist and anarcho/pacifist groups and the principles they impart ... only serve to take more control away from National CND and put it in the hands of the activists". The *Peace News* collective was "of particular influence".

END, the peace movement and Eastern Europe

The transformation of Greenham into an international symbol coincided with what Thompson later judged to have been the "highest tide" of the European movement (1985a: 54). When Pettitt was invited to address a 250,000-strong CND rally on 24 October 1982 (the women had to walk from Greenham to London to extract a two-minute slot, although she spoke for longer), this was part of a massive wave of demonstrations across Western Europe.

This movement comprised national campaigns that evolved autonomously, but END had helped give it a pan-European orientation. After the Appeal was launched in 1980, the Russell Foundation and other British campaigners had helped set up meetings in several major cities, bringing together activists and researchers from across Europe, planning among other things the Copenhagen to Paris march that inspired Pettitt. However, British groups were not the only ones initiating and coordinating. IKV and the Danish group Nej til Atomvaben were also kick-starting European collaboration in 1980, and IKV founded the International Peace Coordination and Communication Centre, another pan-European body, in late 1981 (Kalden 2017: 260).

Nor were END's ideas universally accepted in CND. While END influenced CND's international policy, some leading CNDers were at the time unsympathetic to the convention process and many regarded its East European orientation as marginal. CND had "a limited international perspective", Kent later acknowledged (1992: 174–5). He was always willing to speak up for East European dissidents, but END's linkage of disarmament and human rights had at times "difficult side-effects for CND, by its constitution a single-issue disarmament campaign, not a general human rights movement".

From early in END's existence, Ken Coates mooted a pan-European conference, and in late 1981, it was decided at a meeting in Rome to establish an END Liaison Committee, participation in which was based on support for the Appeal. Seventeen countries were represented, including most of the main peace organizations and many major political parties, demonstrating the breadth of the Appeal's support at this point. The committee organized a convention in Brussels in July 1982, the first of what became annual events until 1992. Ordinary activists took part in the END conventions, and they attracted significant numbers: 1,000 in Brussels and 2,500 in West Berlin in 1983, the largest gathering. As forums for discussion of a wide range of issues – but not decision-making – they helped to build cohesion and momentum. They strengthened and created networks within the movement, including of women, scientists, doctors, nuclear-free towns, unions, churches, soldiers, conscientious objectors and peace educators.

However, the committee represented CND and its equivalents as well as sympathetic political parties and trade unions, rather than grassroots networks. There were long-running arguments about the aims of and participation in the conventions. Many in British END prioritized the grassroots, but Coates countered that "the notion of a nuclear-free Europe did not emerge as an inspiration from the Common at Greenham, but was a political proposal by the Prime Minister of Sweden" (1987: 16). He has been accused of believing in the "Realpolitik" of working through the left organizations (Taylor 2013: 192), but his Russell Foundation colleague Tony Simpson (2014: 78) sees this as a straw man: there were differences of emphasis, but no more than most ENDers did Coates believe it was a choice between the institutions and the mass movement.

What was true was that Coates, like many organizations in the Liaison Committee, regarded the "convention process" as the centrepiece of a European strategy. Programmatically, he emphasized a European nuclear weapons-free zone, which would involve agreement between the blocs. Kaldor, Thompson and the British END committee, in contrast, often together with IKV, the French Comité pour le Désarmement Nucléaire en Europe and the West German Greens, saw the conventions as only one component of a strategy and emphasized the "beyond the blocs" dimension.

There were corresponding disagreements about inviting official East European peace committees. The Soviet Peace Committee wanted a key role in the West European movement and expressed its desire not only to attend but also to co-organize the 1983 convention. It became angry when told that only those who had endorsed the END Appeal could be full participants, and no official committee from any state in the East attended. The issue erupted in the 1984 Perugia convention when it became known that this time all the committees would be represented, but 59 invited independent activists from Eastern Europe had not been given permission to travel. Protestors against their exclusion mounted the stage in the opening session, opening a more serious division within the END current of the movement (Burke 2004: 184–7, 191).

These issues became part of disputes within British END, which also involved the organization of the campaign itself, money and the direction of the *END Bulletin*. In 1982, conflict between the Russell Foundation and the national coordinating committee (hereafter British END) came to a head over the amount of support that the latter was giving to the conventions. The foundation, refusing to allow the committee to control the *Bulletin,* withdrew from it, so the committee set up the *END Journal* with Kaldor as editor. She had wide contacts in Eastern as well as Western Europe and developed a lively publication. However, both groups continued to be represented in the Liaison Committee.

Coates, like many mainstream West European left parties and unions involved in the campaign, saw contacts with official Soviet bloc committees as important in themselves, but others in British END saw them mainly as a tactic to enable access to independents. Coates did not believe that "détente from below" was possible, but for Kaldor it was central; Thompson backed it but found the pro-Western orientation of many independents difficult.

However, END's churches committee attempted to create a European network based mainly on official connections; limited dialogue between

West European peace activists and independent forces in Eastern Europe was already underway by 1981, notably between IKV and the Protestant churches in East Germany. Yet early attempts to engage the Charter 77 human rights group in Czechoslovakia were met with suspicion, and END lacked meaningful dialogue with the Solidarity trade union movement in Poland. Since this was the only independent mass movement in an East European country, it was a significant weakness, but it was not for lack of trying: "extensive enquiries showed that there was absolutely no interest in END among the Polish independent trade unionists" (Coates 1987: 19). However Solidarity's suppression, in a December 1981 coup by the Polish military, would change the situation.

In November 1981, Thompson made a strong new statement of his approach in the banned Dimbleby lecture, *Beyond the Cold War*, delivered in Worcester. Putting "the causes of freedom and of peace back together", he said, was the way the Cold War could end without nuclear war (Thompson 1982a: 31–2). New East–West discussions began in 1982, especially after two spokespersons of Charter 77 issued a Statement on West European Peace Movements. This developed the idea of the "indivisibility of peace": to guarantee peace between states, it was also necessary to have peace within them, by eliminating violence and injustice and guaranteeing human rights (Kavan & Tomin 1983: 22–3).

This statement was promoted in Britain by the exiled Jan Kavan of the Palach Press, who had longstanding links with War Resisters International that went back to protests they had organized against the Soviet invasion of Czechoslovakia in 1968, and with CND from April Carter's period as chair in 1970–1. Michael Randle had gone to Prague and stayed with Kavan's mother, Rosemary, in 1970, and War Resisters International along with others – such as the left-wing *Labour Focus on Eastern Europe* – had continued to support dissidents and publicize their views during the 1970s (Levy 2021: 211–16). In this sense, END was building on links that various activists had developed earlier.

British END also made intensive efforts to connect with an emerging independent peace movement in East Germany, which could be traced back to reactions against the introduction of compulsory premilitary training in schools in 1978 and the Protestant churches' annual "Peace Weeks" from 1980. In 1982, veteran oppositionist Robert Havemann and pastor Rainer Eppelmann launched the Berlin Appeal, eventually

signed by 2,000 people, which demanded free discussion, demilitarization of East German life, a nuclear-free zone in Europe and withdrawal
of "occupation troops" from both Germanies. A church-based Peace
Forum in Dresden was supported by large numbers of young people
(Coates & Meacher 1982: 73–5; Sandford 1983).

In July 1982, Kaldor and the IKV's Mient-Jan Faber managed to
sign a joint statement with representatives of Solidarity in exile, linking peace and human rights, but this caused tensions with Thompson
and Coates, who had reservations about Solidarity's anti-communism
(Rankin 2017: 68–9). Later that year, an independent Peace Group
for Dialogue was founded in Hungary, influenced by END's ideas,
and Kaldor and Faber were able to address a 150-strong audience in
Budapest. In May 1983, about 400 supporters of the group were permitted to march with their own banners in an official Peace Council march
(Köszegi & Thompson nd).

Generally in 1983, the Communist regimes still suppressed independent initiatives and their official committees were hostile to END
and its Appeal; even in Hungary, repressive moves soon followed. The
new beginnings in Eastern Europe that END looked for were real but
still very small in the year when the NATO missile deployments were
to be implemented.

Towards the year of decision

In Britain, it had taken the Conservative government time to take the
movement's measure in 1980. However, it mounted a more aggressive counter-campaign after John Nott was made defence secretary in
January 1981. Believing that the government was losing the argument,
he set up a unit to monitor CND, together with an umbrella group
of anti-movement forces linked to Conservative Central Office. This
eventually included the overtly anti-CND Coalition for Peace through
Security and the Council for Arms Control, which conducted lower-key
outreach, for example in the churches (Salisbury 2021: 150–8).

There were significant changes in the government's discourse, with a
new focus on unilateralism, the use of pejorative terms such as "one-sided
disarmament" and "appeasement", and juxtaposing CND with Nazism
(Garapedian 1987: 349, 352). After Labour's 1980 conference called for

a commitment to unilateralism in the next manifesto and Michael Foot, a veteran CND supporter, was elected leader in November, the government linked CND with Labour. Although the Ministry of Defence's unofficial view was that Labour policy was only "half-unilateralist" and Kent later described Foot as sympathetic to but "distant" from CND by this time (Salisbury 2021: 148, 149), it was exploiting the real tensions that existed in the movement over the extents to which it should stress unilateralism and NATO withdrawal.

Yet these efforts, and those of other NATO governments, showed few results. Thompson's assessment of the strength of the Western peace movement in late 1981 was widely shared: the US political scientist Stanley Hoffman (1981: 328) concluded: "It is a mass movement of continental dimension, which mobilizes and moves people across borders – something quite exceptional even in the partly integrated Western Europe of today."

Fearing this popular opposition, some in NATO circles still hoped that missile deployment might be avoided by a "zero option" in which the USSR would agree to remove its SS-20s. Ronald Reagan had assumed the US presidency earlier that year and his Cold Warrior associates saw "zero" as a win-win, giving the US a military advantage if the Soviets agreed and binding European governments into installing the missiles in the more likely event that they refused. Therefore, on 18 November 1981, Reagan announced a zero-option policy, designed to blunt the peace movement's edge. Its premises seemed "ripped from their banners": no cruise, no Pershing II, no SS-20 (Colbourn 2022: 143). US and Soviet negotiators met a week later to discuss what Western officials now called "intermediate nuclear forces" (INF), but a Soviet counterproposal included British and French weapons, which NATO would not accept. In Britain, the Foreign Office worried that a zero option might create unrealistic expectations, and the government escalated its campaign against the peace movement. However, in December 1981 the Polish coup led Reagan to impose sanctions and talks remained deadlocked throughout 1982. The USSR was unwilling to move partly because the movement might still force NATO to abandon its deployments.

The political situation moved heavily in Thatcher's favour after Argentina invaded the Falklands/Malvinas islands, a small British colony in the South Atlantic, in April 1982, and she compensated for her humiliating failure to prevent the invasion by sending a British naval task force to retake the islands. The ensuing "war of Thatcher's face", as Thompson (1982b) called it, was seen internationally as overkill (255 British and 649 Argentinian service personnel died) but was politically effective.[8] CND organized protests during the 74-day war, but the substantial opposition to it was never fully mobilized (Freedman 1988: 86). *Sanity* (1982, October: 10) reported that three CND membership cards lay at the bottom of the South Atlantic after HMS *Sheffield* was sunk, although the sailors to whom they belonged survived.

Despite the loss of lives, the UK prevailed with covert US support, and tight media management of the war helped maintain majority public backing. Thatcher had risen to the patriotic challenge that Foot posed to her in an emergency debate after the invasion, harnessed the shared "Churchillian" politics of the British elite and, by successfully using British military power, exorcized the ghost of Suez. She emerged greatly strengthened, overcoming the unpopularity of her first years in office (Harris 1983; Glasgow University Media Group 1985: 92–143; Barnett 1982).

"The nuclear issue was almost entirely edged out of public debate", Thatcher herself noted (1993: 267), but the war hardly enabled the government to wave away public concern. The movement was still mobilizing strongly, forcing the cancellation of the Hard Rock civil defence exercise in autumn 1982 after many councils refused to take part, and the GLC opened its secret nuclear bunkers to the public. By October 1982, Nott was urging Thatcher to obtain a new arms control initiative to defuse the growing belief that the government was little more than a "creature of the Americans" (Colbourn 2022: 151). Moreover, the movement was still mobilizing strongly in continental Europe and the USA, where on 12 June 1982 up to a million people participated in a rally for a nuclear freeze, for which polls showed large majority support.

With the government's own research showing that Cruise rather than Trident was the main public concern in Britain, in January 1983 Thatcher replaced Nott with the abrasive Michael Heseltine. Relishing the confrontation and wearing a combat jacket, he took the political battle to Greenham Common the next month. There was "a noisy crush as the women rushed forward and a phalanx of police forced a way through … Heseltine was dragged almost to his knees in the press of bodies – and photographed, just afloat in the sea of helmets" (Fairhall 2006: 52). Although, on the day of his visit, over 100 women entered the base dressed as snakes to show how easy it was to overcome security (Feigenbaum 2008: 137), Heseltine saw this image as the turning point in the campaign against CND. Refusing to debate with it, he easily found allies in the press and right-wing activist groups such as Peace Through NATO. When CND announced a massive human chain to link Greenham, Aldermaston and the Royal Ordnance Factory at Burghfield, the focal points of Berkshire's "Nuclear Valley", on Good Friday 1983, he staged a visit to Berlin the previous day to pre-empt the protest's publicity.

The Falklands had profoundly altered the political situation, and Thatcher had regained her polling lead following widespread enthusiasm for the SDP in 1981–2. After favourable local election results in May 1983, she decided to call an early general election on 9 June, in the expectation that the Liberal-SDP Alliance would damage Labour. This was the first election since the Second World War in which defence was a major political divide: the Conservatives backed Cruise and Trident, while Labour rejected them and set out the aim of non-nuclear defence within NATO. The Alliance position was a compromise between its constituent parties: it said its attitude to Cruise would depend on arms control negotiations and obtaining dual-key operation, an embarrassing issue for the Conservatives because the USA would only "consult" the UK on using the missiles, in contrast to the theoretical veto that it had had over the Thors in the 1950s (Jones 1987).

CND called 1983's poll a "Nuclear Election". It knew that elections, in which broadcasters were required to balance party coverage, worked against single-issue campaigns, but it had begun to discuss the election the previous year and mounted an unprecedentedly professional publicity effort, focused on Cruise and Trident. At the local level, a doorstep Peace Canvass was supposed to be carried out, but this had little effect. CND's fears that it would be frozen out of the national media were realized: once the election was underway its meetings went virtually unreported, as did a Women All Out for Peace Day on International Women's Day.[9]

Although CND's executive had vetoed an explicitly anti-Tory campaign, effectively it was reliant on Labour, but the party barely made the specific case against Cruise; indeed, it "wanted to talk about anything else except defence", Kent complained (Taylor 1986: 208). The other parties attacked Labour's unilateralism while Foot and his deputy,

Healey, expressed contradictory views and the former prime minister, Callaghan, criticized party policy.

Heseltine had circulated Conservative candidates with material linking Labour with CND and the latter with communism and the USSR, and MI5 whistle-blower Cathy Massiter later claimed that she had been asked to pass covert surveillance material on CND members to the Ministry of Defence anti-CND unit (Ponting 1989: 189). But in the event the smears were not needed. Thatcher achieved a commanding plurality (43.9 per cent), while the opposed majority were almost equally divided between Labour (27.6) and the Alliance (25.4). The first-past-the-post system gave her a crushing majority of 144 seats; it was Labour's worst result since 1931 and ended Foot's leadership.

The lessons of the election were a source of controversy at the time and later. While Joan Ruddock claimed that it settled nothing since the majority of voters continued to oppose Cruise and Trident, many activists recognized it as a major reverse, as did sympathetic analysts. For Richard Taylor (1986: 210), the Tories, aided by Labour's anti-CND elements, had managed to "convince the public of their view of the defence debate" as polls showed support for the movement's positions, including on Cruise, falling during the campaign – even if they recovered afterwards. For Adam Roberts (1983: 305), the outcome highlighted the inadequacies of the idea of unilateral nuclear disarmament, which had been shown to be a "blind alley", edging out serious proposals such as those of the Alternative Defence Commission whose report was published just before the election.

Others cast doubt on these interpretations. Brian McNair (1989: 140) showed that the television news had largely bypassed the substantive nuclear issues, focusing instead on Labour's divisions. Analysing the polling, John Curtice (1989: 149) also concluded that the fact of division was more important than its substance. Labour's defence policy appeared "not to have had any particular repellent quality during the election campaign". The voters Labour lost were even more negative about some of its other policies, and Labour supporters actually became more antinuclear. Indeed, there had been a further drift in this direction after 1983, even in support for unilateralism, which was backed by four in ten Labour voters by 1986.

There was, however, no doubting that Thatcher's victory made it much more difficult to stop the missiles. Internationally, the situation had already worsened for the peace movement with the narrower victory of chancellor Helmut Kohl's centre-right coalition in the West German federal election in March, even if, as a result of the movement, the antinuclear Green Party led by Petra Kelly was represented in the Bundestag for the first time. The Italian election, just after the British, also returned a pro-cruise government.

The movement's response during the "hot autumn" of 1983 was a giant wave of protests against the imminent arrival of the missiles. The East–West situation was extremely tense in these months, which "historians routinely describe as the most dangerous point since the Cuban missiles crisis" (Colbourn 2022: 189–90). In September (but unknown at the time), an official in the Soviet early warning system had to override false alarms of US missile strikes to prevent an automatic launch of retaliatory missiles. In November, Soviet officials were unable to exclude the possibility that a NATO exercise, Able Archer 83, involved a real missile strike. (The period has taken on almost mythical status and was satirized in the 2015 television series *Deutschland 83*.)

On 22 October, CND held what was widely believed to be its largest ever rally of several hundred thousand people; the protests in West Berlin, Rome and The Hague were judged to be even bigger. Behind the defiance, however, there were arguments in the leadership about how best to keep the movement going through the inevitable defeat of its prime aim. The longstanding but divisive case for massive mixed action at Greenham as the best way of deterring the government from implementation gained new traction as deployment loomed, the first in any of the five countries. Meg Beresford, backed by some "Greenham heretics", pushed the idea in early 1983, but in April CND's National Council rejected Annie Tunnicliffe's proposal for a mixed action.

During a chaotic few weeks in late October and early November, CND thrashed around trying to find a common response and the movement came close to splitting (Hinton 1989: 192). Some wanted mass civil disobedience in the regions and others outside parliament if and when it made a final decision on Cruise, but the latter was opposed since it might be presented as an antidemocratic siege. Instead (just before the October demonstration), Thompson (1983) insisted privately to Kent and Ruddock, after speaking across the country, that it was at Greenham that activists wanted to protest as the missiles arrived. CND was being held to ransom by a small group of campers, and unless its executive would defy them to organize a protest, he was for a group of individuals including himself issuing a call to action.

Others felt, however, that CND was in danger of accepting the media stereotypes of Greenham. A successful action on 29 October by around 1,000 women, who emerged from the woods around the base to cut the fence, showed the strength of the camp's resistance. Many were dressed as witches; it was Halloween, but they were evoking the idea of witches as proto-feminists that had become common. On 27 October a parliamentary debate had been announced for the 31st, and a small protest blocked traffic at Westminster: but the House of Commons approved the deployment. The CND leadership decided to call a Greenham demonstration and Kent led a delegation there to discuss it with the women, but led by Helen John they wholly rejected any CND action (Pettitt 2006: 273). CND backed off, reluctantly accepting the camp's veto in order to avoid an open confrontation.

On 14 November 1983, the first missiles were flown into Greenham ahead of schedule and moved into their hangars under armed guard. The Bundestag and the Italian parliament had also agreed to deployment, but nowhere had the majority of the public been persuaded. In the Netherlands and Belgium, governments still could not get deployment through parliament; in Greece the Socialist government reversed its support for the NATO decision; and in Denmark the government struggled to get support.

In Britain, a November poll showed 94 per cent supported dual-key operation of the newly installed missiles, which the cabinet had rejected as it would imply that Britain "had lost confidence" in the Americans. In an emergency, they could even be deployed off-base without prior agreement (Michaels 2022: 1020). The USA had invaded the Caribbean island of Grenada, a former British colony of which Queen Elizabeth remained head of state, on 25 October. For many, Reagan's failure to consult Thatcher underlined his lack of interest in British opinion.

Although the peace movement had suffered a serious defeat, the issue of Cruise and Pershing II missiles was far from resolved, not only because in two states missiles were *not* yet deployed but also because arms control (the other track of NATO's 1979 decision) had not been achieved. Four years of intense campaigning had shown that it was possible for a large, diverse, multilevel mass movement to challenge a central strategic policy of both the British government and NATO, and it had not yet run its course.

The movement after the missile deployment

As soon as the Bundestag approved the missile deployment, the Soviets withdrew from the INF negotiations and this appeared to confirm a stalemate between the Cold War rivals. Yet by 1987, it would be agreed that the missiles should be removed; by 1989 – amid mass democracy demonstrations in East European cities that were reminiscent of the peace protests in West European cities a few years earlier – the Cold War was over; and by 1991 the USSR itself would cease to exist.

None of these developments was remotely imaginable as cruise missiles began to arrive in 1983. The movement continued to resist: a national women's protest at Greenham attracted strong support on 11 December 1983 and the camp constantly monitored the missiles. A stretch of fence at "silo corner", closest to where the missiles were kept, was endlessly cut and repaired; it even "assumed a more feminine shape", Ann Pettitt wrote (2006: 307). Indeed, the fence became the "major symbol" of Greenham, Anne Seller (1985: 27) argued: "At the fence you can see the immense might of the nuclear state: acres of coiled barbed wire, immense concrete structures, columns of armed men." The women did much to make it "feel like home" (Feigenbaum 2008: 186).

Similarly, Newbury Magistrates Court, which sat almost every day in 1984 to hear cases against the women, became "a kind of annexe of the Peace-camp" as supporters packed the courtroom and spilled on to its steps (Pettitt 2006: 289). Missiles were tracked whenever they were moved outside; one convoy was stopped for hours after a woman placed a potato in the exhaust pipe of the leading truck. CND started a Cruisewatch network that spread across the dispersal area: 68 convoys were followed between 1983 and 1991.

Protests at Molesworth, where preparations were underway for Britain's second missile deployment, were increasingly important. On 6 February 1985, 1,500 soldiers and hundreds of police, overseen by Heseltine, were used to remove a hundred campaigners from the base, while a barbed wire fence was hastily erected. Soon it too was hung with placards and the base was blockaded. At Easter, a national CND protest was held and even Bruce Kent cut the fence, and a small, mixed peace camp was established.

At Greenham the activities and issues diversified. In 1984, a group of women had filed a lawsuit against the Reagan administration in the New York courts, arguing that the missiles at the base contravened the UN Charter regarding "the threat of use of force, the right to survival, crimes against peace, laws of war and the crime of genocide", but the case was dismissed as a "non-justiciable political question" (Leigh 1985: 746–7). Images of weaving and spider's webs inspired a Widening the Web event in December 1985, connecting nuclear militarism with violence against women, apartheid, imperialism, women in prison, racism and animal liberation. Some women literally learned how to weave, knit and spin wool. Arguments for Black women's autonomy in the peace movement, advocated by the group Wages for Housework (Brown 1984), led to Yellow Gate becoming an antiracist camp.

However, conflicts developed in the camps. At Molesworth in 1985–6, three allegations of rape were made by women members, which escalated into a major crisis for CND. In May 1987, *Sanity*, under the heading "Shame on the Peace Movement", acknowledged the rapes and the organization's failings in dealing with them (Ruddock 1987: 102–4; McDonald 2017: 51–2). At Greenham, accusations of racism within the camp split the remaining women and also spilled over into CND (McDonald 2017: 62–5).

CND remained strong in 1985, when it reached its peak membership of 110,000 and a national protest was estimated at 100,000; but the government's success in installing the missiles caused it to lose momentum; Kent and Ruddock stepped down as general secretary and chair respectively. END supporters highlighted Reagan's proposal for ballistic missile defence, the Strategic Defence Initiative (SDI) known as Star Wars, but CND did not make a major issue of it at this time (Burke 2022). Instead, CND's 1985 conference decided that its main campaign would be on a "Basic Case" centred on the "British Bomb". Local activity was also changing: "nuclear dumping" became a priority in several areas, while many local groups supported mining communities during the 1984–5 strike; this was adopted as a national policy by CND Cymru.

The shock of the US strikes on Libya brought the campaign back to life in 1986. The Chernobyl nuclear disaster the same year reinforced its opposition to nuclear power, and in 1987, CND and Friends of the Earth mobilized an estimated 100,000 for a "No More Chernobyls" protest. But mostly CND settled into a lower-level if still effective routine. In 1988, it returned to Aldermaston for its thirtieth anniversary, although one member complained in *Sanity* about "unproductive nostalgia" (1988, February: 8). It was still able to distribute two million copies of a leaflet against Trident that year (Burke 2004: 109–11; Thompson 1985d; Hudson 2018: 164; Hinton 1989: 192–4). But by now, the movement was clearly receding; at Greenham, the numbers of women were small, although the camp continued for another decade.

Gorbachev and the removal of the missiles

Although cruise missiles were installed at Molesworth in 1986, CND's launch of the Basic Case that year signalled that the active international-ism of the anti-Cruise campaign was giving way to a renewed opposition to British possession of nuclear weapons (Thompson 1985c; Husbands 1989: 66), which would define the movement into the twenty-first cen-tury. The main reason for this was a dramatic turnaround in the argu-ments between the blocs over the missiles, which was mainly the result of the arrival in power in March 1985, after a third elderly Soviet leader had died in three years, of Mikhail Gorbachev.

Up to that point, things had moved slowly in the dealings between the blocs. In the Netherlands, where IKV was still mobilizing strongly, the government proposed their own deal in mid-1984: if the Soviets froze the number of SS-20s, they would not accept the cruise missiles due in 1985. Meanwhile, the USSR proposed new talks on SDI, but the USA linked this to a resumption of talks on strategic and intermediate-range weapons. In March 1985, talks resumed on all three areas, but there was still so little indication of a fundamental shift that immediately after-wards, the Belgian government finally approved its 48 cruise missiles, a third of which were soon deployed.

However, on 7 April 1985, Easter Sunday, Gorbachev made his first initiative designed to appeal to Western opinion, a moratorium on the deployment of medium-range missiles in Europe, followed by one on nuclear tests. He began to use the language, which echoed the END Appeal, of a "common European home". However, his attempt to forestall cruise missile deployment in the Netherlands – opposed by a petition of three-and-a-quarter million signatures – failed when in November 1985 the Dutch government also agreed to proceed with deployment (but only in 1988).

In January 1986, Gorbachev unveiled a more radical plan, aiming for the global elimination of nuclear weapons by 2000, and beginning with the removal of all intermediate-range missiles from Europe. He had adapted the basic premise of Reagan's zero option, and by the time the two met at Reykjavik in October 1986, they were almost ready to agree. Only Gorbachev's insistence that the USA restrict its SDI preparations stopped Reagan from agreeing to abolish nuclear weapons. Thatcher and some other West European politicians again saw a threat to the Atlantic alliance: although they had championed the zero option since 1981, the prospect that the initiative could actually form the basis of an agreement "left allied governments and strategists scrambling" (Colbourn 2022: 227–8).

Despite the apparent impasse, Gorbachev described Reykjavik as a breakthrough. Soviet officials were beginning to question the deployment of SS-20s in Europe – since it had provoked NATO to install the Pershing II missiles that could decapitate the USSR – and also the SDI linkage. The great Soviet physicist and dissident Andrei Sakharov, who Gorbachev freed from internal exile, added his voice, and in February 1987 the Politburo agreed to untie the arms control package so that the superpowers could remove all intermediate-range missiles from Europe (Colbourn 2022: 244).

In April 1987, Gorbachev added in shorter-range INF, more than meeting US demands, which provoked further panic in West European governments. Foreign policy adviser Charles Powell told Thatcher: "Once people in the West have tasted reductions in nuclear weapons, their appetite for more will grow and governments will be unable to resist" (Colbourn 2022: 231). But many in Germany welcomed the inclusion of short-range weapons, and both the West German and British governments reluctantly backed the INF agreement.

Gorbachev and Reagan finalized the deal on 8 December 1987. Four years after its 1983 defeats, the peace movement saw its main short-term goal realized: all land-based missiles with a range of 500–5,500 kilometres were to be dismantled. *Sanity* (January 1988) responded cautiously, but soon Mary Kaldor went to Kazakhstan for END to watch short-range missiles being blown up. She congratulated the Soviet base commander and couldn't help feeling pleased when he replied, "Congratulations to you too" (Kaldor 1988–9: 19).

Gorbachev had been the main mover in this historic turnaround, but the movement played an essential part. The NATO deployments had been proposed to maintain a nuclear defence for Western Europe, but because the movement had exposed the prospect of theatre nuclear war, they had undermined its very basis. Throughout the eight years of the struggle, both NATO and Soviet leaders had constantly retuned their policies with an eye to the movement and its impact on public opinion. Reagan had originally proposed the zero option believing it would not be accepted, and Gorbachev had later reciprocated it knowing that the movement had made it impossible for Western governments to go back on it. Thatcher and Kohl may have faced down the movement in 1983 – although their Dutch counterpart Ruud Lubbers never really did – but in the end they were forced to accept what the movement fought for.

END and the East European upheaval

The battle over the deployments had been fought between the peace movement and European governments, but it had also brought the larger Cold War relationships into play. The movement's issues with the Cold War system itself, which the END Appeal had signalled in 1980, had only begun to be addressed. The 1975 Helsinki Final Act had created new opportunities for social movements in international relations, legitimating human rights monitoring in the Soviet bloc states and improving the conditions for travel and communications, and END activists took advantage of these unless they were blocked.

The linkages that British END campaigners and others had opened up with activists in Eastern Europe assumed a new importance. END had its own dual-track approach, since it was talking to governments and official peace committees at the same time. The officials' willingness to engage varied: meetings took place in East Germany as early as 1982 and in Hungary from 1984, but in the USSR and Czechoslovakia not until 1986 and 1987 respectively. Dialogue with independents was also uneven but developed as they began to show a public interest in the West European peace movement. Immediately after the NATO deployments, the regimes clamped down on independent activists, but this soon began to change (Burke 2004: 156).

Charter 77 played a central role, continuously trying to get the Czechoslovak government to adhere to its treaty commitments, and in 1985 it produced what for END was the most important initiative of the time, the Prague Appeal (Dienstbier, Kanturkova & Sustrova 1985). This proposed to "overcome the superpower bloc structure by way of an alliance of free and independent nations within a democratic and self-governing all-European community living in friendship with all nations of the world", through the "creation of nuclear-free and neutral zones", "renunciation of the use of force or nuclear weapons" and "rapprochement" between the EEC and COMECON, the Soviet bloc economic body. It also contained two taboo proposals: to withdraw US and Soviet forces from Europe and to give Germans in both states the right to decide on unification.

British activists also developed a dialogue with independents in Poland, first with the Committee for Social Self-Defence – although this criticized END and IKV for "one-sidedness" in not recognizing the greater threat of Soviet militarism – and from 1985 with Freedom and Peace (WiP), which also read the superpower conflict differently from END but were more sympathetic. British END members visited East Germany during much of the decade, although its coordinators Barbara Einhorn and John Sandford were often denied access and Einhorn was imprisoned for several days on one trip (Burke 2004: 177–80).

By the 1987 END convention in Coventry (organized by CND), it was clear that Gorbachev represented a major change. Serious numbers of East European independents were able to attend, but the Communist parties and official peace committees had also been invited. A major disagreement broke out over whether a representative of WiP, for whom political change in Poland was the priority, should be a plenary speaker. Many ENDers saw new opportunities for détente from below, but Coates emphasized the fragility of the Soviet changes, arguing that the movement should find common ground with their author. An upheaval in Eastern Europe, he argued, would be "precisely the best way to undermine the Gorbachev revolution" (1987: 9).

There were now two opposed tendencies in the END milieu. A new European Network for East–West Dialogue, established at Perugia but coordinated from West Berlin, became in effect an alternative to the convention process. With strong input from East European exiles, it produced a "Helsinki Memorandum" arguing that citizens should help realize the aims of the Final Act, and attracted some independents, especially East Germans, who had been put off by the conventions. British END was again divided. Kaldor spoke at the European Network's first seminar in Yalta, but Thompson was opposed, believing that it should stick to its strategy of plural dialogue including officials. The conflict exposed the growing tension in END's project between the need for stability in order to achieve disarmament and the inevitable instability of the quickening democratic upheaval in Eastern Europe (Burke 2004: 197, 200–3, 204; Rankin 2017: 110–12, 115–17).

Despite the improving situations over missiles and human rights, END also highlighted troubling new tendencies in US policy. It saw Star Wars as a campaigning priority, since SDI not only carried the arms race into space but was also aimed at restoring US nuclear supremacy, thereby destabilizing arms control. Similarly, the 1986 crisis, in which Reagan used British-based F-111s to bomb Libya, was a harbinger of a "new American unilateralism", exposing the "vulnerability of Britain to American caprice"; the presence of the F-111s had previously "created very little fuss, at least by contrast with … cruise missiles" (Jackson 1986: 125). Presciently, END also saw "terrorism", the pretext for the Libya strike, as a convenient way for the USA to generate a new kind of wartime atmosphere and reimpose allied cohesion (Kaldor 1986: 1–3, 9).

4

Ending the Cold War, facing the fallout, 1987–2001

As the new Network for East–West Dialogue hosted further seminars in Warsaw and Budapest in 1987 and Prague in 1988, a historic upheaval was beginning in Eastern Europe. Barely within a year, the Communist regimes, losing confidence as Gorbachev's withdrawal of support became clear, fell one by one in the face of largely nonviolent revolutions emboldened by the same token. On 9 November 1989, the Berlin Wall was opened. The end of the Cold War, for which the peace movement had fought, was unfolding in front of its eyes. It was a momentous change, with huge ramifications for its future as well as that of Europe and the world.

Western leaders claimed that their 1979 decision had led to this outcome, but they had been forced to abandon it by Gorbachev's bold choices, which reflected the movement's pressure as well as his recognition of the USSR's fundamental weaknesses. After the Cold War ended, researchers discovered that the USSR, despite its monolithic façade, "was rife with debates about foreign policy" (Evangelista 1999: 6). The official peace committees had been listening to END and other Western activists, and much of Gorbachev's new international thinking, one Soviet insider argued, was "simply borrowed" from them (Burke 2017: 243).

In Eastern Europe, a "Helsinki effect" resulting from the 1975 Final Act, which made human rights part of a European settlement, meant that the Soviet leadership had to accept both international and domestic monitoring. But it had taken the activist "Helsinki network" across the bloc, with support from the Western peace movement, to ultimately force the pace, helping generate the mass democracy movements (Thomas 2001; Snyder 2011). NATO would later acknowledge the centrality to the change of the openings for civil society created by Helsinki (Shea 2009).

E. P. Thompson was therefore justified in claiming that END had "prefigured time and time again the events of 1989" (1991: 23). However, in many ways the denouement was unanticipated. He had argued that the Cold War was a self-perpetuating exterminist system that could only be broken from below, but the cycle of military competition had been interrupted from above. Thompson had presented Cold War rivalry as symmetrical, but asymmetry contributed greatly to how it ended. Ultimately it was only one side that broke: as Kaldor (1991: 249) put it, "overcoming socialism, as it actually existed … turned out to be the essential element in overcoming the split in Europe".

The millions on the streets in the 1989 revolutions took change beyond what not only Gorbachev and Reagan but also END and the East European dissidents had envisaged. The uprisings quickly launched negotiated transitions to more democratic institutions. Soon some of END's interlocutors played important roles: Vaclav Havel became president of Czechoslovakia and Jiri Dienstbier its foreign secretary, while Adam Michnik and Jacek Kuron were part of the Round Table Talks that ended Communist rule in Poland and became prominent in the new politics. However, in East Germany oppositionists were eventually swept aside in a stampede towards the unification of the two Germanies, although not before they had achieved their main goal, ending the Soviet military occupation.

The INF deal eliminated only a small part of NATO's arsenals, but it had profound consequences for international nuclear relationships, disrupting the general balance that its strategists aimed to maintain. Flexible response might have been more myth than reality, but it was pivotal to alliance cohesion. After Gorbachev proposed conventional as well as battlefield-nuclear reductions, the changes sweeping the USSR and Eastern Europe did away with the "need" for nuclear modernization. Thatcher, worrying that a creeping nuclear-free Europe would unravel NATO, fought unsuccessfully to save battlefield weapons from becoming the next stage. The doctrine of flexible response, NATO's lodestar for a quarter of a century, was "tossed on the ash-heap of history" (Colbourn 2022: 243–59).

However, it was not only the alliances, governments and East European dissidents who faced novel realities; the West European peace movements also had to deal with a rapidly changing situation. Before long, new conflicts would emerge from changes that the end of the Cold

War produced in the European and global orders, and these would test the movements' unity and coherence. This chapter explores how the movement in Britain adapted and responded to the fallout from its achievement in realizing the "END" that it had fought for.

The end of END

In the aftermath of the INF deal, British END attempted to outline, in a collective submission to a Labour Party policy review, the principles of a new international and security approach. Both Atlanticism and neutralism were, it argued, "outmoded models", and maintaining the opposition between unilateralism and multilateralism was "futile". Instead of the old New Left idea of non-alignment or moving outside the blocs, END proposed the dealignment of states from them, looking for their "evolution and eventual dissolution" through gradual shifts to democracy and demilitarization, rather than "instant abolition" (European Nuclear Disarmament 1988: 18–20).

At the same time, British END activists were involved a project, begun at a seminar in Prague in 1988 and co-organized by Jan Kavan (who had returned to Czechoslovakia and was to become an MP in 1990, and foreign minister of the Czech Republic in 1998), to bring together a European citizens assembly movement. Although the seminar was broken up by the police, after the fall of the Communist regime the activists were able to launch the project, now the Helsinki Citizens Assembly (HCA), in the same city in 1990. Kaldor, who was the driving force of the new body, was co-chair with Faber, and British END transitioned into what became European Dialogue, HCA's British affiliate (Rankin 2017: 118–21). (The Russell Foundation, however, maintained END activity, continuing to publish *END Papers* and *END Info* until 2021.)

In 1988, the geopolitical flux appeared to create space for END's programme of dealignment. Indeed in 1990, NATO invited the USSR and East European states to send representatives to its meetings. However, the rapid disintegration of the Soviet bloc, the political framework of the Warsaw Pact, led to the dissolution of the pact itself in early 1991 and the USSR's own break-up six months later.

These dramatic events appeared to undercut NATO's raison d'être, and it was no longer clear against whom it was directing its nuclear weapons.[1] However, they also undermined END's hopes of a gradual, mutual transformation. Some in Eastern Europe were less optimistic about change in the USSR and were starting to think about NATO membership. Havel was the first to enquire, and Reagan's successor, George H. W. Bush, assured him that the USA had no interest in seeing Czechoslovakia, Hungary and Poland left "in a European no-man's land" (Colbourn 2022: 264–5). END had sought the dissolution of both alliances, but some former dissidents who were now in positions of power were abandoning its "heretical geopolitics" (Szulecki 2015: 32–4). A slow reconsolidation of NATO was beginning.

CND and nuclear politics after the Cold War

CND was also adapting to the changes. In *Sanity* (1988, February: 13), James Hinton, who had chaired CND's projects committee as the missiles arrived in 1983, praised the movement's "resilience" after that defeat and argued that it was in it for the long haul. However, only three months later the magazine's new *Campaign* supplement admitted to a serious downturn: CND was "not the flavour of the month", and members would have to be phoned or visited, as they were not responding to newsletters (*Sanity* 1988, May: xi). The INF deal led to all cruise missiles being removed from Molesworth in October that year and from Greenham Common in 1991.

There was real progress in disarmament, even if the new decade did not turn out as well as was hoped.[2] The pervasive belief that the arms race was over made it difficult for CND to gain traction; it struggled for relevance, and there was a persistent decline throughout the 1990s. Since the friction in the arms control negotiations provided only limited scope, CND focused primarily on the British "deterrent". It demanded a "peace dividend", with money diverted from defence to other public services. It opposed the introduction of Trident, and during its commissioning process backed the Nukewatch network that tracked the convoys that transported warheads from the Atomic Weapons Establishment at Burghfield to Scotland. It protested as each of the four submarines was launched: when the first, *Vanguard*, finally entered service in 1994 – with its missiles detargeted since there was no longer an enemy – CND emphasized that the system, which increased the firepower, range and accuracy of British missiles and the number of targets they could hit, was the UK's own nuclear proliferation in contravention of the NPT.

The INF deal was eliminating cruise missiles in England, but promised little change north of the border. As campaigners prepared to launch a People's Declaration for a Nuclear-Free Scotland, Ian Davison of Scottish CND was quick to proclaim, "Scotland goes it alone", emphasizing "sadness rather than pride" in separating from English colleagues (Davison 1988). The continuing peace camp at Faslane, established in 1982, remained a focal point, and opposition to Trident was widespread almost across the political spectrum in Scotland, where the coming of devolution was deepening the distinctiveness of the country's politics. In this context, the US withdrawal from Holy Loch in 1992 did not have a big impact.

CND worked through international networks to further its demands. In 1994, in the run-up to 1995 NPT review conference, it demanded that the treaty should be extended only for ten years, during which a treaty to ban nuclear weapons should be agreed, rather than indefinitely. When the NPT was nevertheless extended, CND, led by its chair Janet Bloomfield, worked in a new global network, Abolition 2000, to continue to press the case.[3] However, progress was modest. Brazil, which ended its secret nuclear programme after the military regime fell, and South Africa, which abandoned the apartheid regime's equivalent, signed the declaration Towards a Nuclear Weapons-Free World in 1998. But India and Pakistan had become unrecognized nuclear weapons states outside the NPT, alongside Israel, and the five recognized states had no serious programme for the full disarmament to which the NPT committed them.[4]

In 1995 the campaign for the Comprehensive Test Ban Treaty, to replace the partial treaty signed three decades earlier, reached its climax. CND campaigned against the Chinese and especially French resumptions of tests, including a boycott of French goods. This campaign was successful, and the treaty was finally agreed in 1996, although the USA would never ratify it.

CND's membership had slowly declined from its peak a decade earlier to 47,000 in 1995 (NGO UK nd: figure 3), and Glastonbury's profits now went to Greenpeace and Oxfam. CND held its first national demonstration for several years that year, but the attendance of 5,000 underlined how much smaller the campaign was. It continued to oppose nuclear energy but lost the support of some pro-nuclear power trade unionists (Douglass 1995).

The changing left and the peace movement

Longstanding differences on the British left took new forms as the Cold War ended, weakening the broad if loose unity inherited from the early 1980s. Labour's 1983 defeat had seen Neil Kinnock, like Foot regarded as a representative of its broad left, become leader and start to "modernize" the party, which for influential advisers such as Peter Mandelson meant abandoning unilateralism. The party's left had been increasingly divided into a Bennite "hard" left who held to its 1970s programme, including unilateralism, and a "soft" left who were prepared to give Kinnock conditional support.

In the 1987 general election, Kinnock was able to claim that the party was with the grain of Reagan's disarmament ambitions. But Labour still lost, and although Beresford, CND's new general secretary and an END member, argued that this time unilateralism was not to blame, Kinnock was already moving Labour's policy away from it (Hudson 2005: 173; Scott 2012). He succeeded in ending the commitment in 1989 after he made it an issue of confidence; the soft left on Labour's national executive, including Cook, facilitated the policy change.

There was also disagreement about European integration. END's Europeanism had contributed to a shift in attitudes within the Labour movement, which increasingly saw the European Community (EC, formerly EEC) as a bulwark against right-wing governments such as Thatcher's. The shift was symbolized by the welcome the 1988 Trades Union Congress gave to the EC Commission's Jacques Delors. END backed the Labour movement's new direction, arguing that the continent should be reunified through European institutions as well as from below (Thompson & Webb 1988–9). Indeed, Ken Coates and Peter Crampton, Hull END's chair, were both elected as members of the European Parliament in 1989.[5] However, the pro-European stance was not shared by many in the peace movement who maintained the traditional left-wing opposition to the Common Market, including CND supporters such as Benn and Jeremy Corbyn who would oppose the 1992 Maastricht Treaty that transformed the EC into the European Union (EU).

The left outside the Labour Party was also changing in ways that would impact the peace movement. The CPGB's journal *Marxism Today*, which had been the vehicle for Stuart Hall's influential diagnosis of Thatcherism, developed a further New Left project, New Times, but its manifesto saw the movement as part of the left's past (Hall & Jacques 1990). Antimilitarism was more important to those within the CPGB who criticized this approach, who formed a new Communist Party of Britain when the original party dissolved itself in 1991. Indeed Kate Hudson, who joined this (and later became chair of CND), credited the polarization during the 1991 Gulf War with stimulating the new party's formation (2000: 76–7).

From the late 1980s, CND's base again narrowed as it reverted to being a smaller organization. The "hard" Labour left, together with some far-left groups, came to have a strong influence, and their hostility to British, US and NATO militarism struck a chord with CND's continuing pacifist members. As soon became evident, many who remained in peace organizations were deeply opposed to Western military action on principle, whether on anti-imperialist or pacifist grounds. Indeed Labour's rightward shift left Bruce Kent feeling that he was "somewhere on the far left, the far Christian left", as far as it was concerned (Turner 2016: 77).

The divisions within the peace movement over its relationship to the party deepened after Tony Blair became leader (John Smith had replaced Kinnock after Labour lost the 1992 election, but he died suddenly in 1994). Blair had been a member of CND but supported Kinnock's abandonment of unilateralism and made a point, before the 1997 election, of stating that he would be prepared to launch a nuclear strike.

Embarking on a drive to transform the party into "New Labour", Blair was at first little interested in international affairs, and after his landslide victory allowed Cook to make a speech that was reported as committing the UK to an "ethical foreign policy". However, what he actually said was: "our foreign policy must have an ethical dimension and must support the demands of other peoples for the democratic rights on which we insist for ourselves" (Cook 1997). This idea was backed by policies such as banning anti-personnel landmines, supporting the emerging International Criminal Court and restricting arms sales to countries with poor human rights records. By 1999, during the Kosovo war, Blair himself was engaged and made a major speech on "international community" in Chicago, outlining general criteria for "humanitarian" military interventions that came to be seen as his doctrine. However, "dimension" accurately captured the partial role of ethical considerations: they "rarely if ever drove policy in its entirety" (Coates & Kruger 2004: 18).

For HCA, like Labour's "soft" left, Cook's pledge to put human rights at the heart of foreign policy was an opening for progressive internationalism and Blair's doctrine was broadly welcomed. For many others, however, they amounted to little more than what one historian called "a new moral imperialist fantasy" (Edgerton 1998: 123).

Nuclear issues had a low salience in Labour politics as the party finally prepared to return to power. A *New Statesman* conference on Labour's foreign and defence policy that I co-organized in June 1995 – at which Robin Cook spoke after Blair gave him the foreign policy brief – was much more focused on Bosnia and European security. According to my notes, Paul Rogers felt it necessary to remind attendees that "the nuclear age isn't over". For traditional peace organizations such as Pax Christi, too, this was a period in which a broader peace and justice agenda resurfaced after the intense conflict over nuclear weapons.

However, there was significant international recognition of antinuclear campaigning. In 1995, the veteran British scientific campaigner Joseph Rotblat was awarded the Nobel Peace Prize together with the Pugwash conferences that he helped initiate. The following year, the International Court of Justice (1996), after a campaign by the World Court Project that CND supported, gave an advisory opinion that the use or threat of nuclear weapons would be illegal under most circumstances.

In the run-up to the May 1997 election, CND challenged Labour's commitment to retain Trident. The anachronism of the "independent deterrent" had only increased now that there was no Soviet enemy to deter, but the party had reattached itself to that fiction in order to confirm its electability. With a strong momentum for change after 18 years of Conservative rule and popular concern about nuclear weapons at a low ebb, CND made little impact on the election, but after Blair's victory, it transported a 20-foot mock-up of a Trident missile from Faslane to Downing Street and made a detailed submission to the new government's Strategic Defence Review.

Direct action against Trident

Some of the most striking new antinuclear campaigning came from out-side CND. A Ploughshares (or Plowshares) movement, which emerged from the Catholic Worker group in the USA in the early 1980s and focused on "hammering" armaments, had been taken up by British direct actionists. Activists had attacked a nuclear-capable F-111 at Upper Heyford in March 1990, and in January 1996, Seeds of Hope and East Timor Ploughshares disabled a Hawk jet destined for the Indonesian military; with damage estimated at £1.5 million, this was probably the greatest financial cost caused by direct action in modern times.

After being imprisoned for her part in the Hawk attack, in 1997 Angie Zelter – previously known for the Snowball campaign – was inspired by the International Court of Justice's 1996 opinion on the illegality of nuclear weapons use to initiate an ambitious new Scottish-centred but internationalized NVDA campaign. Trident Ploughshares (TP) would undertake civil disobedience to prevent the illegal use of nuclear weap-ons. It wrote to Blair before launching its first actions at Faslane, Coulport and Barrow in the weeks before the launch of the fourth Trident subma-rine in September 1998: these included fence-cutting, blockading and kayaking and swimming to within metres of the submarines.

Zelter's aim was to reclaim the true meaning of international law, integrating it into the heart of the campaign: everyone who took part had to sign a Pledge to Prevent Nuclear Crime. Activists would endeav-our "peacefully, safely, openly and accountably to help to disarm the UK nuclear weapon system", dismantling it "in such a way that it could not be used to threaten or harm living beings" (Trident Ploughshares 2013: 154–5).

Zelter's approach to NVDA emphasized "the real value of an action rather than how popular it might be" (2021: 28). Although this appar-ently contradicted the communicative emphasis of earlier direct action-ists, and was perhaps closer to Gandhi's original concept of nonviolent resistance, law-breaking to uphold the law was another dramatic mode of communication, and TP's willingness to cause serious physical dam-age to nuclear facilities gave it a sharp and controversial edge. In 1999, an "international crime prevention team" emptied the contents of a floating laboratory working on Trident research into Loch Goil, leaving it clean and tidy with copies of TP's publications. Remanded in custody,

Zelter, Ella Moxley and Ulla Røder became the "Trident Three", but they were acquitted by Sheriff Margaret Gimblett who accepted their arguments, ruling that they had not acted illegally in vandalizing the facility. Although the High Court overruled this verdict in 2001, the acquittals stood.

TP's *Tri-Denting It Handbook* (Trident Ploughshares 2013) codified its approach to NVDA, which involved careful training and preparation, including dialogue with the authorities where possible. Their main success, Zelter later claimed (2021: 69), was to disseminate its international law arguments to lawyers and judges as well as the public: they, as well as the activists and their supporters, were getting a free education in international law. Indeed much of TP's action now moved to the courts: in four years, its activists experienced 1,803 arrests, 398 trials and 1,711 days in jail. Although some were acquitted, they recognized the danger of getting bogged down in a legal war of attrition (McKenzie 2003).

As well as Faslane, where the peace camp was 20 years old in 2002, NVDA also continued at Aldermaston, where the camp's Block the Builders campaign opposed the construction of new Trident-related facilities, and Plymouth Devonport naval dockyard, where the submarines were refitted. It also halted warhead convoys on occasion (Trident Ploughshares 2019). The campaign ran alongside CND mass protests and gained support from the General Assembly of the Church of Scotland, and a poll even showed that a majority of Scots approved of NVDA at Faslane. *Peace News* described TP as the "most active nonviolent direct action campaign against British nuclear weapons", and it was presented with the Right Livelihood Award of the Swedish Parliament for being "a model of principled, transparent and nonviolent direct action" (McKenzie 2003).

Campaigners also opposed the Labour government over the USA's National Missile Defence (NMD) system. An updated version of Star Wars that President Bill Clinton approved in 1996, this relied on upgrading the radar systems at Fylingdales and Menwith Hill. Labour had been committed to maintaining the ABM treaty but the governments of Blair and his successor, Gordon Brown – hewing close to the USA and seeking to look strong on defence – incorporated NMD participation into UK defence policy (Simpkin 2023). Protests at the two centres became a focus for a Campaign for Accountability of American Bases, whose regular actions on 4 July – which they dubbed Independence Day *from* America – still continued two decades later. National CND mobilized around these events: in 2000, for example, a campaign was launched with a four-day walk covering the 80 miles from Menwith Hill to Fylingdales. CND (2009) commissioned a national poll showing that 58 per cent agreed that siting NMD components in the UK would contribute to international tension.

Peace campaigners and the new instability

During the 1990s and beyond, however, nuclear issues were often overtaken, for all the main groups of antinuclear campaigners, by the wider political and military consequences of the Cold War's end. In 1990, the Iraqi invasion of Kuwait took their attention: the USA, turning against the dictatorship of Saddam Hussein that it had helped arm during the 1980–8 Iran–Iraq War, secured the support of the UN Security Council for intervention unless Iraq withdrew. To peace campaigners, however, this first Gulf War appeared to vindicate the concerns END had expressed about an increased US willingness to use force. The US-led campaign was only possible because the threat of a Soviet military response had been removed; indeed, Gorbachev unprecedentedly backed the intervention in the UN. The Cold War had helped prevent direct superpower interventions, but now it seemed that war involving major powers could be more rather than less likely.

Peace campaigners were united in opposing military action. CND opposed the sending of troops, arguing that Iraqi withdrawal from Kuwait was essential but war was not the way to achieve it, and urged a worldwide ban on weapons of mass destruction: Saddam had used chemical weapons against Kurds in Halabja in 1988, while the USA had nuclear weapons that it might use against Iraq. Direct actionists were also energized by the threat: Pat Arrowsmith helped set up an international Gulf Peace Team that camped on the Kuwait/Saudi border in an attempt at unarmed "interpositionary peacekeeping" (Weber 1993: 58–9), while at home, a new group, Gulf War Resisters, took action at the Farnborough Air Show. This group came out of the Upper Heyford Ploughshares Support Group, set up for activists who had taken action there in 1990 (Rai 2023b).

CND helped set up a Committee to Stop War in the Gulf, chaired by its vice-chair, Marjorie Thompson, which organized a demonstration of up to 100,000 as a US-led attack loomed in January 1991 (Hudson 2005: 176–82). However, follow-up demonstrations barely mobilized CND's core support, and Thompson expressed concern about the predominance of far-left organizations in them (Shaw 1996: 60–2). CND anticipated a long conflict in which casualties would turn opinion against the war, but the US-led coalition used airpower to destroy Iraqi forces before attacking on the ground and was able to expel Iraq from Kuwait within three months. Although the US-led bombing campaign killed tens of thousands of Iraqi soldiers and 400 civilians in a bombing of a Baghdad shelter that the USA believed was a military target, total direct civilian casualties were estimated at under 4,000 and coalition deaths at fewer than 300.

Thus the war failed to produce the response that CND expected, and effective media management helped maintain support for the war in Britain. The full cost to Iraqi civilians only became apparent when the war was over: many more died from the disruption to water and electricity supplies than were killed by bombing and in the huge humanitarian crises resulting from Saddam's repression of the Kurdish and Shi'ite uprisings – which Bush had encouraged – that followed his defeat. A massive exodus of Kurdish refugees into the mountains was exposed to British viewers by television news, and with Turkey anxious to stem the influx into its territory, the USA, UK and France intervened to create a "safe haven" for the Kurds in northern Iraq (Shaw 1996: 17–26, 62–3, 71–96). This was soon seen as a case of "humanitarian intervention", which became a defining feature of the 1990s and would deeply divide peace campaigners (Wheeler 2000: 139–71).

The peace movement mostly moved on from Iraq after the war, but the Gulf War Resisters, under their new name Active Resistance to the Roots of War (ARROW), started a weekly vigil against economic sanctions against Iraq that lasted until 2003, while a side-project, Voices in the Wilderness UK, broke UN sanctions against Iraq by taking in medicines (Rai 2023b).

Most attention soon returned to Europe, and it was conflict, not democratization, which preoccupied experts and activists alike. Lawrence Freedman, END's critic a decade earlier, argued that Europe was changing from "an oasis of stability" into "the most turbulent of continents" (1991: 23–5). CND seemed to agree, claiming in 1992 that the Cold War had been superseded by "an even more dangerous period in human history" (Hudson 2005: 186).

Kaldor (1991) signalled that "exclusivist nationalism" was the main problem. If the transition in Eastern Europe had been remarkably peaceful, Gorbachev's opening up of the USSR itself was proving less so. Armed conflicts broke out between Armenia and Azerbaijan over Nagorno-Karabakh, in the Baltic states as the Soviet regime tried to stop them becoming independent, and in Moldova and Georgia over attempts at secession from the newly independent republics. Similarly in federal Yugoslavia, democratization was leading to nationalist rivalries within and between the constituent republics.

No one saw these conflicts as raising the danger of nuclear confrontation, but like the Vietnam War in the 1960s they became central concerns of the antinuclear movement. HCA became involved in peace efforts around conflicts in the Caucasus, but it was the wars of Yugoslav succession that gained attention on all sides. These led to an increasing divergence of approaches among British campaigners, in which the consensus on nonviolence was eventually challenged.

When the first Yugoslav crisis developed in Kosovo in 1988–9, after the new Serbian regime of Slobodan Milošević suspended the province's autonomy and deprived its 90 per cent Albanian majority of their influence on government, the Albanian leadership adopted a strategy of peaceful civil resistance, which would avoid war for almost a decade. War Resisters International saw this as a positive example and their coordinator Howard Clark later wrote a full account of the experiment (2000). War Resisters International set up a Balkan Peace Team (nd) to promote wider nonviolent resistance.

In 1991, however, war broke out in Yugoslavia. As the Serbian-dominated federal government attempted to prevent first Slovenian and then Croatian secession, Serbian nationalists forced non-Serbs out of Serbian-controlled territory in Croatia, a process soon known internationally by its local euphemism, "ethnic cleansing", and considered by many to be a form of genocide (Shaw 2015: 66–83). Jill Craigie, supported by her husband Michael Foot, made a film, *Two Hours from London*, exposing the Serbian bombardment of Dubrovnik, a shocking early stage of the war.

When war spread to Bosnia-Herzegovina in April 1992, violence – primarily but not only by Serbian nationalists – was on an even larger scale: two million were terrorized out of their homes and over 100,000 died, mainly in the following year. Bosnia became the principal focus of peace activism, and HCA, working closely with activists in the war zones, initially believed like the Balkan Peace Team that politics from below could curtail the violence. However, it soon argued that international institutions needed to play a major role, launching a campaign to demand that Bosnia or municipalities within it should become "safe havens" in which international organizations, cooperating with civic movements, local non-governmental organizations and councils would ensure demilitarization, reconstruction and the return of refugees.

Kaldor and Faber, the HCA's co-chairs, wrote an appeal that gained support from European parliamentarians including Paddy Ashdown, now leader of the Liberal Democrats, and lobbied Cyrus Vance, a former US secretary of state, and David Owen, the former foreign secretary, who had been commissioned to develop a peace plan. However, Vance and Owen rejected safe havens, proposing instead a form of ethnic partition that would leave the Serbians in control of the areas they had "cleansed" (Rankin 2017: 157–63).

As the war continued, in 1993 Kaldor developed a more ambitious plan for a UN transitional authority, with international troops to protect civilians by force.[6] Finally the UN declared Srebrenica and two other besieged towns safe zones, and with the UN High Commission for Refugees making HCA an "implementing agency", Kaldor was able to work with local civil society activists, providing aid, boosting resilience and refining peace proposals. In July 1993 she was stranded in Sarajevo, the Bosnian capital, after the Serbian siege closed the airport.

However, many in the peace movement were not prepared to countenance any kind of military intervention. War Resisters International argued against it in 1992, and E. P. Thompson (1992), in what was to be one of his last interventions (he died the following year), took a different approach from his HCA comrades. While not disputing Serbian cruelties, he warned that European and US media were on "an emotional trip which utterly lacks even-handedness", designed to open up war against the Serbs. Instead, evoking memories of the youth brigade in which he had taken part in 1947 – which had built a railway to link parts of Yugoslavia under the banner of "brotherhood and unity" – he recommended international mediation to hold Yugoslavia together. For Thompson, the wars were a blow to long-cherished hopes for a reformed socialism: he had long believed that in "an atmosphere of relaxed international tension, the Soviet Union and Eastern Europe [would] prove to be the area of expanding liberty and human fulfilment" (1964: 101).

Many in CND and the wider left agreed that international military intervention was the problem, not the solution. In 1993 Alice Mahon, a Labour MP who later became a CND vice-president, and Carol Turner of Labour CND set up a Committee for Peace in the Balkans to oppose external military involvement and lobby for a continuing UN arms embargo, although in practice this favoured the better-armed Serbians. Tony Benn strongly supported this position in parliament: for him, supplying arms to the Bosnians was a way in which the USA boosted its arms trade (Simms 2001: 279–80). It was NATO's involvement, even under UN auspices, rather than Serbian violence that particularly provoked this camp. Mahon believed that its military operations were designed to move the alliance closer to Russia's borders.

The situation provoked disagreement across the movement. Within HCA, Mark Thompson (1993) argued that E. P. Thompson's idea that Yugoslavia could be resurrected was a "fundamental illusion". There could be no even-handedness between the Serbian regime and its victims; the problem was the EC's *non*-intervention to protect them. For Lynne Jones (2002 [1993]), a former END activist who had been drawn into the movement by Greenham, there was a "moral failure" and "knee-jerk anti-interventionism". She complained that in the winter of 1992, CND's publications had "not one word on the Balkans, not even its humanitarian aspects".

In response Michael Randle (2002 [1994]) argued that civil resistance *could* protect minorities, but he also admitted its difficulties. Even among Quakers, non-pacifist views gained ground (Ceadel 2002: 28). Jones' and Randle's exchange opened up a wider debate on the sufficiency of nonviolence, centred on Bradford Peace Studies. (However, by 2017 Randle was "no longer convinced that it is always possible or likely to be efficacious" in protecting civilians (Levy 2021: 254).)

By 1994, the UN's reluctance to use ground troops to protect civilians left the safe areas exposed, culminating in the Srebrenica massacre of 11 July 1995, in which Bosnian-Serbian forces killed over 7,000 Muslim men and boys, which the International Court of Justice later recognized as genocide. Following this, NATO finally bombed the positions from which Serbian artillery was bombarding Sarajevo. While Kaldor argued that this helped lift the city's three-year siege, the Committee for Peace in the Balkans launched a No Bombing campaign, which CND supported (Rankin 2017: 163–74; Unkovski-Korica 2019; Hudson 2005: 212; Turner 2023). When the war was ended by US-chaired negotiations at Dayton, Ohio, in 1996, the agreement enabled Republika Srpska, established through the forced removal of non-Serbs, to remain an entity within a loose, ethnically divided Bosnian federation under international supervision; far from the plural, multiethnic civil society for which HCA had worked.

The differences within the movement sharpened further in 1999, when NATO launched its first ever full military campaign, extensively bombing Serbian forces in Kosovo, which were attacking Albanian civilians in response to an insurgency.[7] Kaldor helped convince Cook, the British foreign secretary, of the need to intervene, but she believed that NATO's subsequent reliance on high-altitude bombing, as well as causing unnecessary casualties – Albanian as well as Serb – was insufficient to protect civilians, and again called for ground troops.

In contrast the Committee for Peace in the Balkans, supported by CND, completely opposed intervention. Between April and June 1999 it called three demonstrations in London with tens of thousands of participants, condemning "NATO's war on Yugoslavia". When the bombing of Serbian forces in Kosovo failed to force Milošević to withdraw, NATO escalated its attacks to the Serbian capital, Belgrade, including controversial targets such as the television station. Mahon, who had also travelled extensively in former Yugoslavia, visited Serbia during this campaign. Noting bomb damage to civilian facilities, she said she felt as strongly about victims of laser-guided bombs as victims of ethnic cleansing. For CND, the use of depleted uranium warheads was a particular concern as it had been in the Gulf War (Hudson 2018: 183–4).

The movement's divisions were evident when Kaldor and Faber attended an Appeal for Peace conference in The Hague. Their call for ground troops to protect civilians was overwhelmed by passionate demands for an end to NATO bombing, leading them to comment: "what made one feel uncomfortable was that they did not seem to express the same energy and concern about the plight of the Kosovar

Albanians", or even show interest in hearing the latter's views (Rankin 2017: 201–3).

After the war, CND's 1999 conference reinforced its opposition to the transformation of NATO that it saw it as representing. Demanding that NATO pay for the damage its bombing had caused to Serbia, it highlighted the alliance's new Strategic Concept, adopted during the war, which broadened its geographic reach and allowed it to pursue "out of area" operations, and also the dangers of its eastward expansion (Hungary, Poland and the Czech Republic joined NATO just before the war began). CND called once more for Britain's immediate withdrawal from the alliance and its dissolution (Hudson 2018: 185–6).

The HCA, War Resisters International and Committee for Peace in the Balkans all believed they were representing peace and solidarity, but they had very different ideas of what these ideas meant for Kosovo. CND, closely linked to the Committee for Peace in the Balkans, and HCA, the successor of END, were on opposite sides of this defining conflict at the century's end. The alliance of antimilitarism and human rights, at least in the form pioneered two decades earlier, had broken down. As the twenty-first century began, these divisions seemed set to harden. But then events intervened.

5

Afterlife: antinuclear and antiwar activism, 2001–24

Al-Qaida's attacks on New York and Washington, DC on 11 September 2001 (9/11) shocked peace campaigners as much as anyone. As President George W. Bush declared a "global war on terror", which Blair supported, it was soon obvious that activists would continue to be concerned as much with wars as with weapons, and that the wars could be larger and even more consequential than the interventions in former Yugoslavia. In the first years of the new century, while the campaign against nuclear weapons remained politically marginal, an enormous antiwar movement rapidly developed.

In Britain, this movement drew in all shades of antinuclear activists in the build-up to the great demonstration against the Iraq War on 15 February 2003. However, when it subsided, it left effects that persisted during the following two decades. First, it created a lasting alliance of CND with the main antiwar organization, the Stop the War Coalition (StWC). Second, it also consolidated, after considerable turbulence in 2003–4, CND's own internal coalition of Christians and pacifists with the far left that had been reconfigured in the 1990s.

This chapter therefore begins by discussing the roles of antinuclear campaigners in the post-9/11 movement, before turning to the continuing campaign against nuclear weapons by both CND and direct action groups. Further wars often galvanized campaigners more than nuclear developments, but political turbulence within Britain created significant openings to challenge the Trident nuclear system, which remained the main focus of antinuclear campaigning throughout the first quarter of the century.

CND and the new antiwar movement

CND held its annual conference five days after 9/11. The organization was already fielding thousands of calls from people looking for it to take a lead, as Britain's main peace campaign, in opposing Bush's threatened intervention in Afghanistan. Under a newly elected chair, Carol Naughton, and vice-chair, Kate Hudson, it immediately called a "No retaliation, no war" vigil outside Downing Street. Using email, which most activists had by 2001, this mobilized thousands (Sinclair 2011: 105–6).[1]

Others were also organizing. The Socialist Workers Party (SWP) called a public meeting to "stop the war before it starts" on 21 September 2001, which attracted 2,000 people representing a range of left opinion. With their representative Lindsey German in the chair, speakers included Jeremy Corbyn MP and the environmentalist George Monbiot as well as far-left spokespeople. Helen John, who had been at Menwith Hill women's peace camp as news of 9/11 came in, spoke for CND. The meeting set up the StWC, and German, together with Tariq Ali, the former leader of VSC, got it to agree to a minimal three-point platform: stop the war, defend civil liberties and oppose any racist backlash against Muslims (Murray & German 2005: 47–52).

CND then turned a planned demonstration on October 13 into a joint first protest with StWC against the war that the USA and UK was now launching in Afghanistan, and tens of thousands came out. Some felt that as an antinuclear campaign, CND shouldn't be taking a position, but as it had taken stands on Vietnam, the Gulf and the post-Yugoslav wars, there were clear precedents.

StWC quickly became the main antiwar organization, mobilizing in a way that CND could not. The SWP was in pole position, but most of the groups to the left of Labour were involved. Indeed StWC generated remarkably stable partnerships between SWP members and others such as its chair, Andrew Murray, who was a member of the Communist Party of Britain. StWC's core was an alliance of the "anti-imperialist" left – there had even been an unsuccessful proposal to make anti-imperialism a condition of membership – but the organization also included Labour MPs such as Corbyn, Mahon and George Galloway, as well as the Greens, Scottish Socialist Party and some union leaders. Benn, who had retired as an MP, became its president.

The StWC leadership recognized the importance of CND's support. Murray and German would later write (2005: 57) that it was "obvious" that there could be no united antiwar movement "without the involvement of CND, with its prestige, name recognition and national network of committed supporters". Naughton confirmed CND's acceptance of this role: "we could bring a different element to it because of our long history and tradition; we brought a certain historic element in to it" (Sinclair 2011: 110). As an established, relatively well-funded organization, CND also brought practical benefits: for example, marches that it co-sponsored could benefit from its public liability insurance (Gillan, Pickerill & Webster 2008: 117).

StWC quickly became the main coordinating body, at least for England and Wales (north of the border, Scottish CND had taken the initiative), and organized a larger march in November 2001. CND was in an ongoing partnership with the new coalition, but soon found the going difficult. Naughton complained in a report to its December 2001 Council of a "lack of democracy (decisions taken before planning meeting), failure to condemn terrorism and lack of commitment to nonviolence" (Sinclair 2011: 108–9).

Despite pressure for affiliation to StWC, the majority baulked at submerging CND's identity in it. Some were concerned that, with the SWP dominant, StWC would take extreme positions that would alienate potential support (Hudson 2018: 188–9). However, even the SWP's critics later credited it with having worked to make the movement as broad as possible (Sinclair 2011: 313–25). There was more criticism of the SWP's controlling approach. As Mike Marqusee, a veteran activist who was StWC's press officer from 2001 to 2003, later put it: "There was a fear of what [the SWP] considered to be mavericks or loose cannons. What is an anti-war movement without mavericks and loose cannons? I mean please" (Sinclair 2013).[2]

StWC was the catalyst for political mobilization well beyond its far-left core. It filled the space, Murray and German argue (2005: 94–5), of the antiglobalization movement, the first to make widespread use of the Internet, which had emerged after the Seattle meeting of the World Trade Organization in 1999; supporters shared a critique of globalization, neoliberalism and imperialism.

Even more important, this was the first movement to involve Muslims. British Muslim antiwar activism was not entirely new: some had protested against the 1991 Gulf War, with many identifying with Iraq and even Saddam, although the community was divided; but there were no strong links with the secular antiwar movement (Shaw 1996: 65–9). Now most of the enlarged Muslim population perceived themselves as threatened by the US/UK intervention in a Muslim country and by "Islamophobia", which had been supercharged after 9/11. Left-wing Muslims had formed a group, Just Peace, at StWC's inaugural meeting, but support soon spread in the wider community. Murray described speaking at a large rally of Muslims in Batley, West Yorkshire: he was uncomfortable about its gender segregation but was told this was progress, as previously women would not have been allowed to be present at all (Murray & German 2005: 62–3).

The peace movement and the Iraq War

After US and British forces attacked Afghanistan in late 2001, destroying not only al-Qaida's bases but also the Taliban regime that protected them, the Bush administration saw an opportunity to overthrow the Saddam regime in Iraq, which it considered unfinished business from the 1991 war. By late 2002, Bush had decided to attack Iraq and Blair was determined to support him, only trying to persuade him to obtain a UN resolution specifically authorizing force on the grounds of Iraq's possession of weapons of mass destruction (WMD).[3]

As in 1991, the main strands of the peace movement were united in opposing an invasion. All saw the Bush doctrine of pre-emptive war and "regime change" as an aggressive reassertion of US power and recognized that Saddam's human rights abuses, which Blair invoked to justify the war, were not its driver. For HCA, the invasion was certainly a step too far. Kaldor argued that "to expand the very restrictive idea of humanitarian intervention into a general license for war against repressive regimes" was dangerous: "you cannot violate human rights to bring about human rights, you cannot have *wars* for human rights" (Rankin 2017: 212, emphasis in original). However, where Kaldor saw a departure from the Kosovo rationale, Mahon saw continuity: for her, Kosovo had opened a Pandora's box, leading directly to the new invasion (2006: 49103, 49110).[4]

Activists had already built up expertise on Iraq, in campaigns against both post-1991 UN sanctions, which had contributed to a humanitarian catastrophe, and a 1998 US/UK air campaign to contain the Saddam regime, Desert Fox (Sinclair 2011: 62–3). As fears of a new attack grew, events in the Middle East contributed to growing connections between Muslims and the left. In April 2002, the Muslim Association of Britain (MAB), a Sunni Muslim organization with links to the Muslim Brotherhood, organized a protest about Israel's massacre of Palestinians in Jenin. StWC and MAB then co-organized a demonstration on the twin themes of "Don't Attack Iraq" and "Solidarity with Palestine". StWC saw freedom for Palestinians as an essential component of Middle East peace, but critics such as the Board of Deputies of British Jews saw MAB as fundamentalist, antisemitic and misogynist.

By autumn 2002, when it was clear that Bush and Blair were very likely to invade, StWC wanted an even larger joint protest. The case for CND involvement now became even stronger: as Kent later commented, WMD was "the reason for the war" (Sinclair 2011: 108). Hudson wanted CND to co-organize the protest, but Naughton dug in; it would only "support" the No to War demonstration of 28 September 2002.

Meanwhile, Ploughshares and other NVDA campaigners acted independently. They broke into Menwith Hill, disarmed a US warplane at Shannon, Ireland, disabled support vehicles for Stealth bombers at the Fairford airbase and blockaded the armed forces headquarters at Northwood in outer London. Activists, some of them linked to ARROW, also stormed the Confederation of British Industries conference and broke into the chamber of the Welsh Assembly (Trident Ploughshares 2019; Rai 2023b; libcom.org 2016).

However, Ian Sinclair (2013), who interviewed over a hundred activists for an oral history, concluded that "the SWP's domination of StWC led to organized direct action and civil disobedience not being pursued fully by the anti-war movement in the lead up to the invasion of Iraq". (There were also further attempts to have a serious debate on NVDA after 15 February 2003, but according to Marqusee, quoted by Sinclair, the leadership did not favour open discussion of it and "began labelling people who were saying they wanted a different [tactical] emphasis as divisive".)

The mass movement and the 15 February demonstration

As the Iraq crisis escalated, the campaign against intervention grew rapidly into a broad-based mass movement. StWC was its effective centre and there was a de facto "three-way alliance" between it, CND and the MAB, although the latter also remained formally outside the Coalition (Hudson 2018: 189–90; Phillips 2008: 102–5). The momentum was shown when hundreds of thousands came to the September 2002 demonstration, gaining substantial and often supportive media coverage. Although mainstream media remained important, the movement increasingly developed its own media, now that the Internet was widely used: there were extensive flows between the two (Gillan, Pickerill & Webster 2008: 25–40).

The movement gained wide support. StWC held press conferences with celebrities such as Daman Albarn, Bianca Jagger and Ken Loach, while "Poets for Peace" organized and Adrian Mitchell reworked his Vietnam poem as "Tell Me Lies About Iraq". A Cambridge academic, Glen Rangwala, prepared a briefing for Labour Against the War that undermined the government's case over WMD and gave influential evidence in parliament (House of Commons Foreign Affairs Committee 2003). Katharine Hamnett designed "Not In My Name" T-shirts that sold widely.

A major CND contribution was a legal challenge on which it spent £60,000, 12 per cent of its income in 2002. After the UN authorized inspectors to investigate Iraq's alleged WMD, CND established, in an opinion commissioned in November 2002, that an invasion would be illegal without a second UN resolution specifically mandating the use of force, which was the view initially held by Blair's own solicitor-general and supported by 75 per cent in a Channel 4 poll. The Court of Appeal dismissed the case; it was most unlikely, said Lord Justice Brown, that the government had mistaken the law since it had "access to the best advice, not only from law officers but also from a number of specialists on the field" (White 2010: 820). However, CND had brought the international illegality of the war to public attention.

Early 2003 was a period of crisis as war loomed. Blair's pressure for a second resolution failed in the UN, while his culture secretary, Tessa Jowell, failed in her attempt to use the state of the grass in Hyde Park to prevent the February rally there. Michael Foot, now 88, had threatened to chain himself to the park railings, recalling a famous episode in 1867 when over 100,000 people defied the home secretary's ban on a demonstration for electoral reform in the park. Local campaigning reached fever pitch, Blair became "Bliar", school students came out on strike and special trains were organized, including from towns such as Preston with large Muslim populations. An Exeter activist recalled that "the first six weeks of 2003 were a long blur of street stalls, leafleting, visiting people who'd never been on a demonstration before in their lives to deliver bundles of tickets for them and their neighbours, and meetings where everything from sandwich making to the way the world should be was discussed" (Murray & German 2005: 197).

The march on 15 February 2003, which CND co-sponsored, is estimated to have mobilized well over a million people (or 1.6 per cent of the UK population) for what is widely recognized as the largest demonstration in British history (Sinclair 2011: 220; Gordon 2003: 1117). The 41 speakers included Foot, Kent, former cabinet minister Mo Mowlam, US civil rights leader Jesse Jackson, London mayor Ken Livingstone, Benn, Corbyn and Galloway. The singer Ms Dynamite powerfully concluded the rally. For Ian McEwan, who set his novel *Saturday* on the day, with its carnival atmosphere it "seemed more like an Aldermaston march" than the sombre CND protests of the 1980s (Sinclair 2011: 179). Kate Hudson also made this contrast, emphasizing the march's exceptional "mass and spontaneous character": "for huge sections of the demonstration there were no banners, just people in their hundreds of thousands. In other words they were not 'organized' people who had come with a party or union, but people who had just decided, in dialogue with their conscience, that they wanted to be there" (2008a: 379–80).

Although the London demonstration and one attended by tens of thousands in Glasgow were part of a worldwide wave, this was a "decentralized transnationalism"; the British movement was once again predominantly national in character (Gillan, Pickerill & Webster 2008: 123). While there was effective international coordination, the national level was crucial for the movement's political definition, while its mobilizing power and mass participation were largely rooted at another level still, in the localities.

As the movement became massive, its leftist character was partially overtaken: 450 organizations had affiliated themselves to the StWC including Greenpeace, the Greens, Plaid Cymru and the Scottish National Party (SNP). The involvement of the Liberal Democrats under Charles Kennedy, who spoke at the rally (which included a large Liberal Democrat contingent), contributed significantly to its breadth, although they aroused some suspicion in StWC since his position in the event of a second UN resolution was ambiguous. But the leadership was keen to maximize StWC's appeal at a time when the leaders of the Church of England and the Catholic Church, together with prominent Conservatives such as the former Foreign Secretary Douglas Hurd, were coming out against war, although the official Tory opposition remained as devoted to Bush as Blair was. There was also substantial trade union opposition, including after the war started from the Trades Union Congress.

The momentum increased after the demonstration. On "Wobbly Tuesday", 11 March 2003, Blair's defence secretary, Geoff Hoon, even told his US counterpart that the UK might not be able to take part in the invasion (Rai 2012). Blair was forced to concede an unprecedented parliamentary vote, and when this took place on 18 March, one-third of MPs, including a majority of non-payroll Labour members, voted that the case for war "had not yet been established". Robin Cook resigned from the cabinet – most of whom were lukewarm about Blair's policy – making a devastating speech. The following day, Bush's war began with the "shock and awe" bombing of Baghdad, and that weekend StWC organized a further protest, claimed to be the biggest ever during wartime. However, CND, together with a minority of the StWC's steering committee disagreed with its decision to add "Blair Must Go" to the demands (Murray & German 2005: 191–6).

A section of the press fanned the mobilization. The *Daily Mirror* under Piers Morgan sponsored the march, repeatedly used its front page to oppose war and gave substantial space to the antiwar journalist John Pilger, the *Independent* was supportive and the *Guardian* featured antiwar views extensively. Before the war, the movement received more favourable than unfavourable coverage, but as bombing began it saw attention shift to the conflict itself and was increasingly ignored. The polls moved in Blair's favour and parliamentary opposition faded away. A study concluded that a "support our boys" consensus led to the narrowing of the sphere of legitimate controversy, with the antiwar movement relegated to a "sphere of deviance" (Murray *et al.* 2008: 7).

StWC did not stop the war. Its chroniclers, Murray and German (2005: 200–2), seemed divided as to whether the movement's weak implantation in workplaces – which their Marxist approach suggested should have been central – or Labour conformism was to blame. For Milan Rai (2023a), the problem was that while StWC concentrated on marches and direct actionists on military bases, there was insufficient lobbying of the reluctant Labour MPs who could have blocked it in parliament, as happened a decade later over Syria. Activists claimed that the movement may have mitigated the invasion's effects on civilians. Certainly, the little legitimacy the war had was undermined, and Blair's reputation was permanently tarnished.

CND and the left after the demonstration

CND helped fund the February 2003 demonstration and Kent was one of the main speakers up and down the country. Local activists were fully involved up to the outbreak of war, while Hudson and Carol Turner joined StWC's officers group. In late 2003, CND revived its legal attack, supporting a Peacerights tribunal of experts that determined that international law had been violated by the use of indiscriminate weapons. The results were sent to the attorney general, but he refused to act, and then to the prosecutor of the newly established International Criminal Court, who saw the allegations as significant but did not proceed. Nevertheless, the allegation that Bush and Blair were "war criminals" became a powerful motif for campaigners.

However, the antiwar movement was an uneasy alliance. It had united against a particular war, not war as such, and pacifist activists increasingly chafed at StWC's dominance. For Pax Christi, which had sponsored an ecumenical Christian declaration on the Morality and Legality of a War Against Iraq in June 2002, it did not represent the pre-existing peace movement. Pat Gaffney, the group's general secretary, later complained that other faith groups opposed to the war were downplayed in favour of Muslims, questioned StWC's understanding of long-term peacebuilding and criticized people in it for "pushing an extreme political agenda" (Donovan 2003). Sociologists who studied the movement concluded that "few talked to each other across the ethno-religious divide" (Gillan, Pickerill & Webster 2008: 87).

There was also new controversy in CND. In June 2003, Naughton wrote a damning memorandum to its Council members, noting "the different cultural backgrounds" of CND and the MAB, complaining that StWC "did not seem to understand or accept the culture of working in partnership" and even calling its leadership "duplicitous and manipulative" (Sinclair 2011: 318–19). The far left in CND, aiming to restore the relationship with StWC, now attempted to oust Naughton as chair, and in September, Hudson beat her by 167 to 166 votes. Amid claims that members of the Trotskyist group Socialist Action and the SWP had joined in the final days to swing the vote, Kent said the election was "ethically rigged" and predicted a "major fightback" (Carrell 2003; Donovan 2003).

However, Hudson was narrowly re-elected in 2004, when it was reported that 12 out of 15 members of the new national executive shared her views (Day 2007 [2004]). Controversy around the leadership's attitude to authoritarian regimes erupted at the 2005 CND conference, when the Iranian ambassador was invited to speak. Exiled Iranian oppositionists protested, and when they refused a request to stop speaking by Corbyn in the chair, they were asked to leave and escorted out by CND staff and officers (Kilburn 2005).

Despite these controversies, Hudson's position cemented the close alliance between CND and StWC: Murray and German (2005: 218) described her as "the foremost proponent of a united antiwar movement in CND" and a "key member" of their officer group. In the following years, her centrality to CND itself was repeatedly confirmed: she served as chair until 2010 and was then appointed as general secretary, a post she still held in 2024.

This represents by far the longest continuous tenure of high office by a single individual in CND's history. An academic, Hudson had written a book on Yugoslavia (2003) that advocated a position similar to Alice Mahon's and would go on to write or edit others discussing a realignment of the European left (2012a) and defending European freedom of movement (2017). Her position on CND is reflected in her histories (2005, 2018), which emphasize the continuities between the organization today and the earlier movements.

Meanwhile, StWC, with CND's support, still mobilized substantial protests: against Bush's state visit in November 2003, over the Hutton report in January 2004[5] and against US torture of Iraqi prisoners in Abu

Ghraib prison in April 2004. However, while it was soon clear that the US/UK occupation was ill-prepared and widely regarded as illegitimate, the organization was increasingly challenged by the postwar situation.

StWC saw the conflict as defined by US/UK aggression, which Iraqis had the right to resist "by whatever means they find necessary", and therefore refused to take a position on the resisters' politics (Bloodworth 2015). However, some Iraqi exiles had warned of civil war (al-Chalabi 2003), and it soon became clear that the Sunni-based "resistance" was carrying out bloody sectarian attacks on Shi'a Muslims, leading to a low-level war between Sunni and Shi'ite militias during 2005–7 in which each attempted to "cleanse" its areas of Baghdad of the other community. In this context, the priority StWC gave to a "speedy" withdrawal of British troops met with opposition among some previously supportive exiles and Labour movement organizations alike (Murray & German 2005: 205–7). The antiwar movement's connection with political Islam was another continuing source of criticism (Halliday 2006).

The complexities of international intervention that had divided the peace movement over Yugoslavia were now affecting the Iraq movement, and as if to remind it of the earlier divisions, in 2006 Alice Mahon appeared as a witness for Slobodan Milošević at the International Criminal Tribunal for the Former Yugoslavia, saying he had been "the only one trying to keep Yugoslavia together", and claiming that refugees had fled from Kosovo to neighbouring states because of NATO bombing rather than the Serbian campaign of violence (Hudson 2005: 212–16; Mahon 1999; Mahon 2006: 49140, 49107).

CND was also affected by the realignment of left politics that the movement produced. The StWC and CND far left worked closely with a section of the Labour left: for example, Livingstone received a standing ovation at CND's 2004 conference. Yet as StWC shrank closer to its original base, the SWP and George Galloway – who had been expelled from Labour in October 2003 – sought to capitalize on it to create a new electoral force, Respect: The Unity Coalition. Galloway captured a London seat with a large Muslim electorate from Labour in the 2005 general election, but the party peaked and split in 2007.

Respect revived in 2012 when he won a by-election in Bradford, and Hudson, now CND's general secretary (who had left the Communist Party of Britain) briefly joined Respect that year, becoming its candidate for a Manchester by-election. However, she soon resigned after Galloway dismissed rape allegations against the whistle-blower Julian Assange as "bad sexual etiquette" (Hudson 2012b). (After Hudson left Respect, she helped found another new party, Left Unity, in 2014, becoming its national secretary from 2015 to 2017; she remained a member in 2023.)

CND continued to work closely with StWC, organizing protests jointly (sometimes also with the MAB or the Palestine Solidarity Campaign) around combined antinuclear, antiwar and solidarity demands. In 2007, the slogans were "No Trident" and "Troops Out of Iraq". In 2011, CND joined StWC in opposing British and NATO intervention in the Libyan civil war that overthrew the Gaddafi dictatorship.

Most influentially, in 2013 the antiwar movement opposed British participation in US airstrikes against the Syrian dictatorship of Bashar al-Assad, after it committed a chemical massacre of civilians in Damascus. The day after parliament voted by 285 to 272 against intervention, following the decision of the Labour leader Ed Miliband to oppose action, Corbyn, who had taken over as StWC chair in 2011, wrote to supporters: "All of those years marching and working for peace have finally paid off ... Last night we saw the results of the last 10 years of lobbying, and proof that Britain is no longer a plaything of the US military adventure" (2013).

Stop the War coalition march to Downing Street, October 2014.

Source: Mark Thomas / Alamy Stock Photo.

Given the narrow vote, the claim was plausible, and the decision was certainly consequential. The Conservative prime minister, David Cameron, withdrew the UK's proposed involvement, and President Barack Obama, having lost his main ally, cancelled the strikes. They would not have ended Assad's brutal campaign but would undoubtedly have affected the balance in the war. Knowing that Obama would not respond even when his "red line" against chemical weapons had been crossed, Assad gained confidence and Russia increased its involvement, which by 2015 included extensive bombing.

StWC and CND had helped stop Western military intervention but their critics, including some Syrian exiles as well as what they labelled the "pro-war left", argued that they contributed to the continuation of Assad's war in which hundreds of thousands died. StWC's position, implicitly followed by CND, was that as a British campaign, its responsibility was to oppose its own government and its allies. It sometimes criticized other states but did not campaign directly against them, and its support for the right of resistance was sometimes taken by supporters and opponents alike as legitimating repressive actors. It was therefore criticized for selective antiwar politics and a lack of solidarity with the victims of non-Western militarism (Bloodworth 2015).

Nuclear politics and UK political turbulence

After 2003, sociologists who studied the milieu concluded, there were *combined* antiwar and peace movements rather than a united movement; but the combination nevertheless defined the various elements (Gillan, Pickerill & Webster 2008: 74–83). The importance of antiwar issues for both CND and NVDA activists partly reflected a deep downturn in nuclear politics, but both continued dedicated campaigns against Trident, US missile bases in Britain and nuclear power throughout the first quarter of the twenty-first century.

CND as an organization was on a much more secure footing than in the earlier downturn.[6] National membership was sustained at a higher level, 32,000 in 2001 and 2003 and 35,000 in 2009 (NGO UK nd: figure 3). Although subsequent figures were not published, Hudson (2023b) still claimed over 30,000 national, regional and local members. Annual income fluctuated at around £500,000–£800,000, largely reflecting a variable level of legacies. In constant 2009 prices, this was less than 1984's £1,076,000 but much greater than 1979's £102,000 and bigger even than 1962's £374,000, the highest in the first wave (NGO UK nd: figure 1). In most years, a third to a half of the income was spent on direct campaigning and most of the rest on running the organization, which in 2007 had a higher level of staffing (11.9 full-time equivalent) than at its peaks in 1964 (7) and 1984 (9) (NGO UK nd: figure 2). It still had 7.5 staff in 2021. Yet the number of CND "groups" was small compared to earlier periods: in July 2023 the website listed 77, some of them area or regional organizations. Many local groups were in the larger cities and not all of these had one.

By the mid-2000s, activism was "less constituted by public, interpersonal events and more by computer-mediated communication, and the dissemination of news, analysis and imagery online"; it was "difficult to imagine" the movement functioning without its extensive adoption of this technology (Gillan, Pickerill & Webster 2008: 60, 148). National CND developed a professional website, with its chair having final sight of content, while mobile phones became central to direct action, and in the 2010s, campaigning moved into social media. By July 2023, CND had accumulated 85,000 followers on Facebook, 40,000 on Twitter and 5,000 on Instagram, but these numbers were modest compared, for example, to the 946,000, 255,000 and 386,000 respectively of Greenpeace UK.

A near-monthly CND magazine, *Campaign*, kept members informed, but it was written mainly by officers and carried neither the letters nor the reports of internal debates that had made *Sanity* at its best a reflection of the movement. The livelier if less frequent *Heddwch* (Peace) and *Nuclear Free Scotland* suggested greater vigour in the devolved nations. Scottish CND also developed a strong research tradition, notably in the work of John Ainslie over more than three decades until his death in 2016, which is collected in an online archive (Nuclear Information Service 2023).

However, organizational robustness was not fully matched by public impact. CND's profile in the mainstream media was much reduced: its mentions in the *Guardian* and *Times* showed a decline from 389 (1983) to 60 (1989), 32 (1991) and 28 (1999) to fewer than 20 each year in the 2000s, even in 2003, suggesting that CND's supporting role in the Iraq movement gave it little new public recognition (NGO UK nd: figure 4).

The antinuclear campaign now had some legacy characteristics. Activism often reproduced historic modes and commemoration was increasingly important. At Easter 2008, CND commemorated the fiftieth anniversary of the Aldermaston march in Trafalgar Square; only 5,000 came and an annual fixture was not renewed. Hiroshima and Nagasaki days had long been central, and Pax Christi and other Christian groups held an annual Ash Wednesday vigil against nuclear weapons outside the Ministry of Defence, but commemorative activity accelerated around CND's sixtieth anniversary in 2018. The following year, *Peace News*, Housmans Bookshop and War Resisters International also celebrated 60 years' presence at 5 Caledonian Road, London.

Fortieth anniversaries of 1980s events also began to be marked. The 1981 march from Cardiff to Greenham was recreated in 2021, but commemoration of Greenham had actually begun before the camp finally closed in 2000, when it was replaced by a Peace Garden adjacent to the main entrance to the former base, which itself became a business park after the RAF abandoned it. In 2018, Greenham Women Everywhere had started an ambitious online archive, and Thalia Campbell, a prolific maker of the original banners, made a replica of the banner from the 1981 march (Campbell 2019), which hangs in the Amgueddfa Cymru/ Museum Wales, Cardiff. Fortieth anniversaries of the Faslane camp ("the longest-running in the world") and the Upper Heyford blockade were celebrated in 2022 and 2023 respectively.

CND had a strong routine, with regular campaigns around NATO summits, NPT review conferences and the UK's annual Defence and Security Exhibition International (DSEI) arms fair (a focus too for NVDA through Disarm DSEI), as well as activities around the Faslane camp, the monthly part-time women's camp at Aldermaston (established in 1985, in 2009 it resisted a Ministry of Defence attempt to ban it), Menwith Hill and Fylingdales. It also had thriving peace education activities; in Wales, these culminated in 2021 in the launch of Academi Heddwch with funding from the Welsh Labour government, and CND was also regularly at the National Eisteddfod.

CND continued its historic role as a conduit of information on nuclear issues, especially to the left. Its work here was reinforced by the publications of research bodies such as the Oxford Research Group, the British American Security Information Council, the Acronym Institute for Disarmament Diplomacy, British Pugwash and the

Nuclear Information Service, as well as Paul Rogers' column on open-Democracy, published continuously for more than two decades from 2002.

CND also remained the nationally and internationally accepted representative of British antinuclear opinion. Internal conflict died down and the alliance of CND's left and Christian/pacifist tendencies was restored, since both were invested in its historical legitimacy. While Hudson was general secretary, Kent, who symbolized CND's continuity with its past, remained active until his death in 2022; they appear to have worked well together. Other veterans, such as Pat Arrowsmith, John Cox, Christian campaigner Paul Oestreicher, Greenham's Rebecca Johnson and Labour CNDer Walter Wolfgang, also served as honorary vice-presidents alongside MPs such as Benn, Mahon, Corbyn and (from 2017) the first Green, Caroline Lucas, who had been involved in the movement since the Snowball campaign.

The tempo stepped up at key points in nuclear politics. From late 2006 when Blair announced a new generation of submarines, the campaign became one against Trident replacement. At the end of 2007, CND Council reported that the first part of the year had seen a large campaign. A poll showed that 72 per cent opposed replacement; CND claimed that up to 100,000 participated in a No Trident, Troops Out of Iraq demonstration co-organized with StWC and British Muslim Initiative (a split from the MAB); and there was a large Labour backbench rebellion. Hudson (2018: 202) could later quote Blair's comment in his memoirs that non-renewal "would not have been stupid", but he had forced through the decision. Soon "No Trident Replacement" was itself replaced by "Scrap Trident".

The years 2006–7 also saw significant activity around NMD, after the head of the US Missile Defense Agency said that the UK would be on the shortlist to host its interceptors for incoming missiles. The Pentagon then contradicted this, citing British opposition to the Iraq War, but in 2007 Menwith Hill was formally integrated into NMD and Fylingdales was upgraded to support it. CND met with activists from nine concerned European countries in Prague, later co-organizing an international conference opened by the mayor of a Czech town near a radar site for the system (Hudson 2018: 203–4). However, in 2009 Obama cancelled plans for bases in the Czech Republic and Poland. Also in 2007, CND helped set up the International Campaign to Abolish

Nuclear Weapons (ICAN), which would become a major focus and lead to a global treaty a decade later.

TP's campaigns grew in parallel. Thousands were arrested during blockades over several years culminating in Faslane 365, a year-long decentralized protest involving 50 affinity groups, some of them international, launched in October 2006 (Zelter 2008). It even involved an Academics Blockade, which carried out a seminar to block the gates (Gillan, Pickerill & Webster 2008: 126). One of its activists, who described it as a kind of working holiday, commented that NVDA "mostly consists of sitting around drinking tea, eating biscuits and discussing peace, so perhaps it should be called nonviolent direct inaction" (Bateman 2008: xxiii). But the campaign was hardly a vacation: if it did not succeed in blockading the base on each of its 365 days, its legal group (two people) had plenty of work, since there were over 1,000 arrests. In contrast to CND's conventional website, Faslane 365 offered parts of its site to the different affinity groups involved.

Faslane 365 helped put the antinuclear focus on Scotland in order to "break the nuclear chain" in the UK, and TP increasingly focused attention on the role of the Scottish parliament. The SNP formed a Scottish government for the first time in 2007 and soon held a Summit for a Nuclear Free Scotland, as part of preparing the country for independence. TP co-organized an international conference in 2009 to broaden the Scottish as well as international legal case against Trident (Johnson & Zelter 2011).

In the early 2010s, CND linked Trident to the austerity policies of the new Conservative-led coalition, citing a lifetime system cost of £205 billion that could be diverted to socially useful expenditure. It argued for green employment, claiming that the Barrow shipyard could be used to make wave and tidal turbines. It increasingly took part in climate protests, interpreting "antinuclear" as seamless opposition to nuclear power and weapons, and making no concessions to the pro-nuclear energy stance adopted by some environmentalists because of global heating. The Fukushima disaster in 2011, the biggest since Chernobyl, reinforced this position and became a major reference point, especially as the government commissioned a major new station at Hinkley Point, Somerset, where a 1,000-strong demonstration was held in 2012.

However, the politics of Trident replacement, a slow process, were overtaken in the middle of the decade by broader changes as British politics entered a period of crisis linked to international political turbulence. Although this ultimately centred on Brexit, the Scottish referendum of 2014 and the election of Jeremy Corbyn as Labour leader in 2015 were more significant for CND.

The battle over Scottish independence was potentially crucial. After the implementation of devolution in 1999, analysts argued that the Scottish location of the UK's Trident nuclear submarines and the extreme difficulty of relocating them elsewhere meant that the idea of Scottish consent to this situation "could be tantamount to giving Scotland a veto" over the continuation of the independent deterrent (Chalmers & Walker 2001: 4). The SNP had been committed since 1968, when it was becoming a serious political force and the Holy Loch base was newly established, to making Scotland nuclear free. Over half a century, the SNP tied Scottish identity to antinuclear values, so that the removal of Trident had become its most explicit symbol of independence (Lindsay 1983; Ritchie 2010: 655–67). However, in 2012 the party pledged to remain in NATO if it removed nuclear weapons from Scotland.

The stakes were therefore high when a referendum was called for 18 September 2014. Scottish CND had long aligned itself with independence, but "national" CND, mindful of the political situation in England, did not take a position. Scottish CND affiliated to and promoted the Yes campaign, later registering as a campaigning participant, arguing that removing Trident "would probably result in there being no nuclear weapons in Britain" (Ainslie 2013: 2). Given the UK parties' commitment to Trident, the referendum was the only real chance that Scotland had to get rid of it, claimed the SNP's deputy leader Nicola Sturgeon, who had joined CND at age 16. However, during the campaign Yes said little about the fate of the nuclear bases: there was "a tendency to downplay the immensity and complexity" of the task of relocating the nuclear force, indeed "an evasion practised throughout" (Chalmers & Walker 2022: 297–8).

The 55:45 per cent defeat of independence was therefore a setback for Scottish CND, but nationalists did not blame the nuclear issue. In London, CND saw potential if a minority Labour government under Ed Miliband, which was widely expected to result from the UK general election of 2015, needed SNP support. In the event, the Conservatives successfully weaponized English fear of the SNP to secure a narrow overall majority, with the SNP wiping out Labour in Scotland.

However, Labour's defeat created a new twist that unexpectedly opened up possibilities for CND. The leadership election after Miliband resigned was conducted for the first time on the basis of one member, one vote and Jeremy Corbyn, the left's "no hope" standard-bearer, was catapulted into the position as leftists joined or rejoined the party to vote for him. Corbyn had been a CND member since the age of 15, CND vice-chair and chair of Parliamentary CND. Although he resigned as chair of StWC, after he won he became a CND vice-president and addressed its 2015 annual conference and an anti-Trident rally in 2016.

Corbyn's victory raised CND's hopes and, like Labour itself, it experienced a surge in membership. Hudson saw his commitments as promising alongside SNP and Liberal Democrat opposition to like-for-like Trident replacement. For Labour CND's Turner (2016: 117), concluding a book of interviews that surveyed the vicissitudes of the unilateralist cause in the party, scrapping Trident was now "an indivisible part of Labour's forward march".

Yet the new stage of this march proved anything but straightforward. Corbyn lacked support within Labour's parliamentary party and even appointed a shadow defence secretary, Maria Eagle, who quickly dismissed as "unhelpful" his comment that he would not authorize the use of nuclear weapons if he became prime minister. Moreover, his international activities as a backbench MP, which mostly endeared him to CND members, were anathema to Labour's right wing and the press, haunting his leadership from the outset. Despite his reputation as a man of peace, like StWC Corbyn backed the right of armed resistance to imperialism. He had had extensive contacts with Sinn Féin, the party linked to the Provisional IRA, and notoriously met with representatives of Hamas and Hezbollah.

It was soon clear that Corbyn, even with the aid of the new grassroots movement Momentum, would not be able to change the party's position on Trident. In 2016, the majority of Labour MPs voted with the Conservative government for replacement (only 47 voted against), and the party's defence review, which Corbyn hoped would generate an anti-Trident policy, failed to appear. In the 2017 election the party's manifesto dashed CND's hopes, supporting Trident renewal and offering only multilateralist platitudes on nuclear disarmament.

Like much of the left, CND took heart from the unexpected increase in Labour's vote and seats that Corbyn achieved in 2017, which caused a hung parliament and forced the Conservatives into minority government. The summer 2017 issue of *Campaign* claimed the result showed that "a willingness to press the nuclear button was not a vote-winner", and that with Corbyn's stronger position, turning Labour against Trident was back on the agenda. With the final achievement of the Treaty on the Prohibition of Nuclear Weapons, which opened for signature that September (and for which ICAN was awarded the Nobel Peace Prize), there remained a mood of optimism.

However, 2017 proved Corbyn's high point. His and Labour's popularity declined inexorably during the Brexit conflict of the following two and a half years, removing any hope of reversing its Trident stance. A mass pro-European People's Vote movement developed, with protests in March and October 2019 both estimated at around a million participants, making them second in size only to the Iraq march and larger than CND demonstrations in the 1980s. This movement organized the same middle-class radical constituency that CND and StWC had both earlier mobilized, echoed the left Europeanism that END had pioneered and took seriously the idea of the EU as a peace project.

However, CND did not engage with Brexit: it was not even mentioned in *Campaign* or CND's annual reports from 2016 to 2023. CND members were divided: some of the left – but not Hudson – supported "Lexit" (left exit) while others backed the pro-European marches. Brexit did not offer a direct opportunity to influence nuclear policy, and in 2021, the centrepiece of the "Global Britain" that Boris Johnson proclaimed as its outcome turned out to be a new nuclear alliance with Australia and the USA, AUKUS, which CND opposed. However, the UK's departure after almost half a century created a precedent for the exit from NATO that CND had backed for even longer. Its lack of interest in claiming this precedent underlined the differences in the ways that the EU and NATO were perceived on the left.

The wider peace constituency was also largely disengaged. In *Peace News* (June–July 2016), co-editor Milan Rai advocated a Remain vote because Brexit would strengthen anti-immigrant and authoritarian tendencies. However, after the vote (August–September 2016), under the heading "Brexit: Reasons to be Cheerful", the paper welcomed the "wild energy on the loose". In December 2018–January 2019, it reported on a short questionnaire on Brexit to 53 peace groups: it received only four replies.

In a resurgence of direct action in 2017, three members of Nukewatch UK were arrested for blocking a convoy carrying nuclear bombs in Scotland and over 100 were arrested at the DSEI arms fair –some of whom were acquitted after the judge accepted that it was reasonable to cause a certain amount of disruption (*Peace News* 2018, February–March). Amid the Brexit turmoil, CND campaigning against Trident in 2018, including a "Nae Nukes Anywhere" rally at Faslane and a Christian CND protest at a service of thanksgiving in Westminster Abbey for 50 years of "continuous at-sea deterrent", was largely overshadowed.

However, the Extinction Rebellion (XR) climate action group, founded in 2018, attracted NVDA activists and gained media attention, and CND allied itself with this, proclaiming itself "part of the climate movement". XR Peace became a new umbrella for peace action, holding Peace Blockades in autumn 2019, for example blocking the Embankment near the Ministry of Defence in protest at the carbon emissions from military activity, an issue that Scottish CND also raised at the COP26 summit in Glasgow in 2021. "Climate Not Trident" was CND's new banner, while climate activists began to argue for "fossil fuel disarmament" and a Fossil Fuel Non-Proliferation Treaty.

Meanwhile, Corbyn's position deteriorated further as the Brexit polarization reached its climax. Out of sympathy with the pro-European movement and unable to counter Johnson's demand to "Get Brexit Done", he decisively lost the general election of December 2019. This was another election in which defence and Trident played minimal roles, and in which first-past-the-post damned the opposition, who combined had an overall majority of the votes. From CND's point of view, it was disappointing that Scottish Labour, which opposed Trident renewal in 2015, now supported it along with UK Labour (Bella Caledonia 2019).

In 2020 Corbyn was replaced as Labour leader by Keir Starmer, who was elected partly on a platform of "no more illegal wars", introducing a Prevention of Military Intervention Act and reviewing all UK arms sales, but he soon dropped these issues (in 2023 he even refused to call for a ceasefire during Israel's destruction of Gaza). Under his leadership, there was never any question of the party abandoning Trident, let alone returning to unilateralism. Starmer abolished the post of shadow disarmament minister and shadow ministers proclaimed the deterrent part of Labour's "heritage" (Lammy & Healey 2023). The party even banned constituency parties from affiliating to Labour CND.

Although in practice CND maintained considerable Labour support, its hope that the party could be a vehicle for change in nuclear policy had proved even more weakly based this time than it had in 1960 or 1983. CND still possessed some methods of institutionalizing its influence, such as a campaign for councils to back the Treaty on the Prohibition of Nuclear Weapons, which Manchester City Council was the first to support in 2019. By 2023, 33 mostly smaller councils across the UK had become Nuclear Ban Communities, while Scottish CND pressed councils to address the risks of nuclear weapons convoys passing through their areas. But CND's local government impact was a shadow of what it had been.

The possibility that independence would undermine the UK's nuclear weapons became a live issue again after the SNP and the Scottish Greens gained a majority in the Scottish parliament in 2021. In fact the antinuclear majority was even bigger, since some Labour MSPs had also supported the ICAN Parliamentary Pledge. However, the implosion of the SNP and the revival of Scottish Labour in 2023–4 was weakening still further the likelihood of a new referendum.

CND and the global turbulence of the 2020s

The antinuclear campaign was also buffeted by more fundamental global turbulence. When Donald Trump was elected US President, *Campaign* (2016, December) had no hesitation in heralding "exceptionally dangerous times ahead". An obvious target because of his cavalier approach to international order, he figured strongly in CND's campaigning. The organization assessed that his hostility to NATO amounted mainly to pressure on other member states to increase their military spending, and focused instead on his multiple nuclear risks: his access to nuclear codes, his opposition to the Iran treaty and the NPT, and his initially confrontational approach to North Korea.

Trump appeared to threaten a "bonfire of the treaties", undoing much of the progress in managing nuclear weapons that had been achieved over the previous half-century. For the campaign, his February 2019 withdrawal from the INF treaty, the great success of the 1980s, was symbolically the most shocking development. However, the revelation that the chair of the Joint Chiefs of Staff, General Mark Milley, believed he had to prevent Trump from possibly using nuclear weapons after he lost the 2020 election (Pengelly 2021) was even scarier.

After Trump was replaced by Joe Biden, CND continued to argue that the prime threat remained the enhancement of US and UK activities. In 2021, it condemned the UK's decision to increase the cap on its nuclear arsenal by over 40 per cent, commissioning a legal opinion that found that this represented a breach of the NPT. In 2022–3, it opposed the apparent preparations being made to return US nuclear weapons to Lakenheath and explored legal action over this too.

However, like many, CND had failed to take the measure of Russia's new international aggressiveness earlier in the century, maintaining together with StWC that tensions were principally the West's fault. When Russia invaded Georgia following the Georgian government's offensive against South Ossetian separatists, Hudson (2008b) claimed that the USA seemed "hell bent on escalating tensions with Russia". Likewise, when Russia first intervened militarily in Ukraine, StWC's Lindsey German (2014) wrote that while she "did not agree" with the intervention, talk of Russian expansionism took "no note of the far bigger expansionism of the NATO powers and the role played by the world's largest imperialist power, the United States". *Peace News* (2014, April), in contrast, welcomed the removal of Ukraine's pro-Russian president as a victory for civil resistance and drew attention to the "uncomfortable truth" that if Ukraine had kept its nuclear weapons in 1991, it might not have been invaded.

CND even veered into apologies for Russian actions in Ukraine. In *Campaign*, Dave Webb (2019), CND chair since 2010 described taking part in a "study tour" of Russian-occupied Crimea organized by the Global Network against Weapons and Nuclear Power in Space, "to meet people, learn about the Russian annexation and build bridges of friendship and understanding at the citizen level". His article repeated Russian propaganda about how "following a right-wing coup in Kiev, local militia were quickly organized and a referendum held on whether to return to Russia or remain in Ukraine". He reported this vote – almost universally regarded as illegitimate and rigged – completely uncritically, concluded that "the Russian people want peace and security" and called for "the easing of tensions by removing all nuclear weapons from Europe and cancelling intimidating war manoeuvres". This article must have raised eyebrows among CND members, but there does not appear to have been any public pushback.

Two and a half years later, intimidating war manoeuvres were all too evident as Russian troops massed on the borders of Ukraine. Yet as late as 22 February 2022, two days before Putin launched his full invasion, Hudson (2022a) still chided the USA for "refusing to talk to the Russian leadership" and "escalating the conflict". Once the Russian invasion began, CND could no longer maintain this line. On 28 February, she accompanied the 92-year-old Bruce Kent (2022), in one of his last political acts (he died three months later), to deliver a letter condemning the invasion to the Russian embassy. It expressed dismay at Putin's warning of "consequences greater than any you have faced in history", which was "widely interpreted to be a reference to the use of nuclear weapons". CND was disturbed to hear that Russian nuclear forces were being placed on high alert: Putin's actions had "tilted the world towards potential disaster" and "put all of us in peril". CND stood squarely with Russians who protested against the invasion, defending their right to do so. It urged the Russian government to turn its back on its disastrous course, for the sake of Ukrainian children sheltering from Russian missiles, and for all.

CND in the devolved nations expressed solidarity with Ukraine. Scottish chair Lynn Jamieson (2022) urged Scotland to "reject the violations of international law by Russia and the disregard for Ukraine's sovereignty as an independent state". Jill Evans (2022), chair of CND Cymru and a former Plaid Cymru MEP, noted the "tremendous solidarity" of the Welsh people with Ukraine and defended its right to decide its own future. In London, StWC's protest on 6 March 2022, which CND supported, backed the demands of an international "Peace in Ukraine" coalition, including the immediate withdrawal of Russian troops.

As the war continued, CND stepped up its criticism of Russia's nuclear backsliding: its increasingly negative attitude to international nuclear regulation; its suspension of participation in the New Strategic Arms Reductions Treaty (START) treaty; its rescinding of ratification of the Test Ban Treaty; its proliferation of nuclear weapons to Belarus; and its veto of the outcome document at an NPT review conference (Johnson 2022). *Campaign* also publicized the *Bulletin of the Atomic Scientists*' January 2023 decision to move its Doomsday Clock to an unprecedented 90 seconds to midnight, while Scottish CND highlighted the dangers of nuclear power stations in war, which the Ukraine situation demonstrated (Ramsay 2023).

Yet CND's and StWC's settled attitude towards the war itself was antiwar rather than anti-Russian: neither organization followed Kent to the embassy despite the atrocities that Russia committed, and only one out of dozens of local events from the first 18 months of the war, featured on the StWC website in August 2023, was headlined "Russian Troops Out". When Hudson (2022b), spoke for CND at a StWC teach-in, she represented nuclear dangers in Ukraine as resulting from potential NATO actions and directed pressure at Britain and the West to seek a negotiated peace rather than at Russia to withdraw. She also backed StWC's (2023) peace appeal, which failed to demand Russia's withdrawal or oppose its nuclear blackmail. *Campaign* (2023, October) offered solidarity to Ukrainian trade unionists vis-à-vis their government but not to Ukrainian resistance to Russia, even of the civilian variety.

These positions, like the organizations' attitudes to the Syrian civil war a decade earlier, prompted criticism within peace and left circles. In its magazine *Heddwch*, CND Cymru (2022) described how "troops and tanks encircle cities and pound apartment blocks into rubble" and noted that "some commentators blame all this on the 'West'"; it could have been referring to the CND or StWC leaderships. For critics such as Mick Antoniw (2023), a Welsh Labour Senedd member with a Ukrainian background, they represented "a *faux* peace movement", confusing peace with capitulation. An StWC-CND protest marking the anniversary of Russia's invasion was even met with a counterprotest by the Ukraine Solidarity Campaign.

National CND's response to Israel's destruction of Gaza, after the Hamas attacks of 7 October 2023, was, in contrast, one of support for the threatened Palestinians and the Palestine Solidarity Campaign's protests, which were some of the biggest since 2003. CND hailed their "amazing display of solidarity" (2023) and tweeted: "No matter how monstrous or appalling an attack or provocation, genocide is never a permitted response" (2024). Hudson (2023a) commented that "watching this catastrophe unfold on the television screens, in real time, is incredibly distressing – to see people driven from their homes and deprived of the essentials to survive. This is truly a second Nakba."

Challenges and opportunities

As the first quarter of the twenty-first century neared its end, the campaign against nuclear weapons in Britain still mobilized a committed set of activists, but it had not been a mass movement since the 1980s, even if it was part of broader antiwar movements. Neither CND nor the NVDA activists had a road map for British disarmament comparable with the early CND leadership's for converting Labour or the Committee of 100's of levering it through mass direct action. They had international goals, especially to implement legal prohibitions on nuclear weapons, but no strategy for achieving these comparable to END's vision for blocking cruise missiles and ending the Cold War.

CND had attempted to exploit the political opportunities that were offered by the movement against the Iraq War, the climate movement, the referendum on Scottish independence and Corbyn's leadership of the Labour Party, but ultimately none of these had enabled it to make substantial progress. Labour returned to government in 2024, but it seemed improbable that nuclear disarmers would influence its agenda.

Yet there was a sense that the big geopolitical changes that the new wars represented were altering the context of antinuclear politics. The Ukraine War had raised the profile of the nuclear threat but it also appeared to increase the difficulty of the CND's longstanding goal of dismantling or withdrawing from NATO. Despite the contribution of NATO expansion to Russia's aggression, which CND stressed, NATO's support for Ukraine's independence renewed its legitimacy across Europe. Moreover, political uncertainty in the USA was beginning to make Europe's dependence on its nuclear "umbrella" appear problematic, potentially reopening questions that seemed to have been decided decades earlier. Some began to argue again for a European bomb, and developments were starting to bring into question the dependence of the UK's nuclear systems on the USA.

Amid these shifts, the campaign continued its tradition of protest, bearing witness to the deep immorality of nuclear weapons. But it appeared that new issues were emerging that could provide it with both challenges and opportunities.

Conclusion

This has been a short history of a long campaign. Yet after many decades of protest, no end to nuclear weapons is in sight. Most states have signed a treaty against nuclear proliferation and many have signed one to abolish nuclear weapons, but proliferation continues, both horizontally to new states and vertically in the enhanced weaponry of both recognized and unrecognized nuclear powers. In 2023, nine states had over 12,500 nuclear warheads between them, over 11,000 of which belonged to the USA and Russia, and the UK and France remained the only other states to actually deploy the weapons (SIPRI 2023: 248).

Over this time, states have evolved ways of managing war without using nuclear weapons and society has lived with the threat of nuclear annihilation. Although the danger never disappeared – it needs only one sequence of misjudged reactions to cause a global catastrophe – at times even antinuclear activists ceased to believe in it. Bruce Kent, whose campaigning spanned almost the entire period of this book, commented nine years before he died that in the old days, CND used *The War Game* to arouse fear of nuclear weapons, but "nobody believes there's going to be a nuclear war today, so there's no point in playing the fear card" (Kirby 2013: 22).

It is increasingly difficult to remain so sanguine. The idea of a pervasive "nuclear taboo" does not entirely convince (Freedman 2013), and nearly 40 years after the peace movement helped end the Cold War, NATO and Russia have come closer than ever to a hot war in Europe, while something like a cold war is developing between the USA and China. In 2022–3, Russia engaged in nuclear blackmail, and although NATO limited its military support for Ukraine so as not to provoke Russian nuclear use, it was not only CND that said that the danger was greater than for decades.

Weapons technology and strategic thinking are also changing, with some analysts raising the spectre of a "third nuclear age" (Futter & Zala 2021; Crilley 2023). If the first centred on the prospect of mutually assured destruction by the superpowers and the second saw the West countering the proliferation of WMD to hostile regimes, in the third, it is argued, "strategic non-nuclear weapons" will blur the line between conventional and nuclear war. When the Atlantic Council, a US think-tank, can publish a call for the USA to "reconsider its current prohibition on deliberately targeting enemy civilians with nuclear weapons" (Lieber & Press 2023), we should recognize that we have a problem.

Nevertheless, the fact that the antinuclear campaign has been so consistently diverted into antiwar activities, with CND often closely aligned with the StWC, should give us pause for thought about the scope for antinuclear activism. In the years since 1945, while no one has died from a nuclear attack, millions have died in brutal wars and genocides, and outrage has understandably focused on actual rather than the hypothetical atrocities. The fact that nuclear concerns are arising from conventional wars could also suggest that the campaign's pacifists have been right, at least in their diagnosis: the main problem is war itself, and the nuclear danger is a part of that.

So whether there will be a third wave of antinuclear movements, rather than a revival of nuclear concern within antiwar movements, is an open question. If this history has shown anything, it is that while mass mobilization responds to a growing sense of threat, its triggers and forms are difficult to predict. It is a matter of when abstract knowledge crystallizes into urgent perceptions not only of danger but also of the possibilities of action. As in the past, we will probably know only as people come on to the streets.

In Britain, as this book has shown, this happened in 1958 and again in 1980, in each case leading to years of extraordinary activism with manifold impacts. The original antinuclear movement, alongside the civil rights movement in the USA, was one of the first agents of a new middle-class radicalism in Western societies, partly outside the main centre-left parties. These movements broke the confines of 1950s Cold War politics and social conservatism alike, pioneering new types of mass protest and direct action, originally inspired by Gandhi's anti-imperialist struggle, which enabled social movements of many kinds in the following half-century. In Britain, they helped give powerful – if fleeting – political expression to the "alternative nation" of which Edward Thompson spoke at Glastonbury in 1984, as well as to autonomous national identities in Scotland and Wales.

While Michael Hardt (2023) has presented the "subversive" politics of the 1970s, in which violence played a much more serious role, as a paradigm for today's radicalism – faced as it is with the new authoritarianism of the right – there is surely a case to be made that this peaceful resistance could be at least as potent. Indeed, Erica Chenoweth and Maria Stephan (2011) have argued that civil resistance works better than armed struggle against authoritarian regimes. Far from the radicalism of the 1950s and 1960s being a kind of prehistory to be bypassed, it helped inspire the seminal feminist and environmental movements of the 1970s and led directly to the pan-European peace movement of the 1980s that made, as we have seen, an important mark on world history.

Of course, none of these movements can or should be simply reproduced today. But the politics and practices of nonviolent transformation that the antinuclear movement pioneered remain seminal. Without the millions of people in Britain and other countries who have contested nuclear weapons, we would know far less about them, it is more likely that they would have been used and we might not even be here to have a discussion about a better future.

Notes

Introduction

1. Joseph Rotblat, a Polish nuclear physicist working at the University of Liverpool, participated in the project but left it in late 1944 when it became clear that Nazi Germany had abandoned its attempt to build a bomb. He became a British citizen in 1946 and played a major part in the scientific opposition to nuclear weapons.
2. Although "Ban the Bomb" is widely linked to CND, according to the *Oxford Dictionary of Phrase and Fable* it originated in the USA.

Chapter 1

1. This action was led by Universities and Left Review Clubs activists (Young 1977: 435 n9).
2. The DAC organized the 1958 march *to* Aldermaston to take moral responsibility to its scientists and workers; CND reversed the direction, to take the message to the seat of government.
3. Fred Halliday (1983: 1–23) calls 1947–53 the "First Cold War". While "Cold War" can refer to the entire East–West conflict, for him it makes better sense to confine the term to the periods in which war itself was perceived as more likely.
4. US planners estimated in 1949 that England could be quickly destroyed by Soviet bombs: the USA could rely on British bases "for only 60 days" (Duke 1985: 77, 105).
5. The runway-building at Greenham, during which 44 houses were levelled and ancient common land taken over, caused considerable local grievance, but in 1951 it was agreed that the USAF would get a further 26 bases (Jackson 1986: 45; Campbell 1986: 35, 41).
6. By the 1980s there were over 130 US military facilities (Campbell 1986: 16). The "aircraft carrier" idea appears to date from the Second World War, when the then US Army Air Force was first based in Britain.
7. Churchill, when he returned to power, was incensed that Britain had given up the joint control of the atomic bomb that it had enjoyed when cooperating in the Manhattan Project, which developed the bomb during the Second World War. He tried to get the USA to confirm a British veto over nuclear use but without success (Duke 1985: 117–19, 130–7).

8. Brock first knew about Aldermaston because in 1952 "a pacifist whose hobby was bus timetables came across a route from Reading which went to a place called Aere [Atomic Energy Research Establishment]", and he then "took the bus … to the far side of the village of Aldermaston, and found the Atomic Energy Research Establishment" (Driver 1964: 24). The establishment had been founded in 1946 and the linked weapons establishment in 1952.

9. However, it only admitted this, indirectly, in 1955 (Salisbury 2021: 21). Britain already had a nuclear force, the V-bombers, and was building its own intermediate-range ballistic missile, Blue Streak.

10. Raphael Samuel, a Communist student acting outside the party line, instigated the student campaign (Scott-Brown 2017: 48). The Third Camp position of independence and neutrality vis-à-vis the blocs, first proposed in Britain by Common Wealth in 1951, became an ambitious movement bringing together pacifists, anarchists and independent socialists from 1953 to 1958 (Banks 1986).

11. These protests were echoed over sixty years later by the transnational Women in Black movement for peace and justice, which held regular vigils at the Edith Cavell statue in London's West End.

12. The year 1957 also saw the worst nuclear accident in British history, at the Windscale power plant (now Sellafield), which opened the previous year primarily to produce material for the weapons programme, but this was covered up (Cohen 2019: 63–9).

13. British thinking contributed significantly to putting H-bomb threats to Soviet cities at the centre of NATO strategy (Clark & Wheeler 1989: 235), but Sandys was also looking to the day when the USA might not defend the country.

14. The Soviet leader, Nikita Khrushchev, boasted in 1956 that the USSR had perfected one, and the USA, with British assistance, was straining to match it. Yet despite Britain hosting the Thors, the USA refused to repeal the McMahon Act. "Britain it seems, can be trusted to commit suicide in America's defence, but not to share American nuclear secrets", commented the *New Statesman* (Duke 1985: 212).

15. Among other US allies, only Italy and Turkey accepted US intermediate-range missiles, and when Britain's Thors arrived, they were the only ones in Europe.

16. Islanders and servicemen were exposed to radiation from the tests; the resulting health problems led to legal cases including at the European Court of Human Rights in 1998 and the UK Supreme Court in 2012, and were still continuing in 2024.

17. Suez and Hungary are the first historical events of which I was conscious. At age nine, I organized a mini-jumble sale in front of our house in Leeds, raising the sum of £2.1s.8d (£2.08) for Hungarian refugees. Around the same time Maltese refugees from Egypt, who were UK citizens, appeared in my Catholic primary school, and I had my first taste of aggressive nationalism when a fellow pupil voiced the Tory press's characterization of Nasser as a new Hitler.

18. Richard Taylor (1988: 49) names my father, Roy Shaw, as its organizer, but the credit appears to belong to the St Pancras councillor of the same name who was a colleague of Peggy Duff.

19. The election saw the first independent unilateralist candidature, that of the miner Lawrence Daly for the New Left-linked Fife Socialist League, in West Fife; he won a respectable 4,886 votes.

20. Indeed, Britain had become even more important for the USA when its forces were relocated from France, after Charles de Gaulle became president in 1958 and required it to remove them.

21. One of the DAC's final acts was April Carter's organization of the London end of a highly ambitious San Francisco to Moscow Peace March, initiated by US pacifists. There was a CND rally in Trafalgar Square on 4 June 1961 and a vigil at Aldermaston before the small group of marchers left for the continent. Surprisingly they not only made it to Moscow but were able to express their views there, which were very different to the Soviet line (Wernicke & Wittner 1999).

22. The DAC still functioned autonomously in the first half of 1961 and Randle later regarded this as its most important direct action and civil disobedience since North Pickenham. However, it proved to be DAC's swansong: "our job was being done, but on a larger scale" by the Committee of 100, he recalled, so "we decided there was simply no point in having two separate committees" (Levy 2021: 114–15).

23. The Kennedy administration reportedly considered cancelling the basing of its Polaris submarines at Holy Loch, but Macmillan insisted it go ahead out of concern that the movement would have achieved a victory (Randle 1987: 157).

24. However, Collins' attitudes to violence were more complex than might appear: he was prepared to support violent resistance in South Africa (Elias 2020: 288).

25. Driver (1964: 170–81) shows how the imprisoned disarmers continued to challenge authority inside and helped expose prison conditions.

26. Actions continued, of course: 1962 even saw an invasion of the base at Greenham Common, although this history was ignored by the famous 1980s camp, a fact that one participant in both, Diana Shelley, found frustrating (Carroll 2004: 45–6).

27. The military threat was not fundamental since the USSR could already destroy the USA with its nuclear weapons. More important were the perception of Soviet advantage and the risk that if the USA tolerated Soviet missiles in Cuba, other states might be encouraged to host them.

28. Shortly afterwards, this lack of independence was further underlined and the government further humiliated when the US cancelled Skybolt. The crisis this provoked in UK–US relations was resolved in December 1962 at Nassau in the Bahamas, when Kennedy agreed to sell Macmillan the Polaris submarine-based system.

29. Only in recent years have some of the names of those involved been revealed: these now include Nicolas Walter, Ruth Walter, Mike Lesser and Jon Tinker.

30. In another remarkable incident that Easter, 54 campaigners who aimed to join an antinuclear march in West Germany, but were banned from entering the country, hijacked their own charter plane and grounded it at Düsseldorf airport for 48 hours before agreeing to fly home (Phillips 1988).

31. As for attitudes among left-wing academics, John Saville recounted that his wife Constance "was allowed to stay with [his fellow historian] Eric Hobsbawm in London for the Easter March weekend on condition that she prepared meals for him" (Nehring 2011: 125).

32. For the most part, the British Council of Churches and the Church of England, which had both adopted permissive attitudes to nuclear weapons in the late 1940s, stubbornly avoided the arguments against their use, and several bishops even popularized the idea that people were "better dead than red". However, the Methodist Conference became overtly unilateralist in 1959, and Cardinal Godfrey, head of the Catholic Church, said it could never be morally lawful to use nuclear weapons.

33. The Bandung Conference was the meeting of Asian and African states, many of which were newly independent, in Indonesia in 1955, from which the Non-Aligned Movement grew.
34. Gaitskell and CND shared, however, an opposition to the Common Market, which *Sanity* (November 1962: 4) even described as "a new nuclear alliance".

Chapter 2

1. Britain also remained the USA's only European base for long-range "theatre" nuclear forces, but on the surface its presence was reduced in the mid-1960s. With its nuclear systems centred on Polaris at Holy Loch, and with fewer bombers, it acquired new ancillary installations in Scotland but handed back some English bases, including Greenham Common, although it kept Brize Norton and Upper Heyford.
2. Labour's victory in Hull encouraged Wilson to hold a general election in March 1966, which he won by a landslide. In order to win the by-election, Transport Minister Barbara Castle promised to build the Humber Bridge, opened in 1981, across which I would lead Humberside CND's "Bridges not Bombs" march in 1982.
3. Caldwell went on to support the Pol Pot regime in Cambodia and denied its genocide. In 1978 he was murdered in Phnom Penh, in circumstances that have not been fully explained.
4. I arrived at the LSE in 1965, when protests about Rhodesia triggered the conflicts that led to the 1966 sit-in. I joined the Socialist Society in 1966 and took part in the student movement until 1970. Later in 1966, I joined International Socialism, which promoted the libertarian Marxism of Rosa Luxemburg; it started to become more Leninist in 1968 and I left in 1976 as it turned itself into the Socialist Workers Party (Shaw 1978).
5. I took part, carrying a record player while a friend held the Theodorakis records. I was arrested and like other students conditionally discharged.
6. Although Schoenman played a central part in the early years of the Foundation, in 1969 Russell broke with him (Clark 1976: 640–51).
7. I took part in this demonstration, but at a distance from the violence.
8. Ali himself, who had been on the editorial board of *Sanity*, also joined the International Marxist Group.
9. As well as violence, Nigel Young (1977: 342–6), citing these authors, alleges a general intolerance towards opposing opinions; but this view elides the differences among the LSE activists and between the British and US experiences.
10. The Warwick files protests led E. P. Thompson to edit an instant book by academics and students attacking the "business university" (1970).
11. Despite this, the Special Operations Squad, later renamed the Special Demonstrations Squad, was made permanent in November 1968. Conrad Dixon, proposing a template for its permanent operation, observed that "the incompetence of the British left is notorious" and recommended that "officers should take care not to get into a position where they achieved prominence in an organization through natural ability" (Undercover Policing Inquiry 2023a: 17). The squad spied on the legal political activity of the left for the rest of the century, including the peace movement

in the 1980s, leading in the 2010s to the scandal of abusive sexual relationships by undercover officers that produced the inquiry.

12. Olive Gibbs was now "vice-chairman"; the women's movement had not yet altered CND's language.

Chapter 3

1. Erica Chenoweth and Maria Stephan (2011) have argued that success is guaranteed once a movement mobilizes 3.5 per cent of the population of a state in sustained protest. However, this research is based on campaigns against autocratic regimes, not social movements in democracies (Matthews 2020: 592).

2. While the peace movement campaigned against civil defence bunkers because they offered no protection to the population, a private, even DIY, nuclear bunker trend erupted, symbolized by *Protect and Survive Monthly*, founded in January 1981, and a gigantic scheme for a bunker complex in a disused quarry at Eastlays, Wiltshire (Beckett 2016: 97–107).

3. The team involved in the Commission developed a further project on civil resistance, the Social Defence Project, from 1987, and later promoted the idea in a comprehensive global bibliography (Carter, Clark & Randle 2013). However, three decades later Randle reflected: "if I ask myself, 'What is the likelihood, politically, of this method being accepted as a viable option?' I would have to say not very" (Levy 2021: 231).

4. Freedman also argued that in opposing the missiles, END was worrying about the wrong weapons; it was battlefield nuclear weapons that risked a "limited" nuclear war. The commission's report also highlighted these, but it was the strategic systems, rather than tactical missiles and artillery, that preoccupied the movement.

5. Although many from Scotland joined Embrace the Base and other protests in southern England, Helen Steven (2008: 61) complains that when it came to Faslane, many English activists said, "Oh Scotland, that's too far away".

6. In 1981, the Conservative government demanded that local authorities ensure that only heterosexuality was taught in schools and attacked the GLC for funding gay and lesbian groups. Thatcher's notorious Section 28 was still to come.

7. However, local opinion had never been wholly supportive of the base, with intermittent opposition since the original clearance in the 1950s. In 1977–8, when the runways began to be extended for new tanker aircraft, a Campaign Against the Reactivation of Greenham Common Air Base had collected 16,000 signatures and staged a march through Newbury; the government gave in (Jackson 1986: 133–5).

8. On 2 May 1982, when the British task force sank the Argentinian cruiser *General Belgrano*, drowning (it was later estimated) 275 sailors, I was in Rotterdam as part of the peace twinning of the city with Hull. Dutch campaigners and politicians were incredulous at the British action.

9. Three Greenham women spent part of the election period in Russia meeting the independent activists of the Moscow Group for Trust – they had gone independently because END was too busy with Eastern Europe and the relevant CND committee dealing was full of Soviet sympathizers. State media had created "a false Sovietized

image" of Greenham but this gave the women status that they used to secure a meeting with the Soviet Peace Committee. However, they met with hostility when they revealed their contacts with the independent group "that wasn't supposed to even exist" (Pettitt 2006: 245, 244). Some at Greenham were also unsupportive of their trip.

Chapter 4

1.   An early issue was the control of Soviet nuclear weapons, which were based in Ukraine, Belarus and Kazakhstan as well as Russia, as the USSR broke up. The USA helped broker their consolidation in Russian hands, and the UK joined the two powers in guaranteeing the independence and sovereignty of the states that disarmed, in the 1994 Budapest Memorandum. However, Russia would renege on its guarantee to Ukraine in 2014.

2.   Although the implementation of START I culled mainly the older systems, in 1993 the US and Russian presidents signed START II, which banned the use of multiple independently targetable re-entry vehicles on ICBMs. Although the treaty was never fully ratified, the two powers eventually agreed the Strategic Offensive Reductions Treaty, which was implemented in 2003, limiting operationally deployed warheads to 1,700–2,200 each.

3.   In 1999, CND members joined 10,000 people from 100 groups and countries at Time to Abolish War, a gathering in The Hague a hundred years after the 1899 conference that began the process of regulating the conduct of war. Following the meeting, Bruce Kent helped found a Movement for the Abolition of War.

4.   Israel's programme was exposed by the whistle-blower Mordechai Vanunu. In the mid-1990s my father, Roy Shaw, was part of an international delegation led by Bruce Kent that pressed for his release. Kent also went to meet him in 2004 when he was finally freed after 17 years' imprisonment.

5.   Later, in 1999, Cathy Ashton, CND vice-chair in the early 1980s, was made a Labour peer, eventually becoming the first EU high representative for foreign affairs and security policy in 2009.

6.   My own position, in articles for the *New Statesman* (Shaw 1993, 1995) was close to Kaldor's and informed by my increasing interest in genocide.

7.   After the 1996 Dayton talks excluded Kosovo and neglected Albanian grievances, an armed group, the Kosovo Liberation Army, began to carry out guerrilla actions. In response Serbian forces killed over 1,500 and displaced over 300,000 Albanians by 1998. After Milošević refused to sign an internationally brokered agreement in February 1999 (Cook co-chaired the conference at Rambouillet, France), Serbian forces began a bigger campaign of killing, repression and expulsions, which created a large refugee crisis. NATO's intervention was a response to this, but it failed to gain the necessary support of the UN Security Council since Russia and China would not support it. According to the Independent International Commission on Kosovo (2000: 5), this left NATO's campaign "illegal but legitimate".

Chapter 5

1. Bruce Kent did not take email up until a bit later, but "liked it very much" (Gillan, Pickerill & Webster 2008: 158).
2. Sinclair (2013) argues that Marqusee, like other critics of the SWP in StWC, was largely written out of German and Murray's semi-official history.
3. "WMD" had previously been used mainly to refer to nuclear weapons. In 1981 Menachem Begin, Israel's prime minister, had developed a "doctrine" of pre-emptive attacks on potential WMD. Now the term was popularized to indicate Iraq's possible chemical and biological warfare capacity (Kampfner 2003: 191–237; Sands 2005: 182–204).
4. Lawrence Freedman, who advised Blair on the Chicago speech, also emphasizes the difference between his positions in 1999 and 2003 (2017: 109–10).
5. This investigated the circumstances in which Dr David Kelly, a government scientist implicated in disclosures about the "dodgy dossier" the government used to make its case for war, took his own life.
6. The information in this section is based on its documents and publications (CND 2002–21, 2006–21, 2016–23) unless otherwise indicated.

Chronology

1945   USA drops atomic bombs on Hiroshima and Nagasaki.

1947   Attlee government decides to develop British bomb.

1948   Attlee allows US Strategic Air Command to use bases in eastern England.

1949   USSR develops atomic bomb.

        NATO founded.

1952   Pacifists launch Operation Gandhi, first protests against atomic weapons.

        USA tests first H-bomb.

1954   Hydrogen Bomb National Campaign launched.

        Crew members of Japanese fishing boat *Lucky Dragon* die of radiation sickness after US H-bomb tests at Bikini Atoll.

1955   Members of the Cooperative Women's Guild campaign against nuclear tests.

1956   National Council for the Abolition of Nuclear Weapons Tests founded.

        Soviet invasion of Hungary, Anglo-French invasion of Egypt (Suez crisis).

1957   Sandys White Paper shifts British defence policy to primarily nuclear basis.

        Macmillan agrees to allow the USA to install Thor nuclear missiles in England.

        The *New Reasoner* and *Universities and Left Review* founded, leading to the emergence of the New Left.

        Aneurin Bevan attacks unilateral nuclear disarmament at the Labour Party conference.

        Direct Action Committee Against Nuclear War (DAC) formed.

        J. B. Priestley calls for antinuclear campaign in the *New Statesman*, followed by meeting to establish executive for new campaign.

1958   Campaign for Nuclear Disarmament (CND) launched.

        DAC adopts Gerald Holtom's nuclear disarmament symbol.

First Aldermaston march, from London to the Atomic Weapons Research Establishment at former RAF Aldermaston, Berkshire.

First Thor missiles arrive in East Anglia.

DAC protests at North Pickenham, Norfolk, missile base.

1959   DAC campaigns for Voters Veto in Norfolk by-election.

Second Aldermaston march, the first towards London.

DAC decides to oppose French nuclear tests in the Sahara.

Anti-Apartheid Movement founded.

Conservative victory in general election.

1960   Macmillan cancels UK's Blue Streak ballistic weapon programme and agrees to buy US Skybolt missiles and for the USA to base Polaris submarines at Holy Loch, Scotland.

Third, larger Aldermaston march, with estimated 100,000 protestors converging in London.

Committee of 100 founded, with Bertrand Russell as president.

Labour conference adopts unilateralist policy.

1961   Committee of 100 protests, including Whitehall, Holy Loch and RAF Wethersfield.

Berlin Wall erected by East German regime.

Labour conference reverses unilateralist policy.

1962   Official Secrets trial: six Committee of 100 members imprisoned.

Cuban missile crisis.

Steps Towards Peace proposals cause controversy in CND.

1963   Spies for Peace expose Regional Seats of Government (RSGs), secret bunkers from which Britain would be governed after nuclear war.

Further large Aldermaston march, with breakaway to RSG6 at Warren Row.

Protests over visit of king and queen of Greece.

Signature of Partial Test Ban Treaty, establishment of US–Soviet hotline.

1964   Labour wins general election and soon decides to continue UK Polaris system.

Canon Collins resigns as CND chair.

1965   CND helps establish the British Council for Peace in Vietnam.

The War Game banned from being shown on BBC television.

1966   CND becomes membership organization.

1967   Occupation of Greek embassy, the final action of the Committee of 100.

Peggy Duff resigns as CND general secretary.

1968   Vietnam Solidarity Campaign marches against the war.

International year of revolution, peak of student movement.

Soviet invasion of Czechoslovakia.

Nuclear Non-Proliferation Treaty signed.

1970   First National Women's Liberation Conference.

Bertrand Russell dies, aged 97.

1971   Greenpeace founded to protest against US nuclear tests.

1972   Strategic Arms Limitation (SALT I) and Anti-Ballistic Missile treaties agreed.

1973   Bradford University School of Peace Studies founded.

1975   "Nuclear Power – No Thanks" logo designed in Denmark.

Helsinki Final Act on Security and Cooperation in Europe agreed.

1976   Scottish Campaign Against the Atomic Menace founded.

1978   CND campaign against the "neutron bomb", following campaign in the Netherlands.

1979   Conservatives under Margaret Thatcher win general election.

NATO agrees to install Cruise and Pershing II missiles in five European states.

USSR invades Afghanistan.

E. P. Thompson warns in *New Statesman* of theatre nuclear war in Europe.

Bruce Kent appointed general secretary of CND.

1980   Hundreds of local anti-missile groups form, first new mass demonstrations held.

European Nuclear Disarmament Appeal launched.

E. P. Thompson's *Protest and Survive* published.

Greenham Common announced as main base for cruise missiles.

UK's purchase of Trident missile system announced.

Labour adopts unilateralist policy and elects Michael Foot as leader.

1981   First large national CND demonstration against Cruise and Trident held.

Women for Life on Earth march leads to establishment of Greenham peace camp.

First Glastonbury CND Festival.

Joan Ruddock becomes CND chair.

US President Ronald Reagan proposes "zero option".

Military coup suppresses Solidarity movement in Poland.

1982   Falklands/Malvinas War.

First European Nuclear Disarmament Convention held in Brussels.

Nuclear-free councils force cancellation of Hard Rock civil defence exercise.

Establishment of Faslane Peace Camp against Trident.

Peak of Europe-wide peace movement.

Embrace the Base protest makes Greenham an international symbol of the peace movement.

1983   Michael Heseltine becomes defence secretary and confronts women at Greenham Common.

Alternative Defence Commission publishes its report.

Major blockades of Lakenheath and Upper Heyford airbases.

Thatcher wins general election with large majority.

First cruise missiles arrive at Greenham Common.

1984   Snowball Civil Disobedience Campaign founded.

1985   Molesworth, the second cruise missile base, becomes campaign focus.

Mikhail Gorbachev becomes Soviet leader and begins outreach to West.

Charter 77 launches Prague Appeal for nuclear-free Europe.

Bruce Kent steps down as general secretary and Joan Ruddock as chair of CND.

1986   CND begins "Basic Case" campaign focused on opposing the British bomb.

1987   Thatcher wins third general election victory.

Gorbachev and Reagan agree Intermediate Nuclear Forces deal.

1988   Reform politics develops within East European states.

People's Declaration for a Nuclear-Free Scotland launched.

1989   Berlin Wall falls: the end of the Cold War.

1990   Helsinki Citizens Assembly founded, British committee of European Nuclear Disarmament dissolved.

1991	Dissolution of the Warsaw Pact and the USSR.
	First Gulf War and Yugoslav Wars start.
1992	Bosnian War begins, which divides peace movement.
1993	E. P. Thompson dies.
1996	Comprehensive Test Ban Treaty adopted.
	International Court of Justice opinion on legality of nuclear weapons use.
1997	New Labour wins general election and proclaims "ethical dimension of foreign policy".
	Trident Ploughshares direct action campaign founded.
1999	Kosovo War further divides peace movement.
	NATO expands to include Poland, Hungary and Czech Republic.
	Trident Three acquitted after emptying Trident laboratory into Scottish loch.
2000	Greenham Common Women's Peace Camp closes.
2001	9/11 al-Qaida attacks on New York and Washington, DC.
	Stop the War Coalition founded.
2002	Growing movement against wars in Afghanistan and (threatened) Iraq.
2003	Largest ever demonstration in London, against imminent Iraq War.
	Kate Hudson elected chair of CND.
2006	Faslane 365, decentralized protests against Trident, launched.
2007	CND campaign against Trident replacement.
	CND helps establish International Campaign to Abolish Nuclear Weapons.
	New SNP government organizes Summit for a Nuclear Free Scotland.
2010	Kate Hudson appointed general secretary of CND.
2013	UK pulls out of proposed attacks on Syria.
2014	Referendum on Scottish independence.
	Ukraine War begins; Russia annexes Crimea.
2015	Conservatives win overall majority in general election.
	Jeremy Corbyn elected leader of the Labour Party.
2016	Brexit referendum.
2017	Treaty on the Prohibition of Nuclear Weapons adopted, International Campaign to Abolish Nuclear Weapons wins Nobel Peace Prize.

2019   Donald Trump withdraws USA from Intermediate Nuclear Forces treaty.

             Boris Johnson wins large Conservative majority.

2022   New Russian invasion of Ukraine.

             Bruce Kent dies.

2023   Hamas–Israel War in Gaza.

Suggested reading

On the original nuclear disarmament movement of the 1950s and 1960s:

C. Driver, *The Disarmers* (London: Hodder & Stoughton, 1964). The classic account of the first wave, written as it was coming to an end by a sympathetic journalist. Full of wit and irony.

P. Duff, *Left, Left, Left: A Personal Account of Six Protest Campaigns 1945–65* (London: Allison & Busby, 1972). The autobiography of CND's first general secretary, wonderfully written and the best inside account.

C. Hill, *Peace and Power in Cold War Britain: Media, Movements and Democracy, c.1945–68* (London: Bloomsbury, 2018). A challenging reinterpretation of the movements of the 1950s and 1960s, from Gandhian direct action to the Vietnam Solidarity Campaign, centred on their relationships with mass media.

M. Levy, *Ban the Bomb! Michael Randle and Direct Action against Nuclear War* (Stuttgart: Ibidem, 2021). Revealing interviews with a key activist of the original Direct Action Committee and the Committee of 100.

R. Taylor, *Against the Bomb: The British Peace Movement 1958–1965* (Oxford: Oxford University Press, 1988). The essential academic study of the first wave, centred on its politics and strategic dilemmas.

On the 1980s movement:

J. Hinton, *Protests and Visions: Peace Politics in Twentieth Century Britain* (London: Radius, 1989). Written with verve just after the 1980s movement by a historian who took part in it, this book discusses it and its 1960s predecessor in a longer perspective on British peace movements.

J. Liddington, *The Road to Greenham Common: Feminism and Anti-Militarism in Britain since 1820* (Syracuse, NY: Syracuse University Press, 1991). Also written by a participant historian, this book locates Greenham in the history of women's peace campaigns.

A. Pettitt, *Walking to Greenham: How the Peacecamp Began and the Cold War Ended* (Aberystwyth: Honno, 2006). A lively autobiography by the activist whose initiative led to the peace camp being established.

M. Rankin, *The Political Life of Mary Kaldor* (Boulder, CO: Lynne Rienner, 2017). A study of the ideas and initiatives of the activist who was central to British END's European activism.

E. P. Thompson, "Notes on exterminism, the last stage of civilization", *New Left Review* 1/121 (1980): 3–31. Thompson's famous essay on the logics of the arms race and European Nuclear Disarmament.

On the twenty-first century:

A. Murray and L. German, *Stop the War: The Story of Britain's Biggest Mass Movement* (London: Bookmarks, 2005). The semi-official history, analytical and well illustrated, of the campaign that led to the giant demonstration against the Iraq War in 2003.

I. Sinclair, *The March That Shook Blair: An Oral History of 15 February 2003* (London: Peace News Press, 2011). A more critical account, based on interviews with a hundred activists.

A. Zelter, *Activism for Life* (Edinburgh: Luath Press, 2021). Autobiographical reflections of one of the most prolific NVDA activists of our time, the founder of Trident Ploughshares.

References

Ainslie, J. 2013. *Trident: Nowhere to Go.* Glasgow: Scottish CND.

Al-Chalabi, B. 2003. "You should have known we'd fight". *The Guardian*, 25 March.

Ali, T. 1987. *Street Fighting Years: An Autobiography of the Sixties.* London: Collins.

Allison, G. & P. Zelikow 1999. *Essence of Decision: Explaining the Cuban Missile Crisis.* New York: Longman.

Alternative Defence Commission 1983. *Defence without the Bomb.* London: Taylor & Francis.

Alternative Defence Commission 1987. *The Politics of Alternative Defence.* London: Paladin.

Anderson, P. 1965. "The left in the fifties". *New Left Review* 1(29): 3–18.

Antoniw, M. 2023. "An appeal from a life-long trade unionist and socialist to my brothers and sisters in the UK trade union movement". *Labour Hub*, September.

Ashton, C. 1983. "The end of the 1970s: the beginning of the revival". In J. Minnion & P. Bolsover (eds), *The CND Story*, 75–7. London: Allison & Busby.

Aubrey, C. & E. P. Thompson 1982. "Corporate images: Dimbleby, the BBC and balance". In Aubrey (ed.), *Nukespeak: The Media and the Bomb*, 82–93. London: Comedia.

Balkan Peace Team nd. *Nonviolent Intervention in the Conflicts of Former Yugoslavia: Sending Teams of International Volunteers.* https://www.soziale-verteidigung.de/system/files/documents/balkan_peace_team_engl.pdf.

Banks, J. 1986. "The Third Camp Movement of the 1950s (Part 1)". *Discussion Bulletin.* https://files.libcom.org/files/discussion-bulletin-1986-18-jul.pdf.

Barnett, A. 1982. "Iron Brittania". *New Left Review* 1(134), Special Issue.

Bateman, E. 2008. "On vacation". In A. Zelter (ed.), *Faslane 365: A Year of Anti-Nuclear Blockades*, xxxi–xxxiii. Edinburgh: Luath.

Beckett, A. 2016. *Promised You a Miracle: Why 1980–82 Made Modern Britain.* London: Penguin.

Behr, H., N. Megoran & J. Carnaffan 2017. "Peace education, militarism and neo-liberalism: conceptual reflections with empirical findings from the UK". *Journal of Peace Education* 15(1): 76–96.

Bella Caledonia 2019. "Scottish Labour ditches opposition to Trident renewal for UK election". https://bellacaledonia.org.uk/2019/11/26/scottish-labour-ditches-opposition-to-trident-renewal-for-uk-election.

Berrington, H. 1989. "British public opinion and nuclear weapons". In C. Marsh & C. Fraser (eds), *Public Opinion and Nuclear Weapons*, 18–36. London: Macmillan.

Bingham, A. 2012. "'The monster'? The British popular press and nuclear culture, 1945–early 1960s". *British Journal for the History of Science* 45(4): 609–24.

Bloodworth, J. 2015. "The bizarre world of Jeremy Corbyn and Stop the War". *Politico*, 12 December.

Bolsover. P. 1983. "A victory – and a new development". In J. Minnion & P. Bolsover (eds), *The CND Story*, 89–93. London: Allison & Busby.

Booth, K. 1998. "Cold Wars of the mind". In Booth (ed.) *Statecraft and Security: The Cold War and beyond*, 29–55. Cambridge: Cambridge University Press.

Boulton, D. 1964. *Voices from the Crowd: Against the H-Bomb*. London: Peter Owen.

Bove, G. 2007. "Looking back – the Snowball campaign". *Wrexham Peace & Justice News*, April–May, 6–7.

Briggs, R. 1982. *When the Wind Blows*. Harmondsworth: Penguin.

Brocken, M. 2003. *The British Folk Revival, 1944–2002*. Aldershot: Ashgate.

Brown, W. 1984. *Black Women and the Peace Movement*. Bristol: Falling Wall.

Buchan, J. & N. Buchan 1983. "The campaign in Scotland: singing into protest". In J. Minnion & P. Bolsover (eds), *The CND Story*, 52–5. London: Allison & Busby.

Bulkeley, R. *et al.* 1981. "'If at first you don't succeed … ': fighting against the bomb in the 1950s and 1960s". *International Socialism* 2(11): 1–29.

Bunyan, P. 1981. *Nuclear Britain*. London: New English Library.

Burke, P. 2004. *European Nuclear Disarmament: A Study of Transnational Social Movement Strategy*. PhD thesis, University of Westminster.

Burke, P. 2017. "European nuclear disarmament: transnational peace campaigning in the 1980s". In E. Conze, M. Klimke & J. Varon (eds), *Nuclear Threats, Nuclear Fear, and the Cold War of the 1980s*, 227–50. Cambridge: Cambridge University Press.

Burke, P. 2022. "British and international peace campaigning against the Strategic Defence Initiative". In L. Brunet (ed.), *NATO and the Strategic Defence Initiative: A Transatlantic History of the Star Wars Programme*, 221–37. London: Routledge.

Burkett, J. 2012. "The Campaign for Nuclear Disarmament and changing attitudes towards the Earth in the nuclear age". *British Journal for the History of Science* 45(4): 625–39.

Burkett, J. 2016. "Gender and the Campaign for Nuclear Disarmament in the 1960s". In S. Sharoni *et al.* (eds), *Handbook on Gender and War*, 419–37. London: Edward Elgar.

Burns, R. & W. Van Der Will 1988. *Protest and Democracy in West Germany: Extra-Parliamentary Opposition and the Democratic Agenda*. Basingstoke: Macmillan.

Butler, D. & A. King 1965. *The British General Election of 1964*. London: Macmillan.

Butler, D. & R. Rose 1960. *The British General Election of 1959*. London: Macmillan.

Byrne, P. 1988. *The Campaign for Nuclear Disarmament*. London: Croom Helm.

Cadogan, P. 1972. "From civil disobedience to confrontation". In R. Benewick & T. Smith (eds), *Direct Action and Democratic Politics*, 162–77. London: Allen & Unwin.

Campaign 2016–23. London: CND. https://cnduk.org/resource_type/magazine/page/1.

Campbell, D. 1982. *War Plan UK: The Truth about Civil Defence in Britain*. London: Burnett.

Campbell, D. 1986. *The Unsinkable Aircraft Carrier: American Military Power in Britain*. London: Michael Joseph.

Campbell, I. 1983. "Music against the Bomb". In J. Minnion & P. Bolsover (eds), *The CND Story*, 115–17. London: Allison & Busby.

Campbell, T. 2019. "Replica banner made by Thalia Campbell". Cardiff: Amgueddfa Cymru/Museum Wales. https://www.peoplescollection.wales/items/790861.

Carrell, S. 2003. "'Rigged' election row splits CND". *The Independent*, 14 September.

Carroll, S. 2004. "'I was arrested at Greenham in 1962': investigating the oral narratives of women in the anti-nuclear Committee of 100". *Oral History* 32(1): 35–48.

Carroll, S. 2010. "*Danger! Official Secret*: the spies for peace: discretion and disclosure in the Committee of 100". *History Workshop Journal* 69: 158–76.

Carroll, S. 2011. *"Fill the Jails": Identity, Structure and Method in the Committee of 100, 1960–1968*. DPhil thesis, University of Sussex.

Carter, A., H. Clark & M. Randle (eds) 2013. *A Guide to Civil Resistance: A Bibliography of People Power and Nonviolent Protest*, Vol. 1. London: Green Print.

Ceadel, M. 1987. *Thinking about Peace and War*. Oxford: Oxford University Press.

Ceadel, M. 2002. "The Quaker peace testimony and its contribution to the British peace movement: an overview". *Quaker Studies* 7(2): 9–29.

Chalmers, M. & W. Walker 2001. *Uncharted Waters: The UK, Nuclear Weapons and the Scottish Question*. East Linton: Tuckwell Press.

Chalmers, M. & W. Walker 2022. "Preparing for negotiations on nuclear weapons". In G. Hassan & S. Barrow (eds), *A Better Nation: The Challenges of Scottish Independence*, 297–306. Edinburgh: Luath Press.

Chapman, J. 2006. "The BBC and the censorship of *The War Game* (1965)". *Journal of Contemporary History* 41(1): 75–94.

Chenoweth, E. & M. Stephan 2011. *Why Civil Resistance Works: The Strategic Logic of Nonviolent Conflict*. New York: Columbia University Press.

Chilton, P. 1982. "Nukespeak: nuclear language, culture and propaganda". In C. Aubrey (ed.), *Nukespeak: The Media and the Bomb*. London: Comedia.

Church of England Board for Social Responsibility 1982. *The Church and the Bomb: Nuclear Weapons and Christian Conscience*. London: Hodder & Stoughton.

Clark, G. 1972. "Remember your humanity and forget the rest". In R. Benewick & T. Smith (eds), *Direct Action and Democratic Politics*, 178–91. London: Allen & Unwin.

Clark, H. 2000. *Civil Resistance in Kosovo*. London: Pluto.

Clark, I. 1982. *Limited Nuclear War*. Oxford: Martin Robertson.

Clark, I. & N. Wheeler 1989. *The British Origins of Nuclear Strategy 1945–1955*. Oxford: Clarendon Press.

Clark, R. 1976. *The Life of Bertrand Russell*. New York: Knopf.

CND 2002–21. Annual Reports. https://cnduk.org/about/annual-reports-2.

CND 2006–21. CND Conference. https://cnduk.org/about/cnd-conference.

CND 2009. "CND calls 'No to US Missile Defence' demo at Fylingdales radar this Saturday". https://cnduk.org/cnd-calls-no-us-missile-defence-demo-fylingdales-radar-saturday.

CND 2023. Tweet, 11 November. https://twitter.com/CNDuk/status/1723401245203849551.

CND 2024. Tweet, 13 January. https://x.com/cnduk/status/1746156481471246353.

CND Cymru. 2022. *Heddwch*, April. https://www.cndcymru.org/wp-content/uploads/H80-E.pdf.

Coates, D. & J. Kruger 2004. *Blair's War*. Cambridge: Polity.

Coates, K. & M. Meacher 1982. "The independent peace movement in the German Democratic Republic: a dossier". *ENDpapers* 3: 70–95.

Coates, K. 1987. *Listening for Peace*. Nottingham: Spokesman.

Cohen, P. 2019. *Hearts and Minds: The Propaganda War over the British Nuclear Deterrent, 1957–1963*. PhD thesis, University of Hertfordshire.

Colbourn, S. 2022. *Euromissiles: The Nuclear Weapons That Nearly Destroyed NATO.* Ithaca, NY: Cornell University Press.

Cook, R. 1997. "Robin Cook's speech on the government's ethical foreign policy". *The Guardian*, 12 May.

Cook, R. & D. Smith 1978. *What Future in NATO?* London: Fabian Society.

Cook, R. & D. Smith 1979. *Sixth Report from the Expenditure Committee: The Future of the United Kingdom's Nuclear Weapons Policy.* London: HMSO.

Corbyn, J. 2013. "Message from Jeremy Corbyn MP, Chair of Stop the War". https://www.stopwar.org.uk/article/message-from-jeremy-corbyn.

Cox, J. 1977. *Overkill: The Story of Modern Weapons.* London: Peacock.

Cox, J. 1980. "Goodbye to Detente?" *Marxism Today*, September: 5–11.

Crilley, R. 2023. *Unparalleled Catastrophe: Life and Death in the Third Nuclear Age.* Manchester: Manchester University Press.

Curtice, J. 1989. "The 1983 election and the nuclear debate". In C. Marsh & C. Fraser (eds), *Public Opinion and Nuclear Weapons*, 143–62. London: Macmillan.

Daly, M. 1978. *Gyn/Ecology: The Metaethics of Radical Feminism.* Boston, MA: Beacon.

Davison, I. 1988. "Scotland goes it alone". *Sanity*, May: 14–16.

Davison, S. & J. Gilbert 2020. "The new left and its legacies: Michael Rustin talks to Sally Davison and Jeremy Gilbert". *Soundings* 74: 136–63.

Day, A. 2007 [2004]. "Hammer and crescent". *New Humanist* blog, 31 May.

Day, G. & D. Robbins 1987. "The social basis of a local peace movement". In C. Creighton & M. Shaw (eds), *The Sociology of War and Peace*, 218–36. London: Macmillan.

De Graaf, B. 2003. "Détente from below: the Stasi and the Dutch peace movement". *Journal of Intelligence History* 3(2): 9–20.

Dienstbier, J., E. Kanturkova & P. Sustrova 1985. "Introduction: The Prague Appeal (Building a Peaceful Europe)". *END Journal* 15: 2–5.

Donovan, P. 2003. "Stop the War must stop the war within". *The Guardian*, 21 September.

Douglass, D. 1995. "War in the peace movement". *Weekly Worker*, 16 March.

Draper, H. 1965. *Berkeley: The New Student Revolt.* New York: Grove Press.

Driver, C. 1964. *The Disarmers.* London: Hodder & Stoughton.

Duff, P. 1971. *Left, Left, Left: A Personal Account of Six Protest Campaigns 1945–65.* London: Allison & Busby.

Duke, S. 1985. *US Defence Bases in the United Kingdom.* DPhil thesis, University of Oxford.

Durie, S. & R. Edwards 1985. *Fuelling the Nuclear Arms Race.* London: Pluto.

Eavis, M. & E. Eavis 2019. *Glastonbury 50.* London: Orion.

Edgerton, D. 1998. "Tony Blair's warfare state". *New Left Review* 1(230): 123–30.

Elias, H. 2020. "John Collins, Martin Luther King, Jr, and transnational networks of protest and resistance in the Church of England during the 1960s". In T. Rodger, P. Williamson & M. Grimley (eds), *The Church of England and British Politics since 1900*, 279–97. Martlesham: Boydell & Brewer.

European Nuclear Disarmament 1980. "Appeal for European Nuclear Disarmament". In E. P. Thompson & D. Smith (eds), *Protest and Survive*, 223–6. Harmondsworth: Penguin.

European Nuclear Disarmament 1983–9. *END Journal.* London.

European Nuclear Disarmament 1988. "Submission to Labour Policy Review". *END Journal* 34–5: 18–20.

Evangelista, M. 1999. *Unarmed Forces: The Transnational Movement to End the Cold War*. Ithaca, NY: Cornell University Press.

Evans, J. 2022. "The Ukraine invasion has brought us closer to nuclear war than at any time since the 1980s". *Nation Cymru*, 9 March.

Everts, P. 1980. "Reviving unilateralism: report on a campaign for nuclear disarmament in the Netherlands". *Bulletin of Peace Proposals* 11(1): 40–56.

Fairhall, D. 2006. *Common Ground: The Story of Greenham*. London: I. B. Tauris.

Feigenbaum, A. 2008. *Tactics and Technology: Cultural Resistance at the Greenham Common Women's Peace Camp*. PhD thesis, McGill University.

Feigenbaum, A., F. Frenzel & P. McCurdy 2013. *Protest Camps*. London: Zed.

Flessati, V. 1997. *Waking the Sleeping Giant: The Story of Christian CND*. London: Christian CND.

Freedman, L. 1980. *Britain and Nuclear Weapons*. London: Macmillan.

Freedman, L. 1981. "A criticism of the European Nuclear Disarmament movement". *ADIU Report*, 2(4): 1–4.

Freedman, L. 1988. *Britain and the Falklands War*. Oxford: Blackwell.

Freedman, L. 1991. "Order and disorder in the New World". *Foreign Affairs* 71(1): 20–37.

Freedman, L. 2013. "Can the nuclear taboo last?" Jack Ruina Nuclear Age Speaker Series, 25 February. https://web.mit.edu/SSP/news/ruina.html.

Freedman, L. 2017. "Force and the international community: Blair's Chicago speech and the criteria for intervention". *International Relations* 31(2): 107–24.

Futter, A. & B. Zala 2021. "Strategic non-nuclear weapons and the onset of a third nuclear age". *European Journal of International Security* 6: 257–77.

Garapedian, C. 1987. *The Relationship between Media Coverage and Government Policy Presentation: A Study of the Public Debate on Nuclear Defence in Britain, 1979–1983*. PhD thesis, London School of Economics.

German, L. 2014. "Vladimir Putin is the latest 'New Hitler' that the US and its war-making allies keep finding round the world". https://www.stopwar.org.uk/article/ukraine-the-anti-war-movement-and-why-the-main-enemy-is-at-home.

Gillan, K., J. Pickerill & F. Webster 2008. *Anti-War Activism: New Media and Protest in the Information Age*. Basingstoke: Palgrave Macmillan.

Glasgow University Media Group 1985. *War and Peace News*. Milton Keynes: Open University Press.

Gopal, P. 2020. *Insurgent Empire: Anticolonial Resistance and British Dissent*. London: Verso.

Gordon, D. 2003. "Iraq, war and morality". *Economic and Political Weekly* 38(12–13): 1117–20.

Gowing, M. 1974a. *Independence and Deterrence: Britain and Atomic Energy*. London: Macmillan.

Gowing, M. 1974b. *Independence and Deterrence: Policy Execution (Britain and Atomic Energy, 1945–1952)*. London: Macmillan.

Grant, M. 2009. *After the Bomb: Civil Defence and Nuclear War in Britain, 1945–68*. London: Palgrave Macmillan.

Grant, M. 2016. "The imaginative landscape of nuclear war in Britain, 1945–65". In M. Grant & B. Ziemann (eds), *Understanding the Imaginary War: Culture, Thought and Nuclear Conflict, 1945–90*, 92–115. Manchester: Manchester University Press.

Greene, O., I. Percival & I. Ridge 1985. *Nuclear Winter*. Cambridge: Polity.

Hain, P. 1972. "Direct action and the Springbok tours". In R. Benewick & T. Smith (eds), *Direct Action and Democratic Politics*, 192–202. London: Allen & Unwin.

Hain, P. (ed.) 1980. *The Crisis and the Future of the Left*. London: Pluto.

Hall, S. 1960. *NATO and the Alliances*. London: CND London Regional Council.

Hall, S. 1979. "The great moving right show". *Marxism Today*, January: 14–20.

Hall, S. 2010. "The life and times of the first New Left". *New Left Review* 2(61): 177–96.

Hall, S. 2017 [1962]. "The Cuban crisis: trial run or steps towards peace?" In S. Hall, *Selected Political Writings: The Great Moving Right Show and Other Essays*, 70–84. London: Lawrence & Wishart.

Hall, S. & M. Jacques (eds) 1990. *New Times: The Changing Face of Politics in the 1990s*. London: Lawrence & Wishart.

Hall, S. & B. Schwarz 2018. *Familiar Stranger*. London: Penguin.

Hall, S. & P. Whannel 1964. *The Popular Arts*. London: Hutchinson.

Halliday, F. 1983. *The Making of the Second Cold War*. London: Verso.

Halliday, F. 2006. "The left and Jihad". *openDemocracy*, https://www.opendemocracy.net/en/left_jihad_3886jsp.

Halloran, J., P. Elliott & G. Murdock 1970. *Demonstrations and Communications: A Case Study*. Harmondsworth: Penguin.

Haraway, D. 1985. "Manifesto for cyborgs: science, technology, and socialist feminism in the 1980s". *Socialist Review* 80: 65–108.

Hardt, M. 2023. *The Subversive Seventies*. Oxford: Oxford University Press.

Harris, R. 1983. *Gotcha! The Media, the Government and the Falklands Crisis*. London: Faber.

Hetherington, B. 2005. "Review of Kate Hudson, *CND – Now More than Ever, the Story of a Peace Movement*". *Peace News*, October. https://peacenews.info/node/5134/kate-hudson-cnd-now-more-ever-story-peace-movement.

Hill, C. 2016. "Nations of peace: nuclear disarmament and the making of national identity in Scotland and Wales". *Twentieth Century British History* 27(1): 26–50.

Hill, C. 2018. *Peace and Power in Cold War Britain: Media, Movements and Democracy, c.1945–68*. London: Bloomsbury.

Hill, C. 2019. "The activist as geographer: nonviolent direct action in Cold War Germany and postcolonial Ghana, 1957–1960". *Journal of Historical Geography* 64: 36–46.

Hinton, J. 1988. "The second wave: settling in for the long haul". *Sanity*, February: 11–13.

Hinton, J. 1989. *Protests and Visions: Peace Politics in Twentieth Century Britain*. London: Radius.

Hoch, P. & V. Schönbach 1969. *LSE: The Natives Are Restless*. London: Sheed & Ward.

Hoffman, S. 1981. "NATO and nuclear weapons: reasons and unreason". *Foreign Affairs* 60(2): 347–8.

Hogg, J. 2012. "'The family that feared tomorrow': British nuclear culture and individual experience in the late 1950s". *British Journal for the History of Science* 45(4): 535–49.

Holtom, D. 2022. *Gerald Holtom: Designer of the Peace Symbol*. Nottingham: Spokesman.

Home Office 1963. *Advising the Householder on Protection against Nuclear Attack*. London: Stationary Office.

House of Commons Foreign Affairs Committee 2003. *The Decision to Go to War in Iraq: Ninth Report of Session 2002–03*, Vol. 1. London: House of Commons.

Hudson, K. 2000. *European Communism since 1989: Towards a New European Left*. London: Palgrave Macmillan.

Hudson, K. 2003. *Breaking the South Slav Dream: The Rise and Fall of Yugoslavia*. London: Pluto.

Hudson, K. 2005. *CND – Now More than Ever: The Story of a Peace Movement*. London: Vision.

Hudson, K. 2008a. "Reflecting on the recent anti-war movement". *Contemporary Politics* 13(4): 379–88.

Hudson, K. 2008b. "From Georgia to Poland". https://cnduk.org/from-georgia-to-poland.

Hudson, K. 2012a. *The New European Left: A Socialism for the Twenty-First Century?* Basingstoke: Palgrave Macmillan.

Hudson, K. 2012b. "Why I am standing down as Respect Party candidate". http://kate4manchester.org/?p=114. .

Hudson, K. (ed.) 2017. *Free Movement and beyond: Agenda Setting for Brexit Britain*. London: Public Reading Rooms.

Hudson, K. 2018. *CND at 60: Britain's Most Enduring Mass Movement*. London: Public Reading Rooms.

Hudson, K. 2022a. "No nuclear war". https://cnduk.org/no-nuclear-war.

Hudson, K. 2022b. "Ukraine, NATO and the nuclear threat". https://cnduk.org/ukraine-nato-and-the-nuclear-threat.

Hudson, K. 2023a. "Ceasefire now". *Campaign*, November: 1–2.

Hudson, K. 2023b. Interview with the author, 4 December.

Husbands, C. 1989. "SDI and British public opinion". In C. Marsh & C. Fraser (eds), *Public Opinion and Nuclear Weapons*, 57–82. London: Macmillan.

Independent International Commission on Kosovo 2000. *The Kosovo Report: Conflict, International Response, Lessons Learned*. Oxford: Oxford University Press.

Inglis, F. 1995. *Raymond Williams*. London: Routledge.

INNATE 2023. *Peace Groups in Ireland through the Years*. https://innatenonviolence.org/wp/wp-content/uploads/2022/12/Irish-peace-groups-listing-2023.pdf.

International Court of Justice 1996. *Advisory Opinion on the Legality of the Threat or Use of Nuclear Weapons*. The Hague: ICJ.

Jackson, R. 1986. *Strike Force: The USAF in Britain Since 1948*. London: Robson.

Jamieson, L. 2022. "Statement on the Russian invasion of Ukraine". Glasgow: Scottish CND.

Johnson, R., N. Butler & S. Pullinger 2006. *Worse than Irrelevant? British Nuclear Weapons in the 21st Century*. London: Acronym Institute for Disarmament Diplomacy.

Johnson, R. 2022. "Another NPT fails – due to reckless nuclear-armed governments". https://cnduk.org/another-npt-fails-due-to-reckless-nuclear-armed-governments.

Johnson, R. & A. Zelter (eds) 2011. *Trident and International Law: Scotland's Obligations*. Edinburgh: Luath Press.

Jones, L. 1983. "Introduction". In L. Jones (ed.), *Keeping the Peace: A Women's Peace Handbook 1*, 1–6. London: The Women's Press.

Jones, L. 2002 [1993]. "The moral failure of the peace movement". In M. Randle (ed.), *Challenge to Nonviolence*. https://civilresistance.info/challenge.

Jones, P. 1987. "British defence policy: the breakdown of inter-party consensus". *Review of International Studies* 13(2): 111–31.

Kalden, S. 2017. "A case of 'Hollanditis': the Interchurch Peace Council in the Netherlands and the Christian Peace Movement in Western Europe". In E. Conze, M. Klimke & J. Varon (eds), *Nuclear Threats, Nuclear Fear, and the Cold War of the 1980s*, 251–68. Cambridge: Cambridge University Press.

Kaldor, M. 1981. "Why we need European Nuclear Disarmament". *ADIU Report* 3(1): 1–4.

Kaldor, M. 1982a. "Warfare and capitalism". In New Left Review (ed.), *Exterminism and Cold War*, 261–88. London: Verso.

Kaldor, M. 1982b. *The Baroque Arsenal*. London: Deutsch.

Kaldor, M. 1986. "Introduction". In M. Kaldor & P. Anderson (eds), *Mad Dogs*, 1–10. London: Pluto.

Kaldor, M. 1988–9. "Exploding an era". *END Journal* 36: 18–19.

Kaldor, M. 1990. *The Imaginary War: Understanding the East–West Conflict*. Oxford: Blackwell.

Kaldor, M. 1991. "After the Cold War". In M. Kaldor (ed.) *Europe from Below*, 27–42. London: Verso.

Kaldor, M., D. Smith & S. Vines 1979. *Democratic Socialism and the Cost of Defence*. London: Croom Helm.

Kampfner, J. 2003. *Blair's Wars*. London: The Free Press.

Kavan, J. & Z. Tomin 1983. *Voices from Prague*. London: END/Palach Press.

Kent, B. 1992. *Undiscovered Ends: An Autobiography*. London: Fount.

Kent, B. 2022. Bruce Kent at Russian Embassy: full letter text. https://cnduk.org/bruce-kent-at-russian-embassy-full-letter-text.

Kilburn, J. 2005. "A case of my enemy's enemy? Nonsense!" *Peace News*, November. https://peacenews.info/node/5668/case-my-enemys-enemy-nonsense.

King-Hall, S. 1958. *Defence in the Nuclear Age*. London: Gollancz.

Kirby, D. 2013. "Nuclear weapons and the Cold War challenge to the Christian churches: in conversation, Bruce Kent and Brian Wicker". London Metropolitan University, 11 March. https://liverpooluniversitypress.manifoldapp.org/system/resource/fb80a5d9-31a3-4280-8456-08a06a3fc30d/attachment/original-f798e245ef2b81087eeef9135a96452b.pdf.

Kissinger, H. 1988. *The White House Years*. New York: Little Brown.

Knoblauch, W. 2017. "'Will you sing about the missiles?': British antinuclear protest music of the 1980s". In E. Conze, M. Klimke & J. Varon (eds), *Nuclear Threats, Nuclear Fear, and the Cold War of the 1980s*, 101–15. Cambridge: Cambridge University Press.

Köszegi, F. & E. P. Thompson nd [1982]. *The New Hungarian Peace Movement*. London: END/Merlin.

Lammy, D. & J. Healey 2023. "The nuclear deterrent is part of Labour's heritage". *Daily Telegraph*, 27 September.

Leigh, M. 1985. "*Greenham Women against Cruise Missile v. Reagan*. 591 F.Supp.1332". *American Journal of International Law* 79(3): 746–9.

Levy, M. 2021. *Ban the Bomb! Michael Randle and Direct Action against Nuclear War*. Stuttgart: Ibidem.

Levy, M. 2024. *Roundhouse: Joe Berke and the 1967 Congress on the Dialectics of Liberation*. Stuttgart: Ibidem.

libcom.org 2016. "Timeline of direct action against the Iraq War, 2002–2004". https://libcom.org/article/timeline-direct-action-against-iraq-war-2002-2004.

Liddington, J. 1991. *The Road to Greenham Common: Feminism and Anti-Militarism in Britain since 1820*. Syracuse, NY: Syracuse University Press.

Lieber, K. & D. Press 2023. "US strategy and force posture for an era of nuclear tripolarity". Washington, DC: Scowcroft Center.

Lindsay, I. 1983. "CND and the nationalist parties". In J. Minnion & P. Bolsover (eds), *The CND Story*, 134–6. London: Allison & Busby.

Lovell, A. 1959. "Where next for the campaign?". *Universities and Left Review* 7: 5–6.

MacIntyre, A. 1960. "Is a neutralist foreign policy possible?" *International Socialism* 1(3): 26.

McDonald, J. 2017. *"Widening the Web": Greenham Common, the CND and the Women's Movement: The Rise and Fall of Women's Antinuclear Activism, 1958–1988*. PhD thesis, University of Oslo.

McKenzie, D. 2003. "Seeing links and opportunities". *Peace News*, March–May. https://peacenews.info/node/3656/seeing-links-and-opportunities.

McNair, B. 1989. "Television news and the 1983 election". In C. Marsh & C. Fraser (eds), *Public Opinion and Nuclear Weapons*, 124–42. London: Macmillan.

Maclellan, N. 2017. "The pacifist: Harold Steele". In N. Maclellan, *Grappling with the Bomb: Britain's Pacific H-bomb Tests*, 91–104. Canberra: ANU Press.

Mahon, A. 1999. "Public opinion turning". BBC News, 13 May.

Mahon, A. 2006. *Cross-examination, Trial of Slobodan Milošević*. The Hague: International Criminal Tribunal for former Yugoslavia.

Marsh, C. 1989. "Trade unions and nuclear disarmament". In C. Marsh & C. Fraser (eds), *Public Opinion and Nuclear Weapons*, 104–23. London: Macmillan.

Marwick, A. 2005. "The cultural revolution of the long sixties: voices of reaction, protest, and permeation". *International History Review* 27(4): 780–806.

Mattausch, J. 1987. *A Commitment to Campaign: A Sociological Study of CND*. Manchester: Manchester University Press.

Matthews, K. 2020. "Social movements and the (mis)use of research: Extinction Rebellion and the 3.5% rule". *Interface* 12(1): 591–615.

Mattoo, A. 1992. *The Campaign for Nuclear Disarmament: A Study of Its Growth Re-emergence and Decline in the 1980s*. DPhil thesis, University of Oxford.

Membery, Y. 2021. *The Making of Orpington: British Political Culture and the Strange Revival of Liberalism, 1958–64*. Doctoral thesis, Maastricht University.

Michaels, J. 2022. "'No annihilation without representation': NATO nuclear use decision-making during the Cold War". *Journal of Strategic Studies* 46(5): 1010–36.

Mills, C. W. 1958. *The Causes of World War Three*. New York: Simon & Schuster.

Mills, C. W. 1959. *The Power Elite*. New York: Oxford University Press.

Minnion, J. & P. Bolsover (eds) 1983. *The CND Story*. London: Allison & Busby.

Moores, C. 2014. "Opposition to the Greenham women's peace camps in 1980s Britain: RAGE against the 'obscene'". *History Workshop Journal* 78(1): 204–27.

Murray, A. & L. German 2005. *Stop the War: The Story of Britain's Biggest Mass Movement*. London: Bookmarks.

Murray, C. *et al.* 2008. "Reporting dissent in wartime British press: the anti-war movement and the 2003 Iraq War". *European Journal of Communication* 23(7): 7–27.

Nehring, H. 2011. *Politics of Security: British and West German Protests Movements and the Early Cold War, 1945–1970*. Oxford: Oxford University Press.

NGO UK nd. "Figures from a history of NGOs in Britain: chapter 4, Campaign for Nuclear Disarmament". http://www.ngo.bham.ac.uk/appendix/Campaign_for_Nuclear_Disarmament.htm.

Nuclear Information Service 2023. Ainslie Archive. https://www.nuclearinfo.org/ainslie-archive.

Nuttall, J. 1968. *Bomb Culture*. London: McGibbon & Kee.

O'Connell, J. 1986. "The School of Peace Studies at the University of Bradford: the organization of applied research". *Medicine and War* 2(2): 141–7.

Openshaw, S., P. Steadman & O. Greene 1983. *Doomsday: Britain after Nuclear Attack*. Oxford: Blackwell.

Ormrod, D. 1987. "The churches and the nuclear arms race". In R. Taylor & N. Young (eds), *Campaigns for Peace: British Peace Movements in the Twentieth Century*, 189–220. Manchester: Manchester University Press.

Orwell, G. 1949. *Nineteen Eighty-Four*. London: Secker & Warburg.

Parker, T. 2021. *Loose Cannon: Confessions of a Lapsed Activist*. Hythe: Sentinel Publishing.

Parkin, F. 1968. *Middle Class Radicalism: The Social Bases of the British Campaign for Nuclear Disarmament*. Manchester: Manchester University Press.

Payling, D. 2014. "'Socialist Republic of South Yorkshire': grassroots activism and left-wing solidarity in 1980s Sheffield". *Modern British History* 25(4): 602–27.

Peace News 2000–24. London: Peace News. https://peacenews.info.

Pengelly, M. 2021. "Top general feared Trump would launch nuclear war, Woodward book reports". *The Guardian*, 14 September.

Pettitt, A. 2006. *Walking to Greenham: How the Peacecamp Began and the Cold War Ended*. Aberystwyth: Honno.

Phillips, R. 1988. "Hijackers for peace". *Sanity*, July: 17–19.

Phillips, R. 2008. "Standing together: the Muslim Association of Britain and the anti-war movement". *Race & Class* 50(2): 101–13.

Phythian, M. 2001. "CND's Cold War". *Contemporary British History* 15(3): 133–56.

Ponting, C. 1989. "Defence and public opinion". In C. Marsh & C. Fraser (eds), *Public Opinion and Nuclear Weapons*, 177–91. London: Macmillan.

Priestley, J. B. 1957. "Britain and the nuclear bombs". *New Statesman*, 2 November.

Prince, S. 2006. "The global revolt of 1968 and Northern Ireland". *Historical Journal* 49(3): 851–75.

Pugwash Conferences on Science and World Affairs 1955. *The Russell-Einstein Manifesto*. https://pugwash.org/1955/07/09/statement-manifesto.

Rai, M. 2012. "Wobbly Tuesday". *Peace News*, 17 October.

Rai, M. 2023a. "How we nearly stopped the war". *Peace News*, 1 February.

Rai, M. 2023b. "Editorial: a direct action university". *Peace News*, 1 October.

Ramberg, B. 1982. *Power Plants as Weapons for the Enemy: An Unrecognized Military Peril*. Berkeley: University of California Press.

Ramsay, B. 2023. *Castle Zaporizhzhia: War Fighting Implications Linked to the Proliferation of Nuclear Power as Part Solution to Climate Chaos*. Glasgow: SCND.

Randle, M. 1983. "Defenders have 'three to one' advantage". *Sanity*, May: 22–3.

Randle, M. 1987. "Non-violent direct action in the 1950s and 1960s". In R. Taylor & N. Young (eds), *Campaigns for Peace: British Peace Movements in the Twentieth Century*, 131–61. Manchester: Manchester University Press.

Randle, M. 2002 [1994]. "Bosnan dilemmas". In M. Randle (ed.), *Challenge to Nonviolence*. https://civilresistance.info/challenge.

Rankin, M. 2017. *The Political Life of Mary Kaldor*. Boulder, CO: Lynne Rienner.

Rees, D. 1983. "The tide turns". In J. Minnion & P. Bolsover (eds), *The CND Story*, 72–5. London: Allison & Busby.

Ritchie, N. 2010. "Relinquishing nuclear weapons: identities, networks and the British bomb". *International Affairs* 86(2): 465–87.

Roberts, A. 1983. "The trouble with unilateralism: the UK, the 1983 general election, and non-nuclear defence". *Bulletin of Peace Proposals* 14(4): 305–12.

Rochon, T. 1988. *Mobilizing for Peace: The Antinuclear Movements in Western Europe.* Princeton, NJ: Princeton University Press.

Rock, P. & F. Heidensohn 1969. "New reflections on violence". In D. Martin (ed.), *Anarchy and Culture: The Problem of the Contemporary University*, 104–19. London: Routledge & Kegan Paul.

Rogers, P., M. Dando & P. van den Dungen 1981. *As Lambs to the Slaughter.* London: Arrow.

Rogers, P. 2000. "Peace Studies at Bradford: an inside view". *Development Education Journal* 6(2): 19–21.

Roseneil, S. 1995. *Disarming Patriarchy: Feminism and Political Action at Greenham.* Buckingham: Open University Press.

Ross, L. & E. Gibbs 2024. "The making of anti-nuclear Scotland: activism, coalition building, energy politics and nationhood, c.1954–2008". *Contemporary British History* 38(2): 245–69.

Rowbotham, S. 2000. *Promise of a Dream: Remembering the Sixties.* London: Allen Lane.

Ruddock, J. 1987. *CND Scrapbook.* London: Optima.

Russell, B. 1961. *Has Man a Future?* Harmondsworth: Penguin.

Russell, B. 2009 [1967]. *The Autobiography of Bertrand Russell*, Vol. 4. London: Routledge.

Salisbury, D. 2021. *Secrecy, Public Relations and the British Nuclear Debate.* London: Routledge.

Sandford, J. 1983. *The Sword and the Ploughshare: Autonomous Peace Initiatives in East Germany.* London: Merlin/END.

Sands, P. 2005. *Lawless World.* London: Penguin.

Sanity. 1960–91. London: CND. https://www-rockandroll-amdigital-co-uk.

Scalmer, S. 2011. *Gandhi in the West: The Mahatma and the Rise of Radical Protest.* Cambridge: Cambridge University Press.

Schell, J. 1982. *The Fate of the Earth.* New York: Knopf.

Schregel, S. 2017. "Global micropolitics: toward a transnational history of grassroots nuclear-free zones". In E. Conze, M. Klimke & J. Varon (eds), *Nuclear Threats, Nuclear Fear, and the Cold War of the 1980s*, 206–26. Cambridge: Cambridge University Press.

Scott, L. 2012. "Selling or selling out nuclear disarmament? Labour, the bomb, and the 1987 general election". *International History Review* 34(1): 115–37.

Scott-Brown, S. 2017. *The Histories of Raphael Samuel: A Portrait of a People's Historian.* Canberra: ANU Press.

Scott-Brown, S. 2022. "Acting local, *thinking* global in post-war British anarchism". *Global Intellectual History* 1–19. https://doi.org/10.1080/23801883.2022.2136100.

Sedgwick, P. 1959. "NATO, the bomb and socialism". *Universities and Left Review* 7: 7–13.

Seller, A. 1985. "Greenham: a concrete reality". *Frontiers: A Journal of Women's Studies* 8: 26–31.

Shaw, M. 1978. "The making of a party? The International Socialists 1965–76". In *The Socialist Register 1978*, 100–45. London: Merlin.

Shaw, M. 1981. *Socialism and Militarism.* Nottingham: Spokesman.

Shaw, M. (ed.) 1984. *War, State and Society.* London: Macmillan.

Shaw, M. 1993. "Grasping the nettle". *New Statesman and Society*, 15 January.

Shaw, M. 1995. "Cook's chore". *New Statesman and Society*, 16 June.

Shaw, M. 1996. *Civil Society and Media in Global Crises: Representing Distant Violence*. London: Pinter.

Shaw, M. 2015. *What Is Genocide?* 2nd ed. Cambridge: Polity.

Shea, J. 2009. "1979: the Soviet Union deploys its SS20 missiles and NATO responds". Brussels: NATO. https://www.nato.int/cps/en/natohq/opinions_139274.htm.

Simms, B. 2001. *Unfinest Hour: Britain and the Destruction of Bosnia*. London: Allen Lane.

Simpkin, J. 2023. *Labour's Ballistic Missile Defence Policy 1997–2010: A Strategic Relational Analysis*. London: Routledge.

Simpson, T. 1982. *No Bunkers Here: A Successful Non-violent Action in a Welsh Community*. London/Bridgend: Peace News/Mid-Glamorgan CND.

Simpson, T. 2014. "END revisited". *The Spokesman* 124: 77–80.

Sinclair, I. 2011. *The March That Shook Blair: An Oral History of 15 February 2003*. London: Peace News Press.

Sinclair, I. 2013. "The Stop the War Coalition, The Socialist Workers Party and Iraq". https://ianjsinclair.wordpress.com/tag/andrew-murray.

SIPRI (Stockholm International Peace Research Institute) 2023. *SIPRI Yearbook 2023*. Stockholm: SIPRI.

Smith, D. 1980. *The Defence of the Realm in the 1980s*. London: Croom Helm.

Snyder, S. 2011. *Human Rights Activism and the End of the Cold War: A Transnational History of the Helsinki Network*. Cambridge: Cambridge University Press.

Solidarity 1968. *The Death of CND as Performed by the Grosvenor Square Demonstrators under the Direction of Themselves Alone*. https://libcom.org/article/death-cnd-performed-grosvenor-square-demonstrators-under-direction-themselves-alone.

Stein, W. (ed.) 1961. *Nuclear Weapons and the Christian Conscience*. London: Merlin.

Steven, H. 2008. "A history of Scottish anti-nuclear protest". In A. Zelter, *Faslane 365: A Year of Anti-nuclear Blockades*. Edinburgh: Luath.

StWC 2023. "Peace Now! Stop the War in Ukraine". https://actionnetwork.org/petitions/peace-now-stop-the-war-in-ukraine.

Szulecki, K. 2015. "Heretical geopolitics of Central Europe: dissident intellectuals and an alternative European order". *Geoforum* 65: 25–36.

Tannenwald, N. 2006. "Nuclear weapons and the Vietnam War". *Journal of Strategic Studies* 29(4): 675–722.

Taylor, R. 1986. "CND and the 1983 election". In I. Crewe & M. Harrop (eds), *Political Communications: The General Election of 1983*, 207–16. Cambridge: Cambridge University Press.

Taylor, R. 1987a. "The Labour Party and CND: 1957–64". In R. Taylor & N. Young (eds), *Campaigns for Peace: British Peace Movements in the Twentieth Century*, 100–30. Manchester: Manchester University Press.

Taylor, R. 1987b. "The Marxist left and the peace movement since 1945". In R. Taylor & N. Young (eds), *Campaigns for Peace: British Peace Movements in the Twentieth Century*, 162–88. Manchester: Manchester University Press.

Taylor, R. 1988. *Against the Bomb: The British Peace Movement 1958–1965*. Oxford: Oxford University Press.

Taylor, R. 2013. "Thompson and the English peace movement: from CND in the 1950s and 1960s to END in the 1980s". In R. Fieldhouse & R. Taylor (eds), *E. P. Thompson and English Radicalism*, 181–204. Manchester: Manchester University Press.

Taylor, R. & C. Pritchard 1980. *The Protest Makers: The British Nuclear Disarmament Movement 1958–1965*. Oxford: Pergamon.

Thatcher, M. 1993. *The Downing Street Years*. London: HarperCollins.

Thomas, D. 2001. *The Helsinki Effect: International Norms, Human Rights, and the Demise of Communism*. Princeton, NJ: Princeton University Press.

Thompson, E. P. 1947. *There Is a Spirit in Europe … : A Memoir of Frank Thompson*. London: Victor Gollancz.

Thompson, E. P. 1958. "NATO, neutralism and survival". *Universities and Left Review* 4: 49–51.

Thompson, E. P. (ed.) 1960. *Out of Apathy*. New Left Books. London: Stevens.

Thompson, E. P. 1963. *The Making of the English Working Class*. London: Gollancz.

Thompson, E. P. 1964. "The New Left". In D. Boulton (ed.), *Voices from the Crowd: Against the H-Bomb*, 96–105. London: Peter Owen.

Thompson, E. P. (ed.) 1970. *Warwick University Ltd: Industry, Management and the Universities*. Harmondsworth: Penguin.

Thompson, E. P. 1979. "The doomsday consensus". *New Statesman*, 20 December.

Thompson, E. P. 1980. "Notes on exterminism, the last stage of civilization". *New Left Review* 1(121): 3–31.

Thompson, E. P. 1982a. *Beyond the Cold War*. London: Merlin/END.

Thompson, E. P. 1982b. "The war of Thatcher's face". In Thompson, *Zero Option*, 189–98. London: Merlin.

Thompson, E. P. 1983. Letter to Bruce Kent and Joan Ruddock, 17 October. Modern Records Centre, University of Warwick, MSS.343/10/6.

Thompson, E. P. 1984. Speech. Glastonbury, 23 June. https://www.youtube.com/@e.p.thompson.

Thompson, E. P. 1985a. *Double Exposure*. London: Merlin.

Thompson, E. P. 1985b. "The liberation of Perugia". In E. P. Thompson, *The Heavy Dancers*, 182–201. London: Merlin.

Thompson, E. P. 1985c. "Folly's comet". In E. P. Thompson (ed.), *Star Wars*, 93–149. Harmondsworth: Penguin.

Thompson, E. P. (ed.) 1985d. *Star Wars*. Harmondsworth: Penguin.

Thompson, E. P. 1991. "Ends and histories". In M. Kaldor (ed.), *Europe from below*, 7–26. London: Verso.

Thompson, E. P. 1992. "Excuse me if I DISSENT". *HCA Newsletter* 5: 3–4.

Thompson, M. 1993. "No more even-handedness". *HCA Newsletter* 6: 11–12.

Thompson, E. P. & D. Smith (eds) 1980. *Protest and Survive*. Harmondsworth: Penguin.

Thompson, M. & B. Webb 1988–9. "Simple: profound" (editorial). *END Journal* 36: 2.

Tønnesson, S. 2022. "The peace policy maker: Dan Smith". In S. Tønnesson (ed.), *Lives in Peace Research: The Oslo Stories*, 189–222. Oslo: Peace Research Institute Oslo.

Trident Ploughshares 2013. *Tri-Denting It Handbook: An Open Guide to Trident Ploughshares*. 3rd ed. http://tridentploughshares.org/wp-content/uploads/2013/01/intro.pdf.

Trident Ploughshares 2019. "Trident Ploughshares Chronology: 1996–2019". http://tridentploughshares.org/trident-ploughshares-chronology.

Tunnicliffe, A. 1983. "Let's get on with it together". *Sanity*, March: 10–11.

Turner, C. 2016. *Corbyn and Trident: Labour's Continuing Controversy*. London: Public Reading Rooms.

Turner, C. 2023. "Alice Mahon obituary". https://cnduk.org/alice-mahon-an-example-to-all.

Undercover Policing Inquiry 2023a. *Tranche 1 Interim Report*. London: House of Commons.

Undercover Policing Inquiry 2023b. *Special Branch Threat Assessment: Support from London for the Four Day Blockade of Upper Heyford US Air Force Base (May 31st 1983 to June 3rd 1983)*. London: House of Commons.

Undercover Policing Inquiry 2023c. *Special Branch Report on the Greenham Common Women's Peace Camp and the Use of NVDA*. London: House of Commons.

Unkovski-Korica, V. 2019. "From the Cold War to the Kosovo War: Yugoslavia and the British Labour Party". *Revue d'Etudes Comparatives Est-Ouest* 1(1): 115–45.

Wainwright, H. & D. Elliott 1982. *The Lucas Plan: A New Trade Unionism in the Making?* London: Allison & Busby.

Walter, Natasha 2023. *Before the Light Fades: A Memoir of Grief and Resistance*. London: Virago.

Walter, Nicolas 1962. "Disobedience and the new pacifism". *Anarchy* 14: 97–113.

Wayne, M. 2007. "Failing the public: the BBC, The War Game and revisionist history, a reply to James Chapman". *Journal of Contemporary History* 42(4): 627–37.

Webb, D. 2019. "Building bridges". *Campaign*, Summer: 8.

Weber, T. 1993. "From Maude Royden's peace army to the Gulf peace team: an assessment of unarmed interpositionary peace forces". *Journal of Peace Research* 30(1): 45–64.

Weir, J. & The Angry Brigade 1985. *The Angry Brigade: Documents and Chronology, 1967–1984*. https://theanarchistlibrary.org/library/various-authors-the-angry-brigade-documents-and-chronology-1967-1984.

Wernicke, G. & L. Wittner 1999. "Lifting the Iron Curtain: the peace march to Moscow of 1960–1961". *International History Review* 21(4): 900–17.

Whannel, P. & S. Hall 1961. "Direct action?". *New Left Review* 1(8): 16–27.

Wheeler, N. 2000. *Saving Strangers: Humanitarian Intervention in International Society*. Oxford: Oxford University Press.

White, N. 2010. "International law, the United Kingdom and decisions to deploy troops overseas". *International and Comparative Law Quarterly* 59(3): 814–23.

Whiteley, G. 2011. "Sewing the 'subversive thread of imagination': Jeff Nuttall, bomb culture and the radical potential of affect". *The Sixties: A Journal of History, Politics and Culture* 4(2): 109–33.

Widgery, D. 1976. *The Left in Britain, 1956–1968*. Harmondsworth: Penguin.

Williams, R. 1962. *Communications*. Harmondsworth: Penguin.

Williams, R. 1980. "The politics of nuclear disarmament". *New Left Review* 1(124): 26–42.

Wittner, L. 2000. "Gender roles and nuclear disarmament, 1954–1965". *Gender & History* 12(1): 197–222.

Wittner, L. 2009. *Confronting the Bomb: A Short History of the World Nuclear Disarmament Movement*. Stanford, CA: Stanford University Press.

Women for Life on Earth 1982. "Women for Life on Earth say 'No Cruise Missiles at Greenham Common'". Greenham Common Women's Peace Camp, 14 October.

Worsley, P. 1960. "Imperial retreat". In E. P. Thompson (ed.), *Out of Apathy*, 101–40. London: Stevens.

Young, A. 1990. *Femininity in Dissent*. London: Routledge.

Young, K. 2007. "US 'atomic capability' and the British forward bases in the early Cold War". *Journal of Contemporary History* 42(1): 117–36.

Young, N. 1977. *An Infantile Disorder? The Crisis and Decline of the New Left*. London: Routledge.

Zelko, F. 2013. *Make It a Green Peace! The Rise of Countercultural Environmentalism*. Oxford: Oxford University Press.

Zelter, A. 2021. *Activism for Life*. Edinburgh: Luath Press.

Zelter, A. (ed.) 2008. *Faslane 365: A Year of Anti-Nuclear Blockades*. Edinburgh: Luath Press.

Index